INTRODUCTION TO THE COMMON LAW

VOLUME II

Portuguese

DR. PATRICK B. GRIFFIN

Published in 2018 by
English Language Solutions for Law and Business Ltd

Layout design by Gough Typesetting Services, Dublin

ISBN: 978-1-911404-24-8 (ePub)
ISBN: 978-1-911404-33-0 (Print)

A catalogue record for this book is available from the British Library

CONTENTS

HOW TO USE OUR BOOKS

Each book is broken-up into 10 chapters and each chapter is divided into five parts:

- Part 1 allows the student to increase his/her knowledge of a specific area of law and to develop his/her technical vocabulary.
- Part 2 concentrates on the area of grammar revision.
- Part 3 allows the student to work on his/her listening and speaking skills.
- Part 4 encourages the student to work on his/her translation skills and is made up of translation exercises focused on the theme of each chapter.
- Part 5 allows the student to access more in-depth information on the theme under discussion in each specific chapter.

If possible each chapter/course segment should be completed over a one-week period in order to achieve maximum benefit.

We believe that Mylegalenglish books can have a major impact on the ability of students to use and understand legal English. However, to ensure positive results, it is necessary that students apply the system relied on in the books and actively make use of the book's interactive character, discussed immediately below.

Mylegalenglish books have an interactive content that can be accessed on Mylegalenglish channels located on YouTube.com:

- Part 1 of each Mylegalenglish book has both a vocabulary pronunciation support (with a separate channel for each language version) and a presentation video:
  - Language pronunciation videos are located on Mylegalenglish Youtube channel – *Mylegalenglish **French** vocabulary support* – **(insert appropriate language to find the video of your choice: Chinese, French, Italian, Japanese, Polish, Portuguese, Russian, Spanish, Turkish)**;
  - Presentation videos are located on Mylegalenglish Youtube channel – *Mylegalenglish Videos **Introduction to the Common Law Vol 2**.*
- Part 3 of each Mylegalenglish book allows students to work on listening and speaking skills with the help of recorded conversations. Conversation videos for each chapter are located on Mylegalenglish YouTube channel – *Mylegalenglish **Introduction to the Common Law Vol 2** – Conversations*.

To access the Mylegalenglish channel of your choice:

- search **Youtube.com**;
- on the *left hand* column (2/3 down the screen) click on **"Browse channels"**;
- then in the search box write in the name of the *Mylegalenglish channel* you wish to access, for example *Mylegalenglish French vocabulary support* and press return
- then on the *right side* of the screen immediately below the *search box* click on **"Filter"**;
- then go to the column headed **"Type"** and click on **"Channel"** (second option on the list);
- then click on the Mylegalengish channel (identifiable by the Mylegalenglish logo);
- finally click on **"Created playlists"** and choose the playlist for the book or chapter that you are using.

NOTE TO TEACHERS

As regards teachers with a non-legal background, one is not expected to have a complete understanding of all the legal terminology. The meaning of legal words and their equivalent in the students' own language *should be a source of class discussion and in this regard there are no absolute meanings*. Legal terms are used to describe concepts not necessarily having defined limits or having exact legal equivalents in the students' legal system. These books represent the first step of a *fabulous learning process* and full appreciation of all the legal terminology will in most cases require further study by students with teachers specialized in the area of law. Our courses serve as a gateway to introduce students to the legal English applicable in a specific area and should they wish to facilitate subsequent law studies in English. In this regard, the role of the language teacher is to offer linguistic support and *not to be an expert in law.*

Chapter one

WHAT IS A CONTRACT?

PART 1 – TEXT 1 – INFORMATION

To facilitate understanding of both the text and the technical English contained in Part 1 and Part 5 of each Chapter, it is recommended that the student access the video presentation available on the relevant Mylegalenglish learning channel (see instructions at the beginning of the book).

Introduction to contracts

A contract can be distinguished from a simple agreement by the fact that its **terms** are enforceable **in law**. Consequently, **failure** by one **party** to **respect** the terms of a contract will give the other **party to the agreement** a **right of action** before the courts.

Four basic **requirements** are needed for a contract to come into existence:

- *offer* There must be an **offer** made by the **offeror** to another party referred to as the **offeree**;
- *acceptance* There must be clear and **unqualified acceptance** of the offer by the offeree;
- *consideration* Each party must offer the other party a benefit in return for entering into the agreement; that benefit is referred to as **consideration**;
- *intention to create legal relations* The parties must demonstrate that they had an **intention** to create legal relations between them.

Can everyone enter into a contract?

Only parties **possessing** the necessary **capacity** are thought to be able to enter into a contract. In most common law jurisdictions, only people over the age of eighteen[1] and in **sound** mental health are capable of entering into a contract. **Minors** and the **mentally ill** are not normally considered to have the necessary capacity to enter into a contract, as they do not have a sufficient **understanding** of the consequences of their acts.

What is an implied contract?

Even though the parties have not expressly entered into an agreement, the courts sometimes nonetheless consider that they are contractually bound. They are said to be in an **implied contract**. As we have seen, an implied contract is **deemed** to

---

[1]   21 years of age in some common law countries.

exist even though the parties did not **expressly** agree to enter into an agreement. The common law recognizes two principal categories of implied contract:

- contracts **implied by fact** *resulting from the* **behavior** *of the parties* For example, where the parties continue to perform a **previously** existing contract that has officially come to an end, the court may consider that the parties have entered a new *implied in fact* contract, based on their behavior. The terms of the new implied contract will normally be the same as the previous express contract that came to an end;

- contracts **implied by law** A contract implied by law, also known as a **quasi-contract**, may be implied by the courts as a means of **preventing unjust enrichment** by one party over another. In such cases, it is not the behavior of the parties that brings the contract into effect; rather the contract is implied because the courts consider that in the circumstances of a particular case, a party should be required to act in a certain way.

Are there any restrictions concerning the subject matter of a contract?

In most western democracies, the parties to a contract are free to make any agreement they wish, as long as the **subject matter** of the contract is not illegal. If the content of the agreement is illegal, the contract will be thought to have no existence **in the eyes of the law**.

Classification of a contract

Depending on the status of its legality, a contract can be classified as a(n):

- *enforceable contract* An **enforceable contract** is one that is **valid** in law **meeting all the requirements** of a legally binding agreement;

- *unenforceable contract* An **unenforceable contract** is an agreement between parties which is not considered to be **binding** as one or more of the four ingredients necessary for the formation of the contract are not present. For example, an agreement where one of the parties fails to provide consideration in return for the promise of the other party;

- *void contract* A **void contract** is one that is validly constructed, i.e. all the four ingredients necessary for a contract are present; however its subject matter is not valid. For example, the case of an illegal contract in which the parties agree to **defraud** the tax authorities. In such a case, it does not matter that an otherwise legally formed contract exists between the parties as such agreements are considered void and have no existence in the eyes of the law;

- *voidable contract* A **voidable contract** is a contract that is effectively binding on only one of the parties to the contract and where the other party has the choice to enforce it or not. For example, a contract entered into by a minor. In the case of such contracts, the minor has the right either to enforce the agreement or to repudiate it on grounds of his/her incapacity; the other contracting party is dependent on the minor's choice.

Vocabulary

Term – *disposição, cláusula*
In law – *em direito*
Failure – *falha, incapacidade*
Party – *parte*
To respect the terms of a contract – *respeitar as disposições do contrato*
A party to the agreement – *uma das partes do acordo*
Right of action – *direito de ação (na justiça)*
Requirement – *condição*
Offer – *oferta*
Offeror – *oferente*
Offeree – *destinatário da oferta*
Unqualified acceptance – *aceitação incondicional*
Consideration – *contrapartida*
Intention – *intenção*
To possess – *possuir*
Capacity – *capacidade*
Sound – *são (mentalmente)*
Minor – *menor*
Mentally ill – *doente mental*
Understanding – *compreensão*
Implied contract – *contrato tácito*
To deem – *considerar, julgar*
Expressly – *expressamente*
Contract implied by fact – *contrato tácito resultante do comportamento das partes*
Behavior – *comportamento*
Previously – *anteriormente, previamente*
Contract implied by law/quasi-contract – *contrato de direito, quase–contrato*
To prevent – *impedir, evitar*
Unjust enrichment – *enriquecimento sem causa*
Subject matter – *objeto do contrato*
In the eyes of the law – *aos olhos da lei, segundo a lei*
Depending on – *dependendo de*
Enforceable contract – *contrato exeqüível*
Valid – *válido*
To meet the requirements – *atender às condições*
Unenforceable contract – *contrato não exeqüível*
Binding – *juridicamente exigível, compulsório, obrigatório*
Void contract – *contrato nulo*
To defraud – *fraudar*
Voidable contract – *contrato anulável*

PART 1 – TEXT 1 – EXERCISES

1. Vocabulary test

Fill in the missing words using the vocabulary in Text 1

a)   A contract will not be considered _____ by the courts if one of the four basic _____ necessary for a contract is missing.

b)   Even where the parties have not expressly agreed a contract between them, the _____ may find that an _____ contract exists between them.

c)   When a contract is _____ ab initio it is said not to exist in the eyes of the _____.

d)   There are two types of _____ contract, contracts implied by law and contracts implied by _____. The former are also known as _____.

e)   Minors and the mentally ill are not thought of as having the necessary _____ to enter into a contract and thus, they are not _____ by the agreements they make.

f)   A contract is said to be _____ when it meets all the conditions necessary to be considered a valid agreement. Where it does not, the contract is said to be _____.

g)   For a contract to be valid, it is necessary that the _____ to the contract exchange _____ between them, i.e. that each one receives a benefit in return for entering into the agreement.

h)   A contract is said to be _____ if it is void for one of the parties but may be _____ by the other party to the agreement.

i)   The courts will _____ a contract to exist in law in order to prevent unjust _____ by one of the parties.

j)   Once the _____ has made an offer to another party, there must be clear and unqualified _____ of the offer by the _____.

2. Vocabulary test

Write sentences with the following pairs of words. Your sentence should demonstrate your knowledge of the relationship between the words

a)   Valid/enforceable
b)   Consideration/benefit
c)   Capacity/intoxicated
d)   Void/voidable
e)   Implied contract/express
f)   Offer/offeree

3. Knowledge test

Each of the following statements is false; do you know why? Write a sentence stating why it is false

a)   The courts will consider an implied in fact contract to exist in order to prevent unjust enrichment by one party over another.

b)   An agreement without consideration is classified as a void contract.

c) Once a person is intoxicated, it is impossible for them to be deemed capable of entering a contract.

d) The offeror is the person to whom an offer is made.

e) Another name given a contract implied by fact is a quasi-contract.

Access answers at the end of the book.

PART 1 – TEXT 2 – MORE INFORMATION

Introduction to contracts

In the common law, a contract can be compared to a form of private law, **whereby the signatories** to the agreement **undertake** to **carry out acts** or **duties in anticipation** of the **rewards set out therein**[2]. A contract can be distinguished from a simple agreement between friends by the fact that it is **enforceable in law**. Indeed, the **failure** by one party to **respect the terms** of the contract will give the other **party to the agreement** a **right of action** before the courts. However, for an agreement to be considered a contract and thus enforceable in law, it must respect certain rules and conditions. It is for this reason that businesses normally request a lawyer to **draft** important agreements for them. Under the common law, four **basic requirements must be met** in order for a contract to come into effect. There must exist:

- an **offer made** by the **offeror**;
- **acceptance** of the offer by the **offeree**;
- **consideration**, i.e. some kind of payment or exchange of value, not necessarily money **provided** by both parties in return for their respective promises; and
- an **intention to create legal relations**, i.e. proof that the parties intended to enter into a legally binding contract.

When these four elements are present, a **meeting of the minds** is said to have occurred between the parties, resulting in the creation of a binding agreement.

What is an offer?

The first requirement for the formation of a contract is the existence of an offer made by the offeror to the offeree. An offer must be distinguished from an **invitation to treat**. An invitation to treat is **merely** an indication by one party that they are interested in doing business with the other party, but it **falls short** of being an actual offer. Often this is because it lacks sufficient detail to allow a real acceptance by the offeree. For example, if X, who has three cars, offers to sell Y *his/her car* without specifying which of the three cars (s)he is referring to, it will be impossible for Y to accept this offer, as (s)he does not have enough information for real acceptance to take place. In a case such as this, X will be said to have made an invitation to treat.

For example, calls for **tender** are normally **classified** as invitations to treat; thus,

---

[2] The rewards set out by the terms of the contract.

the party replying to the tender will be considered to have made an offer, which may then be accepted by the party that issued the tender. In the same way, at an **auction**, when the auctioneer places the goods for auction, he is said to be making an invitation to treat and it is the party who makes the **bid** and not the **auctioneer** that is thought to make the offer; the offer may then be accepted or not by the auctioneer. Thus, by presenting the goods for auction the auctioneer is normally thought to be making an invitation to treat. However, if the auction is advertised as being *without reserve*, i.e. that there is no established reserve price *below* which the goods will *not* be sold, then case law suggests that in such cases the auctioneer is making an offer to whoever makes the highest bid during the subsequent auction[3].

It is important to remember that there is no **hard and fast rule** distinguishing an offer from an invitation to treat, and each situation is decided on its facts. For example, it is a general rule of the common law that an advertisement offering something for sale is not an offer but merely an invitation to treat. However, an advertisement *may* **be construed** as an offer, where there is sufficient certainty in the advert. For example, where the following conditions are met an advertisement may be thought to amount to an offer, where the advertisement is:
- precise **as to the price** and quantity of the goods for sale; and
- definite **insofar** as the offeror clearly indicates his/her willingness to be bound by the offer in the advertisement, and a timeframe is specified as regards the duration of the offer.

In distinguishing between an offer and an invitation to treat, the courts look to the facts of each case and apply an objective test, asking themselves what a reasonable person would consider to have occurred, i.e. whether an offer or an invitation to treat has been made. Where the transaction is occurring between professionals, normal industry practice will be significant, i.e. whether people in the relevant industry would consider an offer or an invitation to treat to have been made.

If an offer has been made, the general rule is that it may be withdrawn by the offeror at any time prior to acceptance by the offeree. However, the **revocation** of the offer must be communicated to the offeree; if not, then the offer will remain **operative**.

Acceptance

Once an offer is made by the offeror to the offeree, there must be clear and **unqualified** acceptance of the offer by the offeree, if a contract is to come into effect. It is for the offeror to **prescribe the manner** of acceptance.

However, the offeror is not allowed to force a contract into existence. For example, imagine X writes an e-mail to Y:
> *"I offer you my car for sale. If I do not hear from you within ten days, I will presume that you have accepted the contract".*

---
[3] See discussion in translation section.

Will Y **be bound** by contract with X if he does not contact X in the prescribed ten-day period? The answer is that he will not be bound. X has no right to force a contract on Y and make Y perform an act in order to **avoid** its formation. Thus, Y may ignore such an e-mail without **incurring** any **legal liability** toward X.

Moreover, if the offeree (Y) seeks to modify the terms of the offer made by X, (s)he is said to have made a **counteroffer,** which will bring X's original offer to an end. For example, X might offer to sell his/her car to Y for €5,000. If instead of accepting the offer Y **chooses** to offer X €4,500 for the car, (s)he is said to have made a counteroffer. The effect of a counteroffer is to bring X's original offer to an end. Thus, if X refuses Y's new counteroffer of €4,500, Y cannot then go back and seek to accept X's original offer at €5,000, as it has been **extinguished** by Y's counteroffer. Y's **belated** acceptance of X's offer to sell the car for €5,000 is considered to be a new offer made by Y to X, an offer that X is free to accept or reject. Thus, attempts by Y to seek a better **bargain** by automatically offering X less money for the car can **cost Y the deal**.

However, it is important to distinguish between a counteroffer and a **request for information** concerning the original offer made by X. For example, Y has the right to inquire as to whether or not delivery of the car to Y's home by X is included in the offer to sell the car for €5,000. A request for information by Y seeking to clarify the offer that has been made, but not seeking to change the terms of that offer, is not considered to be a counteroffer and thus does not bring X's offer to an end.

Consideration

Consideration is the exchange of value or benefit that each party gives the other in return for their **respective promises** under the contract. **Frequently**, the consideration people offer is money, but it can be anything on which **a value can be placed**. People normally enter into a contract in order to receive something from the other party and whatever it is that they receive will be the consideration. If consideration is only **flowing** from one of the parties and not from the other, then the courts may well believe that an offer of a gift has been made and thus will refuse to enforce it. Consequently, if X offers Y his/her car and Y accepts without offering any consideration in return, X will not be bound by the offer. Without consideration from both parties, an agreement is not considered to be a **binding contract**.

Imagine that X wins the lottery and immediately promises to give Y €10,000. Two weeks later, Y asks X for the money and X refuses, saying that (s)he has changed his/her mind. Can Y sue X for the €10,000? No, because Y has offered X nothing in return for the €10,000, i.e. (s)he has offered him no consideration and as a result there is no binding agreement between them. In legal terms X is said to have made Y a **bare promise** that is not enforceable in law. In fact X has made Y a promise of a gift, which (s)he is free to withdraw at any time[4].

---

[4]   There are exceptions to the consideration rule but the requirement of consideration is nonetheless a cornerstone of common law contract law.

However, once the existence of consideration between both parties is established, it is a general rule of the courts not to concern themselves as to whether the consideration given by each party is **adequate**. People are free to do business on the terms of their own choosing. Thus, if A wants to sell B his/her convertible Rolls Royce for a reduced price of €5,000, the common law courts will not **prevent** the contract coming into effect. The €5,000 offered by B will be considered sufficient consideration to enforce the contract. Thus, the law requires the existence of consideration but is not inclined to ask whether it represents good value.

For the consideration offered by the parties to be considered **valid**, it must not be something that a party is already bound to do. For example, a policeman who arrests a criminal may not normally collect the reward offered for finding the criminal. Why? Because a policeman/policewoman is already under a duty to find criminals and is already paid to do this job. However, if (s)he dedicated his/her free time to finding the criminal, then (s)he probably would be able to receive the reward, as (s)he will have gone beyond the duty for which (s)he is paid.

The common law rule requiring the existence of consideration has been slightly modified by the courts **ruling in equity**. Under the equitable doctrine of **promissory estoppel**, an offer made by X to Y may be enforceable by Y, even where Y fails to provide consideration. However, for promissory estoppel to apply, it is necessary for Y to show that:
- X, the offeror, knew that Y, the offeree, would rely on his/her promise; and that
- reliance by Y on X's promise was reasonable in the circumstances.

Where these criteria are fulfilled, the court applying promissory estoppel *may* decide that it is not necessary for Y to have provided consideration for X, in order for Y to **enforce** X's promise. However, it is important to remember that the doctrine of promissory estoppel is an equitable remedy and its application remains in the discretion of the courts. Indeed, the doctrine of consideration is fundamental to common law contract law and exceptions to its application are unusual.

Intention to create legal relations

Finally, in order for a contract to come into effect between the parties, the courts require that the parties **demonstrate** that when entering the agreement they had an intention to create legal relations.

If there is a dispute between the parties as to whether this intention existed, the courts will look to the:
- **context of the agreement**, for example whether it was a business agreement or an agreement between friends; and
- **subject matter** of the agreement, i.e. the object of the agreement. For example, whether it is an agreement to meet for a drink or an agreement to **guarantee a loan**.

Moreover, there is a **rebuttable presumption** of an intention to create legal relations as regards agreements of a commercial character. In the case of domestic agreements, for example an agreement between a married couple, there is a corresponding rebuttable presumption of no such intention.

Can everyone enter a contract?

Only parties **possessing** the necessary **capacity** are able to enter into contracts. In most jurisdictions, only people over the age of eighteen and in sound mental health are thought to have the necessary capacity to enter into a contract. Companies having a recognized separate legal personality are also considered as having the capacity to enter into contracts **in their own name**. Minors and the mentally ill are not normally thought to have the necessary capacity to enter into a contract, as the law believes that they do not have sufficient **understanding** to appreciate the consequences of their acts. However, a minor will be liable in contract for goods that are deemed to be necessary for his/her everyday life; for example, food, water, electricity, etc. People under the influence of drugs will not be considered as capable of entering a contract where the **level of their intoxication** is such that they do not understand the nature of the contract.

What is an implied contract?

An **implied contract** is a contract that is **deemed** to exist by the courts even though the parties did not expressly agree to it. There are two types of implied contract:

- *contract implied by fact* Such contracts result from the behavior of the parties. For example, where the parties continue to perform a fixed-term contract that has actually come to an end, the courts would probably imply a contract to exist between the parties, based on the fact of their continued performance;
- *contract implied by law* A contract implied by law, also known as a **quasi-contract**, is implied to exist because the courts consider it to be appropriate. For example, a contract may be implied to exist as a means of preventing **unjust enrichment** by one party over another. Thus, if a doctor finds an injured person by the side of the road and gives them medical assistance, the courts will imply a contract to exist between the patient and the doctor as regards the doctor's reasonable medical expenses and **fees**.

Are there any restrictions on the subject matter of a contract?

In most common law countries, the parties to a contract are free to make any agreement they wish between them, as long as the subject matter of the contract is not illegal. If X agrees to pay €100 to Y **under the table** in return for Y painting his/her house, the contract will be illegal as it is an **attempt** to **defraud** the tax authorities. As a result, **despite** having painted the house for X, Y will not be able to **sue** X for payment for the work done, as the agreement will be thought to be illegal and thus will have no existence **in the eyes of the law**. The subject matter of a contract will be illegal in two circumstances, where it violates:

- *the provisions of case law or statute* For example, an agreement between **undertakings** to restrict competition, violating the US **Sherman Act** or the **provisions** of both United Kingdom and European Union **competition law**; or more generally
- *public policy* For example, a contract that discriminates against people of a specific racial background.

Depending on its status, a contract can be classified as a(n):

- *enforceable contract* An enforceable contract is one that is valid and **meets** all the requirements of a legally binding agreement;
- *unenforceable contract* An unenforceable contract is an agreement between the parties where one of the four ingredients necessary for a contract is not present; for example an agreement in which one of the parties fails to provide consideration. In this case, although there is an agreement between the parties, it will not be considered enforceable by law;
- *void contract* A void contract is an agreement that has no **standing** in law and thus in reality is not a contract at all. For example, an illegal contract is void *ab initio*[5] despite the fact that it is validly constructed, i.e. all the four ingredients necessary for a contract are present[6];
- *voidable contract* This is a contract that is non-enforceable for one of the parties to the agreement, depending on the choice of the other contracting party, who is free to enforce it or not. For example, if a record company enters into a contract with Y, a sixteen-year-old singer, the contract will be considered voidable. Thus, for the record company the agreement has no legal force unless the minor decides to enforce it. For the minor the agreement is voidable, i.e. Y may choose to enforce the agreement or not after receiving advice from a qualified advisor/parent.

VOCABULARY

Whereby – *através do qual*
Signatory – *signatário*
To undertake something – *comprometer–se a fazer algo*
To carry out – *realizar, cumprir*
Act – *ato*
Duty – *dever*
In anticipation – *antecipadamente*
Reward – *recompensa*
To set out – *estabelecer*
Therein – *neste*
Enforceable agreement in law – *acordo exigível em direito*

---

[5]   Void from the beginning, i.e. from the moment the agreement was made.
[6]   The four ingredients necessary for the formation of a contract being offer, acceptance, consideration and an intention to create legal relations.

Failure – *falha, incapacidade*
To respect the terms of a contract – *respeitar as disposições do contrato*
A party to an agreement – *uma das partes do acordo*
Right of action – *direito de ação (na Justiça)*
To draft – *redigir*
Basic requirement that must be met – *condições básicas que devem ser satisfeitas*
Offer – *oferta*
Acceptance – *aceitação*
Offeror – *oferente*
Offeree – *destinatário da oferta*
Consideration – *contrapartida*
To provide – *fornecer, prover*
Intention to create a legal relation – *intenção de criar uma relação jurídica*
Meeting of the minds – *acordo de vontades*
Invitation to treat – *convite para negociação*
Merely – *simplesmente, apenas*
To fall short – *estar aquém das expectativas*
Tender – *proposta*
To classify – *classificar, categorisar*
Auction – *leilão*
To bid – *ofertar, propor*
Auctioneer – *leiloeiro*
Without reserve – *sem reservas*
Hard and fast rule – *norma estrita*
To be construed – *ser interpretado*
As to the price – *no que diz respeito ao preço*
Insofar – *na medida em que*
Revocation – *revogação, retratação*
Operative – *em vigor*
Once – *uma vez que, assim que*
Unqualified – *incondicional*
To prescribe the manner – *prescrever a forma*
To be bound (to bind) – *estar ligado, estar obrigado*
To avoid – *evitar*
To incur – *implicar, incidir*
Legal liability – *responsabilidade jurídica*
Moreover – *ademais, além disso*
Counter offer – *contra proposta*
To choose – *escolher*
To extinguish – *extinguir, eliminar*
Belated – *atrasado*
Bargain – *negócio*
To cost somebody the deal – *fazer alguém perder um negócio*
Request for information – *pedido de informações*
Respective promises – *respectivas promessas*
Frequently – *freqüentemente*
A value can be placed on something – *objeto cujo valor pode ser estimado*
To flow – *fluir, circular*

Binding contract – *contrato juridicamente exigível, compulsório, obrigatório*
To imagine – *imaginar*
Bare promise – *promessa unilateral (sem promessa da outra parte)*
Adequate – *adequado*
To prevent – *prevenir, evitar*
Valid – *válido*
To rule in Equity – *estabelecer em eqüidade*
Promissory estoppel – *preclusão de promissória*
To enforce – *aplicar, colocar em prática*
To demonstrate – *demonstrar*
Context of the agreement – *contexto do acordo*
Subject matter – *objeto (do contrato)*
To guarantee a loan – *ser fiador de um empréstimo*
Rebuttable presumption – *presunção refutável*
To possess – *possuir*
Capacity – *capacidade*
In their own name – *em seu próprio nome*
Understanding – *compreensão*
Level of intoxication – *grau de intoxicação*
Contract implied by fact – *contrato tácito*
To deem – *jugar, estimar*
Contract implied by law/quasi-contract – *contrato de direito, quase–contrato*
Unjust enrichment – *enriquecimento sem causa*
Fees – *honorários*
Under the table – *informalmente*
Attempt to defraud – *tentativa de fraude*
Despite – *apesar de*
To sue – *processar*
In the eyes of the law – *aos olhos da lei*
Undertaking – *empresa. Undertaking pode também significar comprometer–se a fazer algo*
Sherman Act – *lei Sherman antitruste*
Provision – *disposições (de uma lei)*
Competition law – *direito da concorrência*
To violate public policy – *perturbar a ordem pública*
Depending on – *dependendo de*
Enforceable contract – *contrato exeqüível*
To meet (the conditions)– *preencher (as condições de um contrato)*
Unenforceable contract – *contrato não exeqüível*
Void contract – *contrato nulo*
Something has standing in law – *algo que é juridicamente exigível (no standing – juridicamente não exigível)*
Voidable contract – *contrato anulável*

To improve pronunciation and understanding of technical vocabulary, the student is advised to listen to the vocabulary recording on the relevant Mylegalenglish learning channel (see instructions at the beginning of the book).

1. Definitions

Write a sentence defining each of the following terms – one sentence per term

a)   Quasi-contract
b)   Consideration
c)   Counteroffer
d)   Enforceable agreement
e)   Voidable contract
f)   Capacity
g)   Liability
h)   Invitation to treat

2. Sentences

Write sentences with the following pairs of words demonstrating your knowledge of the relationship between them

a)   Offeror/offeree
b)   Consideration/binding
c)   Invitation to treat/offer
d)   Acceptance/counteroffer
e)   Implied in law contract/equity
f)   Enforceable/sue
g)   Revocation/offer
h)   Voidable/enforce
i)   Minor/capacity
j)   Intention to create legal relations/subject-matter

3. Fill in the missing words

Using the vocabulary in Text 2, fill in the missing words

a)   An offer may be revoked by the _____ as long as it has not been accepted by the _____.
b)   Minors do not normally have the necessary _____ to enter into contracts and thus any agreement that they make is not considered to be _____.
c)   If an agreement has an illegal subject matter it is said to be _____ and if it can only be enforced by one of the contracting parties but not the other it is said to be _____.
d)   Should the offeree make a _____ in place of accepting the offer made to him, the original _____ will be brought to an end.
e)   Even where there is no express agreement between the _____, the courts are sometimes willing to find that there is an _____ contract between them. Such contracts can be implied in law or depending on the behavior of the parties, sometimes they may be said to be _____.

4. Knowledge test

The following questions may be answered in writing or by way of discussion

a)   Does the law in your jurisdiction require consideration? If not, is there any equivalent to the consideration requirement?

b)   Why do you think a counteroffer by the offeree has the effect of extinguishing the first offer? What is the situation in your jurisdiction?

c)   Explain what you understand by the notion of an invitation to treat.

d)   Do you think it is unfair that a person who performs work pursuant to an illegal contract has no right to be paid for the work (s)he has done?

Access answers at the end of the book.

PART 2 – QUICK LOOK GRAMMAR REVISION

Modal auxiliaries

1. Modal auxiliary + the base form of the verb

Can: I can drive a car.
Could: I could do it tomorrow.
May: It may snow tomorrow.
Might: It might rain today.
Should: Michael should speak English.
Must: I must study harder.
Will: I will go to London to live.
Would: Would you telephone me later today?

> **Note:**
>
> Most modal auxiliaries are single words: can, could, may, might, should, must, will, would are all invariable and are followed by the base form of a verb.
>
> **They are not followed by "to":**
> –   I can speak English = correct
> –   I can *to* speak English = not correct
>
> "to" appears however in three modal auxiliaries – *ought to, be able to* and *have (got) to.*
>
> *Ought to* is invariable, like the other modal auxiliaries listed above; *be able to* and *have (got) to* must be conjugated to correspond to the subject:
>
> –   *Have to*: I have to work today/(s)he has to work today;
> –   *Have got to*: I have got to work harder/(s)he has got to work harder;
> –   *Able to*: (S)he is able to do the job;

– *Ought to*: I ought to work harder.

2. Expressing ability: can and could

Can expresses *a general ability to do something in the present*
John can speak English.

> **Note:**
>
> The negative form of CAN may be written in the following way:
> – can't: but not for formal writing and normally only in speech;
> – cannot: for written English.

> **Note:**
>
> John can speak English = correct
> John can *to* speak English = incorrect
> John can *speaks* English = incorrect

Could is used to express such ability in the past
John could speak English when he left school; however, now he has forgotten how!

> **Note:**
>
> The negative form of COULD may be written in the following way:
> – *couldn't*: but not for formal writing and normally only in speech;
> – *could not*: for written English.

3. Expressing possibility: can and could, may and might

i) Expressing possibility: can and could

Can and *could* may be used in general statements to say that a situation is (can) or was (could be) possible.
You *can* learn English by attending this school.
The judge *could* be a bit of a bore at times.

ii) Expressing possibility: may and might

May and *might* can be used to express possibility in the present or future.
John may/might go to court tomorrow.
Why is John not in court today? I do not know; he *may/might* be sick.

It is only possible to use *may* to say that a situation is usual or common:
Contracts *may* be written or oral

Might is the past form of *may*, so it is used in indirect speech:
I *may* be late. (S)he said (s)he *might* be late.

Note:

The negative form of MAY is only written in the following way:
John *may not* go to the court today.

The negative form of MIGHT is:
mightn't: but not for formal writing and normally only in speech and even then
it may be better to say *might not*;
might not: for written English.

Note:

MAYBE spelt/spelled as one word is an adverb, for example:
maybe it will rain tomorrow;
maybe John is working.

MAY BE spelt/spelled as two words is the auxiliary with the verb, for example:
John *may* be sick.

4. Expressing permission: can and could, may and might

Can and *could* may be used to ask for permission, could being a politer way of so doing. *Can (not)* – and not *could (not)* – is used to refuse permission:
Can I have a bonus this year? Yes, you can. No, you can't.
Could I have a bonus this year? Yes, you can. No, you can't.
You cannot have a bonus this year unless you earn more money.

May can be used in more formal situations to ask for or give permission:
May I have a bonus this year? Yes, you may. No, you may not.

Might can be used to ask for, but not to give permission:
Might I borrow your pen for a few minutes, please? Yes, you may. No, you may not.

PART 2 – GRAMMAR EXERCISES

1. "To" or not "to"

Add "to" where necessary

I have *to* go to work tomorrow.
John has *to* plead before the courts.

a)   Could you please _____ open the window?
b)   The lawyer must _____ learn all of the case tonight.
c)   Barbara has _____ do her work today.
d)   I think you should _____ take better care of your clients.
e)   I ought _____ go to the courthouse this evening.

f) Would you _____ speak more slowly please?
g) We may _____ bring the case before the court.
h) John and I might _____ go to the courthouse tomorrow.
i) I have got _____ go to the court tomorrow.

2. Oral or written exercise

Answer the following questions using **could** *......*

a) What could you do when you were a school child that you cannot do now?
b) What could you do when you were living at home that you cannot do now?
c) What did you want to do last Saturday that you were not able to do? Why were you not able to do it?
d) The last time you missed work, why were you not able to go?
e) What sports were you able to practice when you were young that you cannot do now?

3. Making sentences

Make sentences with may, might and maybe

Do you have any plans for the weekend?
I may go to see my parents.
I might go to the cinema.
Maybe I will (I'll) do some work.

a) It is nearly midday and your secretary is not here. Where is she?
b) You are finishing an important business meal and you realize you forgot your wallet in the office. What are you going to do?
c) You have an important court case tomorrow but you are feeling ill. What will you do?[7]
d) It is late at night and you are alone in your office when you hear a strange noise. What would/will you do?

Access answers at the end of the book.

PART 3 – AUDIO AND ORAL – LISTENING AND SPEAKING

Listen to the following conversation, make notes of all the relevant facts and then answer the questions below. If you have trouble understanding, follow the conversation while also reading the text. Access the conversation on the relevant Mylegalenglish learning channel (see instructions at the beginning of the book).

Conversation between Frank, a solicitor and his client Alessandra

Frank: "Hello Alessandra, nice to meet you."

---

[7] An *adjournment* describes the fact of postponing a case that is due to be heard before a court. A lawyer is said "to ask the court for an adjournment".

Alessandra: "Hello Mr. Fall, thank you for agreeing to see me so quickly."

Frank: "No bother at all, it's a pleasure and please call me Frank."

Alessandra: "OK, Frank, thank you."

Frank: "So what can I do for you?"

Alessandra: "Well, I entered into a contract with Mr. Rodgers, who turned out to be really dreadful and did not do half the things he promised to do and now he wants me to pay him money."

Frank: "OK, let's go slowly here. What exactly did you agree to do with Mr. Rodgers?"

Alessandra: "Well I am a singer and he agreed to be my manager; he said he would promote me and get me a record deal and everything. However, he only arranged a couple of shows for me in a local bar and he kept all the money; and that was a year ago. I stopped working with him afterwards and found a new manager. Now I have a record deal and suddenly Bob, or Mr. Rodgers has reappeared and he says he wants 10% of the money I received from the record company. That was the deal we made, he was to receive 10% of everything I made."

Frank: "And tell me, did you record the contract with Rodgers in writing?"

Alessandra: "Yes, he had his solicitor draw up or draft the agreement and unfortunately I signed it. Oh I am such a fool."

Frank: "And when you began to use your new manager, did you end your agreement with Mr. Rodgers?"

Alessandra: "Well no, you see he effectively stopped being my manager, he said I was no good. And at the time he refused to pay me the money I made, claiming that it was money he had invested in promoting me. But in fact he never did anything."

Frank: "And did he actually write to you officially informing you of the fact that he would no longer be your manager?"

Alessandra: "No, I never heard from him, up until last week that is."

Frank: "OK, do you have a copy of the agreement that you made with him?"

Alessandra: "Yes, I brought it with me, here it is."

Frank: "Good, just give me a couple of minutes to quickly read it over."

Alessandra: "Well, what do you think?"

Frank: "Mmnnn the contract at clause 10 does actually require written notice if the agreement is to be brought to an end; however, if Rodgers stopped working for you, we might have a case for constructive termination, whereby he has brought the contract to an end as a result of his behavior. Sometimes the courts are willing to imply that a contract exists or no longer exists based on the behavior of the parties. But we would have to prove that. Has Rodgers actually done anything for you over the last nine months?"

Alessandra: "No, nothing at all."

Frank: "And may I ask you your age Alessandra?"

Alessandra: "Yes, I'm seventeen years old."

Frank: "So when you entered into the agreement with Rodgers you were a minor?"

Alessandra: "Well I'm not yet eighteen years of age, if that is what you mean."

Frank: "Wonderful Alessandra, I don't think you will have any problem as a contract made with a minor is considered to be voidable and thus cannot be enforced by Rodgers. Only you can choose to enforce it, which I presume you do not wish to do?"

Alessandra: "Certainly not."

Frank: "OK, I think I know how to deal with Mr. Rodgers. I will write him a letter explaining the situation to him."

Alessandra: "Oh Frank, you are my hero!"

PART 3 – AUDIO COMPREHENSION – EXERCISES

1. Comprehension

From the notes you have taken, answer the following questions

a) Who did Alessandra enter into a contract with?

b) What does Alessandra do exactly?

c) Did Alessandra have a written agreement with Mr. Rodgers?

d) What does Frank mean when he talks of *constructive termination* of the contract?

e) Why does Frank ask Alessandra her age?

f) What was the deal that Alessandra had with Mr. Rodgers?

2. Speaking practice

In the following series of conversation couplets develop suitable responses to the questions asked

a) Frank: "Hello Alessandra, nice to meet you."
   Alessandra: "_____"

b) Frank: "OK, let's go slowly here. What exactly did you agree to do with Mr. Rodgers?"
   Alessandra: "_____."

c) Frank: "And tell me did you record the contract with Rodgers in writing?"
   Alessandra: "_____"

d) Frank: "OK, do you have a copy of the agreement that you made with him?"
   Alessandra: "_____."

e) Frank: "And may I ask you your age Alessandra?"
   Alessandra: "_____."

f) Frank: "When you began to work with your new manager, did you end the agreement with Mr. Rodgers?"
   Alessandra: "_____"

g) Frank: "So when you entered into the agreement with Rodgers you were a minor?"
   Alessandra: "_____."

h) Frank: "And did he actually write to you officially informing you of the fact that he would no longer be your manager?"
   Alessandra: "_____."

3. Speaking practice continued ......

Create five other conversation using in each couplet at least one word from the vocabulary found in Part I, Text 1 or Text 2

4. Speaking practice continued ......

Listen to the suggested replies and repeat

a)   Frank: "Hello Alessandra, nice to meet you."
       Alessandra: "Hello Mr. Fall, thank you for agreeing to see me so quickly."

b)   Frank: "OK, let's go slowly here. What exactly did you agree to do with Mr. Rodgers?"
       Alessandra: "Well I am a singer and he agreed to be my manager; he said he would promote me, get me a record deal and everything."

c)   Frank: "And tell me, did you record the contract with Rodgers in writing?"
       Alessandra: "Yes, he had his solicitor draw up or draft the agreement and unfortunately I signed it."

d)   Frank: "OK, do you have a copy of the agreement that you made with him?"
       Alessandra: "Yes, I brought it with me, here it is."

e)   Frank: "And may I ask you your age Alessandra?"
       Alessandra: "Yes, I'm eighteen years old."

f)   Frank: "And when you began to use your new manager, did you officially end your agreement with Mr. Rodgers?"
       Alessandra: "Well no, you see he stopped being my manager months ago."

g)   Frank: "So when you entered into the agreement with Rodgers you were a minor?"
       Alessandra: "I wasn't yet eighteen years of age, if that is what you mean."

h)   Frank: "And did he actually write to you officially informing you of the fact that he would no longer be your manager?"
       Alessandra: "No, I never heard from him, up until last week that is."

5. Associated questions

Discuss the following questions

a)   How would Alessandra's case be dealt with in your country?
b)   Does the notion of constructive termination exist in your legal system?
c)   Is it possible for a minor to enter into a contract in your legal system?
d)   If Alessandra had been over eighteen years of age when she entered into her agreement with Mr. Rodgers, would she have had to respect her agreement with him?

PART 4 – TRANSLATION EXERCISES

When carrying out a translation it is not necessary to translate directly word for word; rather the emphasis should be on translating the sense of the text. Language is not directly interchangeable and so direct translations do not always convey the meaning in the text.

Translate the following texts from English to Portuguese

A. Is it possible to accept an offer that is made to another person? – Boulton v Jones, 1857

Facts: Mr. Boulton bought a builders' supply business from Mr. Brocklehurst. Mr. Jones, a customer of the business before it was sold, was owed money by its previous owner Brocklehurst. Prior to selling the business, Brocklehurst had agreed with Jones that he would pay him back the money he owed him by supplying Jones with free building goods. On the basis of that agreement, Jones addressed an order to Brocklehurst for some piping, not knowing that the business had been sold to Boulton. Boulton, the new owner, supplied the piping even though the order was not actually addressed to him, and billed Jones for the goods supplied. Jones refused to pay indicating that he had made his offer to Brocklehurst, with whom he had a set-off *contra* account[8]. Boulton sued Jones for payment for the amount of the goods supplied.

Held: In the opinion of the court, Jones specifically addressed the order to Mr. Brocklehurst and not Boulton. Consequently Jones was not liable to Boulton for the goods that Boulton mistakenly supplied.

B. The distinction between an offer and an invitation to treat – Heathecote Ball & Co. v Barry, 2000

Facts: Barry, an auctioneer, advertised an auction offering to sell *without reserve*[9] two new engines. The manufacturer's list price[10] for the two engines was £14,000. At auction a representative of the claimant Heathecote Ball & Co. bid £200 and, as it was the only bid that was made, considered that he had accepted the auctioneer's offer to sell the goods without reserve, i.e. he had made the highest offer. The auctioneer claimed that in putting the machines up for auction, he had made no offer to sell the goods but had merely made an invitation to treat. Consequently, in his opinion, it was the claimant that had made the offer to buy the machines at £200 and he was free to refuse this offer or not and was thus free to withdraw the goods from sale. The complainant argued that use of the words "without reserve" turned what would normally have been considered an invitation to treat into an offer.

Held: In the Court's view, the use of the words "without reserve" amounted

---

[8] A set-off contra account means that goods will be supplied free by the debtor until his debt is paid.

[9] Without reserve means that there is no reserve price, i.e. no minimum price.

[10] The term "list price" refers to the manufacturer's recommended sale price.

to an offer by the auctioneer Barry to sell to the highest bidder, no matter the amount of the actual bid.

C. Going beyond one's normal duty is good consideration – Glasbrook Bros. v Glamorgan County Council, 1926

Facts: The owners of a coalmine requested police protection during a strike. The police agreed to patrol the premises but the owners, afraid for their property, requested that the police stay at the site of the mine and offered to pay for the extra cost of this service. However, the mine owners subsequently refused payment on the basis that the consideration offered by the police, staying at the mine, was not good consideration, as they were only doing their duty. In the opinion of the mine owners, the police already had a duty to protect the premises.

Held: According to the Court, performance of an existing duty will not be considered as good consideration to create a binding contract. However, on the facts of the present case, the Court was of the opinion that the police went beyond their duty by actually billeting police officers on the premises. Consequently, the mine owners had to pay for the extra service provided.

Translate the following texts from Portuguese to English

A. Uma contrapartida anterior não é uma contrapartida válida, ReMcArdle

Fatos: Um marido e sua esposa estavam morando na casa da mãe daquele. O filho/marido fez diversas reformas na casa, e a mãe prometeu o pagamento de certa quantia em dinheiro após a sua morte. Depois da morte da mãe, o filho procurou o pagamento do dinheiro prometido. Entretanto, o executor do testamento se recusou a pagar a quantia prometida ao filho, alegando que o espólio da mãe não poderia ser alterado pela promessa. Na opinião do executor, a contraproposta oferecida pelo filho foi uma contrapartida anterior, uma vez que as obras foram realizadas antes que a mãe fizesse a promessa de pagamento em dinheiro.

Julgado: O Tribunal concordou com o executor, considerando que a promessa de fazer algo em troca de uma ação já realizada não cria relação contratual. Dessa forma, o espólio da mãe não estava juridicamente obrigado pela sua promessa, e, conseqüentemente, o filho não poderia receber o dinheiro.

B. Os Tribunais às vezes estão dispostos a incluir cláusulas e obrigações tácitas a um contrato, levando à existência de um quase-contrato

Fatos: O requerente celebrou um contrato para utilizar o cais do requerido, que se localizava no rio Tâmisa, perto do mar. Por isso, quando a maré baixava, os barcos atracados no cais encalhavam no leito no rio. O leito do rio na região do cais do requerido era acidentado e irregular e, por esse motivo, o barco do requerente partiu-se em dois quando a maré baixou. O requerido alegou que não era responsável pela reparação do dano do requerente, uma vez que ele não forneceu alguma garantia com relação às condições do leito do rio. O requerente processou o requerido alegando a existência uma cláusula implícita que assegurava que o leito do rio deveria estar em boas condições para o cumprimento do contrato.

Julgado: Quando necessário, os Tribunais incluirão cláusulas deste tipo para assegurar a eficácia do negócio. Conseqüentemente, no presente caso, foi julgada existência da cláusula tácita que assegurava que o leito do rio deveria estar em boas condições para o cumprimento do contrato[11].

C. O que é lei Sherman?

A lei Sherman antitruste autoriza o governo federal dos Estados Unidos a investigar empresas suspeitas de comportamento anti-competitivo. A lei Sherman foi a primeira lei nacional de direito da concorrência que tinha como objetivo limitar cartéis e monopólios, e hoje forma o modelo utilizado pela maior parte das autoridades de direito da concorrência. Aprovada em 1890, a lei Sherman proíbe:

- acordos ou conspirações entre empresas com o intuito de restringir o comércio.
- monopolizar ou tentar monopolizar o comércio.

Access answers at the end of the book.

PART 5 – ADVANCED READING

What is consideration?

Consideration is anything of value promised to another party when making a contract. It can take the form of money, a service or a promise to do or not to do *something*. In common law it is a prerequisite that both parties offer some consideration before a contract can be thought of as binding. If A signs a contract to buy a car from B for €50,000, A's consideration is the €50,000, and B's consideration is the car. If one of the parties fails to supply the other with good consideration, then, although there may be an agreement between the parties, there is no binding agreement, i.e. no contract.

Consequently, the offer of a gift that has been made by one party to the other may normally be withdrawn at any time without legal consequence. However, once the presence of consideration is shown to exist, the courts are not inclined to inquire into whether either of the parties received good value. The reason for this is that each party is free to enter into the contract of their choice and it would be inappropriate for the courts to begin to decide for the parties the terms of the agreements they choose to enter into. Prior to considering the different theories explaining consideration, it is worthwhile remembering the fundamental rule that both parties to a contract must supply consideration. If they do not,

---

[11] Thus a clause was implied into the contract guaranteeing the "suitable" condition of the river bed for mooring boats. As the river bed was not in a suitable condition in the present case, the court considered that the defendant had breached the clause it implied into the contract.

then the party that has failed to provide consideration will not be able to sue the other under the contract.

The traditional theory explaining the requirement of consideration is the *benefit-detriment theory*. According to this theory, a contract must involve a benefit for the promisor and represent a detriment for the promisee in order for an agreement to be binding in law. However, this theory has been replaced in many common law jurisdictions by *the bargain theory*, pursuant to which the parties subjectively view the contract to be the product of an exchange or bargain. Frequently, these theories overlap, as in the normal purchase contract there will be a(n):

- objective benefit and detriment, i.e. the buyer experiences a benefit by acquiring the product in question, whilst the seller experiences a detriment by handing over the product; and
- subjective notion of entering into a bargain.

The main reason behind the shift from the benefit-detriment theory to the bargain theory is to allow the court to avoid inquiries into whether the consideration supplied is adequate. Although the courts, as we said, do not inquire into the adequacy of consideration, some common law jurisdictions require that it be sufficient, i.e. be something that has a tangible commercial value.

Under the doctrine of promissory estoppel, equity may consider a promise for which no consideration was received to be binding, in circumstances where it would be unfair not to enforce the promise. Consequently, negotiation documents, such as letters of intent or comfort letters, may be viewed as binding on the issuer – even if the recipient has not given any consideration in exchange – where it is felt that the promissory character of the letter is such that it would be unfair for the promisor not to perform the *promise*, the subject of the letter. This is controversial and renders the sending of such letters dangerous for the issuer, as (s)he may be considered contractually bound by a document that may have been issued so as to avoid this very consequence. Normally letters of intent are issued with the express purpose of avoiding making a formal legally binding offer, i.e., so as to limit contractual liability.

Chapter two

VITIATING FACTORS AND THE MEETING OF THE MINDS

PART 1 – TEXT 1 – INFORMATION

When a meeting of the minds does not occur

As we have already seen, for a contract to come into existence it is necessary to have a **meeting of the minds** between the parties. This meeting of the minds will not be considered to occur in certain circumstances.

- *Mistake:* A **mistake** is deemed to occur when the parties **entered into the contract** on the basis of an error. In the presence of such a **misunderstanding** or mistake concerning the **subject matter** of the contract, the courts may find that there has been no meeting of the minds between the parties. However, in order for a mistake to **invalidate** a contract, the mistake must **concern** a **material** or **fundamental element** of the contract. Thus, the mistake must **go to the heart of the contract**. If the mistake concerns a **trivial** question of minor importance, then the contract will be considered valid and will continue **in force**, **notwithstanding** the mistake that has occurred.
- *Misrepresentation* **Misrepresentation** occurs when X induces Y into a contract on the basis of a statement that is untrue, i.e. (s)he *misrepresents* the truth to Y. However, the statement although significant is not considered important enough to be an actual term of the contract. If it were a term of the contract Y would have an action in breach of contract. For example, if X claims to Y that the car (s)he is selling has only had one owner when it had two, X will be said to have misrepresented this fact to Y. In the case of **innocent misrepresentation**, i.e. where X does not know that what (s)he is saying is untrue, normally Y can **repudiate** or reject the contract and in many common law jurisdictions (s)he may not receive damages[12]. However, if it concerns a case of **fraudulent misrepresentation**, where X knows what (s)he is saying to Y is untrue, it is possible for Y to:
  - request damages from the court equivalent to the amount of loss caused by the misrepresentation; and also
  - repudiate the contract incurring no **liability toward** X.
- *Undue influence* **Undue influence** occurs where one of the **parties to**

---

[12] For example, in the United States it is not possible to receive damages for innocent misrepresentation; however, in the United Kingdom a limited indemnity payment (a very direct form of damages) may be available.

the contract induces the other to enter the agreement by **exercising** an excessive or *undue* influence over that party. Certain types of relationships, for example, a doctor and patient relationship, are considered to automatically create a presumption of undue influence. Thus, if a doctor benefits from entering a contract with one of his patients, the **burden of proof** is on the doctor to **rebut** any allegation of undue influence that may subsequently be made by the patient or eventually by members of the patient's family.

- *Duress* **Duress** occurs where one of the parties to a contract **robs** the other party of his **freedom of choice** and forces him/her to enter the agreement. Duress is defined as ***coercion**, either physical or mental, **administered** by one party thereby **depriving** the other party of his/ her free will.* An obvious example of duress would be if X held a gun to Y's head and **forced** him/her to sign a contract. It is important to note that the simple fact that there has been duress involved in the *negotiation* of the contract is not sufficient to subsequently invalidate the contract. It is necessary for the claimant or plaintiff to demonstrate that the duress was the actual **cause** or part of the cause behind the decision to enter into the contract.
- *Unconscionability* **Unconscionability** occurs when a party in a **superior negotiating position** imposes excessively unfair conditions on the other party to the contract. For example, X finds Y lost in the desert and agrees to give Y a drink of water in return for €10,000. To invalidate a contract on grounds of unconscionability, it is necessary to show that one of the parties was in a greatly superior bargaining position to the other party and that (s)he exploited this position by imposing remarkably severe and unconscionable terms. Unconscionability is normally restricted to cases of consumer contracts and in particular **adhesion contracts**, i.e. **standard form contracts**, which leave the consumer no room for negotiation.

VOCABULARY

Meeting of the minds – *acordo de vontades*
Mistake – *erro (to make a mistake – cometer um erro)*
To enter into a contract – *celebrar um contrato*
Misunderstanding – *equívoco*
Subject-matter – *objeto (do contrato)*
To invalidate – *invalidar*
To concern/involve – *dizer respeito, concernir/implicar*
Material/fundamental element – *elemento fundamental*
To go to the heart of the contract – *própria essência do contrato*
Trivial – *trivial*
In force – *em vigor*
Notwithstanding – *contudo, não obstante*
Misrepresentation – *deturpação dos fatos por um dos contratantes; informação falsa*

Innocent misrepresentation – *erro de fato escusável*
Fraudulent misrepresentation – *erro provocado por fraude*
To repudiate – *repudiar*
Liability – *responsabilidade*
Toward – *em direção a*
Undue influence – *influência indevida*
Party to the contract – *parte do contrato*
To induce – *persuadir, induzir*
To exercise (influence) – *exercer (influência)*
Burden of proof – *ônus da prova*
To rebut – *refutar*
Duress – *coação*
To rob – *privar (furtar)*
Freedom of choice – *liberdade de escolha*
Coercion – *coerção*
To administer – *administrar*
To deprive – *privar*
Free will – *livre arbítrio (voluntariamente)*
To force – *obrigar, forçar*
Cause – *causa (to cause – causar)*
Unconscionability – *iniquidade*
Superior negotiating position – *posição de superioridade na negociação do contrato*
Adhesion contract/standard form contract – *contrato de adesão*

PART 1 – TEXT 1 – EXERCISES

1. Vocabulary test

Fill in the missing words using the vocabulary in Text 1

a) Where one party is in a _____ negotiating position, it is possible that the courts will make a finding of unconscionability, especially in the case of _____ contracts.

b) Where a meeting of the _____ has not occurred between the _____, a binding contract will not come into effect.

c) If one party exercises _____ influence over another party, it is possible that any contract between them will be classed as voidable; this is especially true in cases where there is a special _____ between the parties, such as doctor and patient.

d) There are three types of _____: _____, _____ and negligent misrepresentation. The former occurs where one party deliberately misrepresents the truth to the other.

e) If one of the parties enters into the agreement as a result of coercion exercised by the other party, the courts may make a finding of _____, considering that the victim was prevented from exercising his _____ when deciding to contract.

f) In the case of a _____ or misunderstanding between the parties concerning a _____ element of the contract, the contract between the parties may not be enforced.

g)   In the case of a finding of _____ misrepresentation, the aggrieved party may not only apply to have the contract _____ but may also make a claim for any damages (s)he suffered.

h)   The _____ of undue influence that applies when the parties are in a fiduciary relationship may be _____ by the stronger party, if he/she can demonstrate that the other party acted of his/her own free will.

2. Vocabulary test

Write sentences with the following pairs of words. Your sentence should demonstrate your knowledge of the relationship between the words

a)   Adhesion contract/unconscionability
b)   Duress/choice
c)   Misrepresentation/mistake
d)   Rebut/burden of proof
e)   Fraudulent misrepresentation/innocent misrepresentation
f)   Meeting of the minds/contract

3. Knowledge test

Each of the following statements is false; do you know why? Write a sentence stating why it is false

a)   There is a presumption of undue influence in all contracts.
b)   Once a party establishes innocent misrepresentation, it is possible to both receive damages and apply to have the contract rescinded.
c)   Once the existence of duress is established, the contract between the parties will be automatically invalidated.
d)   In the area of unconscionability, once a party is in a superior negotiating position to the other, it is possible for the weaker party to automatically repudiate the agreement between the parties.
e)   When the existence of a mistake is revealed by one of the parties to a contract, no meeting of the minds will be deemed to have occurred and the contract will be invalidated.

PART 1 – TEXT 2 – MORE INFORMATION

When a meeting of the minds does not occur

As we have already seen, for a contract to come into existence it is necessary to have a **meeting of the minds** between the parties. A meeting of the minds is said to occur when the parties to a contract have the same understanding of the terms of the agreement. Such a mutual comprehension is essential to the formation of a valid contract in the common law. This meeting of the minds will be considered flawed where one of the parties can demonstrate the presence of the following vitiating factors: **mistake, misrepresentation, duress, undue influence** or **unconscionability** at the time of the formation of the contract.

Mistake

The presence of a **misunderstanding** or mistake at the time of entering into the contract *may* lead the courts to find that there has been no meeting of the minds between the parties. However, for a mistake to **prevent** a contract from coming into existence it must **concern** a **material** or **fundamental element** in the contract, i.e. the mistake must go right to the **heart of the contract**. If the mistake concerns a **trivial** question of minor importance or an **error of judgment**, it will not **invalidate** the contract. For example, if X sells his replica Ferrari to Y and Y, mistakenly thinking it to be a genuine Ferrari, pays X more money than the car is worth, such a mistake will not invalidate the contract on the grounds of mistake. Should Y be able to demonstrate that X **deceived** him into thinking the car was a real Ferrari, then Y can seek to invalidate the contract on the grounds of **fraudulent misrepresentation** rather than mistake.

There are three different categories of mistake recognized by the law:
- *unilateral mistake* Unilateral mistake is said to occur when only one of the parties to the contract makes an error. In the absence of fraud, the courts are not normally willing to consider a contract unenforceable **on the grounds of** unilateral mistake;
- *common mistake* Common mistake occurs when both parties are mistaken about the same issue. For example, in the case of *Couturier v Hastie*, the parties agreed to the sale of a **cargo** of **corn**, which at the time of the agreement they both mistakenly thought was being transported by ship. However, **unknown** to both of them, the captain of the ship had already sold the corn to someone else. As neither of them could have reasonably been expected to know that the corn was already sold, the contract between them was considered void on the grounds of their common mistake;
- *mutual mistake* Mutual mistake occurs when the parties are **at cross purposes**. For example, in *Raffles v Wichelhaus* the parties agreed to the sale of a load of cotton onboard a ship called the Peerless, leaving Bombay in October. However, **unbeknownst** to the parties, there were two ships called Peerless leaving Bombay that October: one at the beginning of the month and the other at the end of the month. As one party thought that their agreement concerned the Peerless ship leaving early in the month, and the other that it concerned the Peerless leaving at the end of the month, the Court declared the contract void and unenforceable, as a result of the parties' mutual mistake.

Misrepresentation

Misrepresentation occurs when one party (X) makes an incorrect statement to the other party (Y) that **induces** Y to enter a contract. The statement, although significant and helped to convince Y to enter the agreement, is not considered important enough to be an actual term of the contract. If it were a term of the contract Y would have an action in breach of contract. An example might be if X claimed to Y that the car (s)he was selling had only had one owner when in fact it had two; X might be said to have misrepresented this fact to Y.

There are three different types of misrepresentation.

- *Fraudulent misrepresentation* Fraudulent misrepresentation occurs where one party, X, **knowingly** misrepresents an important or material fact that induces another party, Y, to enter into a contract. For example, taking the example above, if X knows that the car has had two owners, (s)he will be **guilty** of fraudulent misrepresentation and Y may repudiate or reject the contract and seek damages for any loss (s)he has suffered. Even if X is only **reckless** with the truth, (s) he will be considered guilty of fraudulent misrepresentation. For example, imagine X does not actually know anything about the age of the car, but decides **nonetheless** to tell Y that it is two years old, so as to induce him into the contract, X will be considered to have been reckless with the truth. For a finding of fraudulent misrepresentation against X, Y must demonstrate to the court that:
  - X misrepresented a material fact to the plaintiff;
  - the misrepresentation was made knowingly or recklessly with the intent to defraud; and
  - Y relied on the misrepresentation when entering into the contract and suffered loss as a result.

  Once fraudulent misrepresentation is established, the victim may immediately repudiate the contract without the need to inform the other party. Alternatively, (s)he may apply to the courts for an order of **rescission** and also request damages. However, instead of applying to have the contract rescinded, the injured party may choose to **affirm** the contract but request monetary compensation for any loss (s)he suffered as a result of the misrepresentation.

- *Innocent misrepresentation* **Innocent misrepresentation** differs from fraudulent misrepresentation as the party making the misrepresentation does not know that the representation is false. Thus, the statement is not made with the intention to **defraud** the other party. Innocent misrepresentation occurs when X states that the car is two years old because that is what (s)he reasonably considers to be the truth. In other words, (s)he makes the misrepresentation innocently. In the US, innocent misrepresentation does not **give a right** to damages and the only remedy **available** to the victim is rescission of the contract. However, in the United Kingdom, under the 1967 Misrepresentation Act, the courts may decide to award limited damages, referred to as an indemnity payment for any **direct damages** suffered by the plaintiff resulting from the misrepresentation.

- *Negligent misrepresentation* In the 1960s, the courts recognized the existence of negligent misrepresentation[13]. Negligent misrepresentation occurs where one party unknowingly makes an untrue statement to

---

[13]   To be negligent with the truth is not the same as being reckless. Being reckless with the facts, which amounts to fraudulent misrepresentation, is saying a thing, which, had one taken any care at all, one would have realized, was untrue. Negligent misrepresentation occurs when X misrepresents the facts unknowingly but, had (s)he taken reasonable care, (s)he would have known what (s)he said was untrue. Unlike fraudulent/reckless misrepresentation, there is no real desire to misrepresent the facts.

the other, which, had they taken reasonable care, would have known to be untrue, i.e. they were negligent. Developed under the heading of tort law, the area of negligent misrepresentation is now governed in the UK by the 1967 Misrepresentation Act.

Duress

Not surprisingly, if Y agrees to enter into a contract with X because the latter is holding a gun to his/her head, the courts will probably be of the opinion that there has not been a true meeting of the minds. This is an example of duress, which is defined as ***coercion,** either physical or mental, **administered** by one party **depriving** the other party of their **free will,** as regards the decision to enter a contract.* In the United Kingdom, contracts entered into under duress are voidable and not void. Thus, the party claiming duress must inform the other party that they are **repudiating** the contract. Interestingly, the simple fact that there has been duress involved in the **negotiation** of the contract is not by itself sufficient to invalidate the contract. It is necessary for the plaintiff to demonstrate that the duress was the cause, or at least one of the **causes**, behind the plaintiff's decision to enter into the contract.

Undue influence

When one party takes advantage of another by reason of their being in a superior influential position, it is considered to be a case of undue influence. When this occurs, the contract is said to be voidable and the weaker party/victim has the right to repudiate the contract entered into with the stronger party. Cases coming under the heading of undue influence can be broken up into two categories.

- *Where the parties are in a **fiduciary** relationship* Where the parties are in a fiduciary relationship, there is a presumption of undue influence and the courts will not hesitate to **set the contract aside**, where it is clearly disadvantageous for the weaker party. As there is a presumption of undue influence, the **burden of proof** is on the stronger party to prove that the weaker party entered the transaction of their own free will and with a full understanding of the nature of the agreement. Fiduciary relationships are said to **arise** *inter alia* in cases of agreements between a parent/child, lawyer/client, religious advisor/believer, **investment advisor**/client, and **trustee/beneficiary**. A husband and wife are not considered to be in a fiduciary relationship.
- *Where the parties are not in a special fiduciary relationship* In cases where the parties are not in a special fiduciary relationship, the burden of proof falls on the alleged victim of the undue influence to establish that the other party was:
  - in a dominant position; and that
  - they exercised that undue influence to convince them to enter into the agreement.

Unconscionability

In certain limited circumstances, the courts are willing to accept that a person is not bound by their contractual obligations, when at the time the contract was entered into there was excessive inequality concerning their respective bargaining positions. Preventing a contract coming into effect on the grounds of unconscionability **flies directly in the face** of the **laissez faire** economic system, as well as the notion of freedom of contract. As a result, unconscionability is not easy to establish before the courts. To begin with, the burden of proof is high. The common law courts consider that the business world is a harsh environment where frequently good business involves the exploitation of the other's weakness. However, the courts do not want to promote the creation of an **economic jungle** and thus are prepared to make an exception in certain limited circumstances. In order for the defense of unconscionability to succeed, it is necessary to show that one of the parties was in a greatly superior bargaining position to the other and that this position was exploited by the imposition of **unconscionable terms**. The terms imposed must be **shocking** in their **extremity** and clearly **offensive**. Unconscionability has been applied most frequently in the case of consumer contracts, where businesses have imposed unfair terms on consumers, especially in the case of **adhesion contracts**, also referred to as **standard form contracts**.

VOCABULARY

Meeting of the minds – *acordo de vontades*
Mistake – *erro (to make a mistake – cometer um erro)*
Misrepresentation – *deturpação dos fatos por um dos contratantes; informação falsa*
Duress – *coação*
Undue influence – *influência indevida*
Unconscionability – *iniquidade*
Misunderstanding – *equívoco*
To prevent – *evitar*
To concern/involve – *dizer respeito, concernir, implicar*
Material, fundamental element – *elemento fundamental*
To go to the heart of the contract – *própria essência do contrato*
Trivial – *trivial*
Error of judgement – *erro de julgamento*
To invalidate – *invalidar*
To deceive – *ludibriar, enganar*
Fraudulent misrepresentation – *induzir a erro de forma fraudulenta*
Unilateral mistake – *erro unilateral*
On grounds of – *em razão de*
Common mistake – *erro comum às partes contratantes*
Cargo – *carga*
Corn – *milho*
Unknown – *desconhecido*
Mutual mistake – *erro de ambas as partes contratantes que induz à fins divergentes*
To be at cross purposes – *compreender outrem de forma equivocada*
Unbeknownst – *desconhecido*

To induce – *persuadir, induzir*
Knowingly – *conscientemente*
Guilty – *culpado*
Reckless – *imprudente*
Nonetheless – *contudo, entretanto*
Rescission – *rescisão do contrato*
To rescind – *rescindir, anular*
To affirm – *firmar (contrato)*
Innocent misrepresentation – *erro de fato escusável*
To defraud – *fraudar*
To give a right – *conferir um direito*
Available – *disponível*
Direct damages – *danos diretos*
Coercion – *coerção*
To administer – *administrar*
To deprive – *privar*
Free will – *livre arbítrio (voluntariamente)*
To repudiate – *repudiar*
Negotiation – *negociação*
Cause – *causa (to cause – causar)*
Fiduciary – *fiduciário*
To set aside – *deixar de lado, anular*
Burden of proof – *ônus da prova*
To arise – *surgir, resultar de*
Investment advisor – *consultor de investimentos*
Trustee, beneficiary – *fiduciário, beneficiário*
To fly in the face – *ir contra*
Laissez faire market – *mercado regido pela lei da oferta e da procura*
Economic jungle – *lei da selva no que diz respeito à questão econômica*
Unconscionable term – *cláusula iníquia, abusiva*
Shocking – *chocante*
Extremity – *extremismo*
Offensive – *ofensivo*
Adhesion contract, standard form contract – *contrato de adesão*

PART 1 – TEXT 2 – EXERCISES

1. Definitions

Write a sentence defining each of the following terms – one sentence per term

    a)   Misrepresentation
    b)   Free will
    c)   Mutual mistake
    d)   Unconscionable
    e)   Duress
    f)   Meeting of the minds
    g)   Undue influence
    h)   Fiduciary relationship

2. Sentences

Write sentences with the following pairs of words demonstrating your knowledge of the relationship between them

    a)   Deceive/misrepresentation
    b)   Undue influence/relationship
    c)   Common mistake/parties
    d)   Burden of proof/rebut
    e)   Adhesion contract/unconscionable
    f)   Duress/free will
    g)   Meeting of the minds/binding
    h)   Reckless/fraudulent misrepresentation
    i)   Intention to create legal relations/subject-matter

3. Fill in the missing words

Using the vocabulary in Text 2, fill in the missing words

    a)   Fraudulent misrepresentation occurs when one contracting party _____ misrepresents a _____ fact to the other party.
    b)   _____ involves depriving one party of their free _____, as regards their decision to enter a contract.
    c)   Unconscionability, which involves the _____ of contracts terms that are shocking in their extremity, normally concerns _____ contracts made with consumers.
    d)   In cases of fraudulent misrepresentation, it is possible for the victim to both _____ the contract, as well as asking the court for _____.
    e)   In order for _____ to be actionable, it is necessary that the error concern an issue of importance going right to the _____ of the contract.

4. Knowledge test

The following questions may be answered in writing or by way of discussion

    a)   Do you think that mistake should be actionable as a means of preventing the formation of a contract? After all, mistakes are ultimately a personal matter under the control of those who make them, even when both parties make the mistake in question.
    b)   Why should a party be denied the right to damages in the case of innocent misrepresentation?
    c)   Is it correct to consider contracts that impose unconscionable terms as potentially void; surely parties should be free to enter into any contract of their choice, whether good or bad.
    d)   What is the approach in your jurisdiction to the issue of whether a meeting of the minds has occurred in the context of the doctrines of mistake, misrepresentation, duress, undue influence and unconscionability?

PART 2 – QUICK LOOK GRAMMAR REVISION

Modal auxiliaries continued......

1. Making a request

People can make a request by using various modal auxiliaries:
- *Would* you please telephone John?
- *Could* you please telephone John?
- *Will* you please telephone John?
- *Can* you please telephone John?

Note:

Would, could, will and *can* are grammatically interchangeable when used in a sentence making a request, but modify the degree of politeness and the underlying meaning of the request.

Although they can all be used to make a request, *could* is considered politer than *can*; and *would* is politer than will.

Can and *could* focus on whether doing what is requested is possible; *will* and *would* lack this dimension, and simply request that someone do something.
Can/Could you get this letter posted before 17h?
=
Is it possible for you to post the letter before 17h?

English speakers frequently give instructions in the form of a question, so as not to be perceived as being too "bossy". However, even if the instruction is phrased in a polite way, if it comes from your boss you are expected to say "yes"!

In order to decide whether a statement using *would, could, will* or *can* is either a genuine request or an instruction, it is necessary to look at the:
- relationship between the parties;
- tone of voice used by the *requesting* party; and
- subject matter of the request.

Note:

Positive answers to a request:
- Yes, of course …
- Yes, certainly …
- I'd be happy/glad/delighted to …
- Sure …
- My pleasure …
- Certainly …
- No problem …

Note:

Negative answers to a request:
- I'd like to but I can't as I have to wash my hair ...
- Sorry but unfortunately I don't have enough time ...
- Sorry, no can do ... (*no can do = informal response meaning that a person cannot do what they were asked*)

Note:

Normally when making a request, do not use *may*:
  May you please pass me the file? = ***incorrect***

Use may when asking for permission to do something
  May I leave the room?

2. Expressing advice or an opinion

People express advice/opinion using a number of different terms:
- I *should* go to work;
- I *ought* to go to work;
- I *had better* go to work.

The negative forms are:
- I *should not (shouldn't)* go to work.
- I *ought not to (oughtn't)* go to work.

The interrogative forms are:
- *Should* I go to work?
- *Ought* I to go to work?

Should is used when the speaker feels personally involved in the advice (s)he is giving:
- You *should* go to see the doctor.
  =
- If I were you, I *would* go to see the doctor.

Ought to expresses a more general obligation:
- You *ought* to go to see the doctor.
  =
- Everyone *would* agree that given your state of health, it *would* be advisable to go to see the doctor.

Had better may also be used. It is used when the speaker wishes to warn against the dangers of doing something, or to show a strong recommendation:
- You'*d better* go to see the doctor.
  =
- You are strongly advised to see the doctor, otherwise you will end up in hospital!

- You'd better not eat that pizza, otherwise you'll get food poisoning.

Note:

Had better is an idiom; it is invariable, and functions like the other modal auxiliaries without "to".

Note:

When using *had better* in spoken English, you normally contract "had" to "d" for example:
- **I'd** better, **you'd** better, **(s)he'd** better, **we'd** better, **they'd** better go to work today.

In negative forms:
- **I'd** better not go; **(s)he'd** better not come, etc.

3. Expressing necessity

People express necessity using a number of different modal auxiliaries:
- I *have to* go to work today;
- I *have got to* go to work today;
- I *must* go to work today.

Have to expresses necessity over which the subject has little or no control:
- He *has to* wear glasses for driving.
- He *has to* appear in court today.

Have got to expresses the same as above, but in an informal manner. It should not be used in written English.

Must indicates that the subject acquiesces in the necessity.

Contrast:
- He *must* go to work today.
=
- He believes that it is necessary for him to go to work today.

- He *has (got) to* go to work today.
=
- He is obliged to go to work today.

Note:

Have to changes to: *has to* in the third person singular: I *have to*, you *have to*, John **has to**, we *have to*, they *have to*

Note:

When talking about what was required or necessary in the past, it is not possible to use *must*.

Similarly, when reporting speech, *must* is transposed into *had to*.
He *had to* go to court yesterday.
"I *must* go to court today". What did he say?
He said he *had to* go to court today.

Note:

In spoken English, the vowel sound in the word "to" is often unstressed. This means that its pronunciation changes from the standard strong pronunciation, written phonetically as /tu/ and pronounced as the double "o" in "boot", to the weak form, written as /tə/ and pronounced like the "a" in "about".

Has to /hæz tu/ becomes /hæztə/ (hasta)

Phonetically, "v" and "f" are very close. Both are labiodental (or labial) fricatives.
"V" is a *voiced* labiodental fricative, whereas "f" is a *voiceless* labial fricative.
When speaking, the voiced "v" sometimes becomes an unvoiced "f", if the sound that follows is also unvoiced, which is the case with "t".

"Have to" /hæv tu/ therefore sounds like /hæftə/ (hafta)

"Have got to" can also be pronounced in a weak form, which is sometimes written as "gotta", with the final "a" pronounced as schwa – phonetically this is written /gɒtə/.

"I've gotta go now" or even "I *gotta* go now" are the written transcriptions of what is sometimes heard in casual conversation. These forms should never be used for written work.

PART 2 – GRAMMAR EXERCISES

1. Develop the dialogue

Using the sentences below make a request and respond……

Close the door.
Would you close the door please?
Sure, no problem.
Thanks.

a) Send me an e mail by way of confirmation of your request.
b) Represent me in court.

c)   Ring the client and confirm the time for the meeting.
d)   Come into my office.
e)   Pass me the file.
f)   Repeat what you said.

2. Develop the dialogue continued......

*Complete the dialogue using **should**, **ought to** or **had better**:*

- *making a positive statement*
- *making a negative sentence*
- *asking a question*

a)   Call his lawyer and complain.
b)   Send another bill to the client.
c)   Ask the court for an adjournment.
d)   Draft new pleadings[14].
e)   Translate the contract into English.

3. Develop the dialogue continued......

Complete the sentences using have to, has to, had to ......

I went to work this weekend because (client's case) ...... *because I had to work on my client's case.*

a)   John cannot go to court today (meeting) ......
b)   If you want to join an international law firm (speak English) ......
c)   I need to use the office car because (court) ......
d)   My client could not come to the meeting because (work) ......
e)   When I was a law student (study) ......

PART 3 – AUDIO AND ORAL – LISTENING AND SPEAKING

Listen to the following conversation and make notes of all the relevant facts and then answer the questions below. If you have trouble understanding, follow the conversation while also reading the text.

Conversation between businessmen Frank and James

Frank: "Hello James, I was hoping I might bump into you."
James: "Really, why?"
Frank: "Well you know the car you sold me last week?"
James: "Yes, the Spyder, she is a super little model isn't she? I always loved Italian sports cars; they are so chic ......"
Frank: "Well the police called to the house yesterday and took possession of it."
James: "What?"
Frank: "Yes apparently it was stolen."

---

14   The name given to the document setting out a lawyer's arguments and that is submitted to the judge prior to the trial. The term *submissions* can also be used in this context.

James: "Stolen by who? I certainly didn't steal it. I bought it from a chap a bit down on his luck. Apparently he had a publishing business that went bankrupt and had creditors snapping at his heels."

Frank: "Well, he is the guy who stole it apparently."

James: "I don't believe it, I really felt sorry for the guy. He told me this big sob story and I fell for every line of it. I even paid him more than I normally would … he spoke about having a baby …… I guess you could say he really got me."

Frank: "Got you! Got me more to the point; the police have repossessed the car."

James: "But how did he rob the car?"

Frank: "Apparently the scam works like this. First he stole the identity of a man named Michael Hunt."

James: "What do you mean he stole his identity?"

Frank: "What, you never heard of identity theft? It is rampant[15] now. First he robbed this chap's house, the real Michael Hunt. Took his identity papers and then turned up at an Alfa Romeo garage, pretending to be Mr. Hunt"

James: "So what, he still had to buy the car."

Frank: "He bought it alright …… but on hire purchase[16] from Alfa Romeo Hire Purchase Ltd. in the name of Michael Hunt."

James: "Wow, what a thief."

Frank: "Yes and then he drove the car down to you and sold it to you telling you his story about his business going bankrupt."

James: "Oh no …… and I fell for it *hook, line and sinker*[17]."

Frank: "Yes, but I bought the car from you and now Alfa Romeo have taken it back."

James: "But you did not know that the car had been stolen?"

Frank: "No I didn't. Just like you and Alfa Romeo I made a mistake."

James: "So if we all made a mistake, why do you have to give back the car?"

Frank: "Well I was talking with my solicitor this morning and according to him, because the hire purchase contract entered into between Alfa Romeo and the supposed Mr. Hunt was based on mistaken identity, that contract was never valid. So Hunt, whose real name is John Smith by the way, did not at any time actually own the car. As a result, the contract under which he sold the car to you was also invalid, as he had no title[18] in the car to transfer. That means you had no title to transfer and so I do not own the car, even if I paid for it. Alfa Romeo is the legal owner apparently."

James: "So what are you going to do?"

Frank: "Well that is why I wanted to talk to you. I was hoping you'd give me back all or at least part of the purchase price I paid to you."

James: "What!"

---

[15] Rampant in this sentence means it happens all the time.

[16] Hire purchase is a type of leasing contract whereby a party rents a car from the seller with an option to buy the car.

[17] This is a fishing metaphor and it means that a party "swallowed" the whole story, i.e. believed everything they were told …… like a fish that swallows the hook, the weight and all the fishing line.

[18] Title means ownership.

PART 3 – AUDIO COMPREHENSION – EXERCISES

1. Comprehension

From the notes you have taken, answer the following questions

- a) Who did James enter into a contract with?
- b) What was the contract for?
- c) Who does Frank think owns the car?
- d) Who is John Smith?
- e) How did John Smith buy the car?
- f) What does Frank want from James?

2. Speaking practice

In the following series of conversation couplets develop suitable responses to the questions asked

- a) Frank: "Hello James, I was hoping I'd bump into you; I've had a problem with the car you sold me last week."
  James: "_____"
- b) Frank: "Could you tell me from whom you bought the car?"
  James: "_____."
- c) Frank: "Did you notice anything suspicious about the man who sold you the car?"
  James: "_____"
- d) Frank: "So will you refund me all or part of the purchase money I paid you for the car?"
  James: "_____."
- e) James: "So who is this guy Michael Hunt?"
  Frank: "_____."
- f) James: "What was the agreement between the supposed Michael Hunt and Alfa Romeo Hire Purchase Ltd.?"
  Frank: "_____."
- g) James: "So who is the owner of the car?"
  Frank: "_____."
- h) James: "How did John Smith steal Michael Hunt's identity?"
  Frank: "_____."

3. Speaking practice continued ......

Create five other conversation couplets using in each couplet at least one word from the technical vocabulary found in Part I, Text 1 or Text 2

4. Speaking practice continued ......

Listen to the suggested replies and repeat

- a) Frank: "Hello James, I was hoping I'd bump into you; I've had a problem with the car you sold me last week."

James: "Really? I can't imagine you having any problem with the Alfa Romeo, they are wonderful little cars."

b)   Frank: "Could you tell me who it was you bought the car from."
     James: "Sure no problem ….. I bought it from a guy called Michael Hunt."

c)   Frank: "Did you notice anything suspicious about the man who sold you the car?"
     James: "No nothing at all, he is a businessman in a bit of financial trouble and had to sell the car in a hurry."

d)   Frank: "So will you refund me all or part of the purchase money I paid you for the car?"
     James: "Well I sold you the car in good faith, I am not sure I can afford to pay you back the money now, these are tough economic times you know."

e)   James: "So who is this guy Michael Hunt?"
     Frank: "Apparently his real name is John Smith, he is a conman and has done this sort of thing before."

f)   James: "What was the agreement between the supposed Michael Hunt and Alfa Romeo?"
     Frank: "He bought the car from Alfa Romeo Hire Purchase Ltd".

g)   James: "So who is the owner of the car?"
     Frank: "Alfa Romeo retained ownership of the car."

h)   James: "How did John Smith steal Michael Hunt's identity?"
     Frank: "Simple, he broke into his house and stole his wallet."

5. Associated questions

Discuss the following questions

a)   How would Frank's case be dealt with in your country?
b)   Does the notion of mistake exist in your legal system?
c)   What would happen to John Smith in your jurisdiction?
d)   Do you think that Alfa Romeo should be held liable for the mistake?

PART 4 – TRANSLATION EXERCISES

When carrying out a translation it is not necessary to translate directly word for word; rather the emphasis should be on translating the sense of the text. Language is not directly interchangeable and so direct translations do not always convey the meaning in the text.

Translate the following texts from English to Portuguese

A. Mistake as to the identity of a person may lead to a contract being considered void – Cundy v Lindsay & Co, 1878

Facts: A certain Mr. Blenkarn, a thief, ordered goods by mail from Lindsay & Co.[19], forging the signature of one of Lindsay's valued customers. Lindsay sent the goods to Blenkarn who immediately sold them on to Cundy. Lindsay & Co.

---

[19]   The wording "& Co." indicates that Linsday & Co. was a business taking the form of a

sought to recover the goods from Cundy, claiming that the original contract for the sale of the goods between Lindsay and Blenkarn was void, as a result of the case of mistake provoked by Blenkarn's fraud. If the contract was void, Blenkarn would not have had the necessary title to sell the goods to Cundy and consequently Cundy could have no title/ownership in the goods.

Held: According to the Court, Lindsay's contract with Blenkarn was void as a result of the mistaken identity provoked by the fraud. Thus, Cundy had received no title to the goods from Blenkarn and so had to return the goods to Lindsay.

B. In order to be considered fraudulent, a misrepresentation must be made knowingly – Derry v Peek, 1889

Facts: The Plymouth Tramways Co. was authorized by an Act of Parliament to make tramways. Under the provisions of the Act the firm was authorized to:
- immediately start making trams to be pulled by horse power; and
- *if they received the special agreement of the Board of Trade* to also make trams powered by steam.

However, the company issued a prospectus stating that one great feature of their business was that *"the company has the **right** to make trams using steam"*. The plaintiff bought shares based on this statement/representation, which was however untrue as the Company needed the prior permission of the Board of Trade to make steam trams. The Board later refused its permission and as a result the company was wound up[20] on grounds of insolvency. However, at the time of issuing the prospectus, the company honestly believed that the consent of the Board of Trade would be given. The plaintiff brought an action for fraudulent misrepresentation.

Held: In the opinion of the court, the Plymouth Tramways Co. was not guilty of fraudulent misrepresentation, as it entertained an honest and reasonable belief that what it said was true.[21]

C. For a finding of fraudulent misrepresentation it is necessary that the statement concern a fact and not an opinion – Bisset v Wilkinson – 1927

Facts: Wilkinson was selling land to Bisset. During the negotiations Wilkinson said to Bisset that the land could easily support 2,000 sheep. At the time of making the representation the land was not used for sheep farming and Bisset knew that Wilkinson had no expertise in this area. After buying the farm Bisset realized that the farm could not support 2,000 sheep and brought an action to rescind the contract on the grounds that Wilkinson had fraudulently misrepresented the farm's capacity for sheep farming.

---

company, i.e. having a separate legal personality from its owners. "Co." is an abbreviation of *company*.

[20] The business was brought to an end.

[21] Had the defense of negligent misrepresentation existed at the time, presumably the plaintiff would have succeeded under this heading.

Held: Bisset's action failed as the Court considered that Wilkinson's statement was only an opinion and not a statement of fact.

Translate the following texts from Portuguese to English

A. Para que uma ação impetrada por coação seja pertinente, é necessário que a coação tenha sido a causa da decisão de firmar o contrato: Barton contra Armstrong, 1975

Fatos: Armstrong era o presidente da empresa Landmark Corporation. Barton era o diretor administrativo, que, além disso, possuía uma grande quantidade de ações da empresa. Havia um histórico de desentendimentos entre as duas partes. Armstrong queria deixar a empresa e fez várias ameaças de morte a Barton para pressioná-lo a comprar as suas ações da empresa. Conseqüentemente, Barton concorda em comprar as ações de Armstrong, em parte por causa das ameaças e também porque ele desejava se livrar de Armstrong para obter total controle da empresa. Tempos depois, a empresa se torna insolvável e Barton tenta invalidar o contrato relativo à venda das ações sob o argumento de que ele havia firmado contrato sob a coação das ameaças de morte proferidas por Armstrong. Armstrong afirmou que Barton assinou o acordo não por causa das ameaças de morte mais porque ele gostaria de obter controle sobre a empresa.

Julgado: Numa apelação que modificou a decisão da instância inférior, o Tribunal determinou a anulação do contrato devido à coação. Segundo o julgamento do Tribunal de apelação, o fato das ameaças de morte terem contribuído em parte para a decisão de firmar o contrato eram o suficiente para provar a coação.

B. Quando os tribunais reconhecerão a existência de influência indevida? Lloyds Bank contra Bundy, 1975

Fatos: O senhor Bundy era um venho fazendeiro que, durante alguns anos, confiou a administração de seus bens financeiros ao gerente de seu banco, o Lloyds Bank. O filho do senhor Bundy também era cliente do banco e devia dinheiro a este. O gerente convenceu Bundy convenceu Bundy a hipotecar a sua casa para pagar a dívida de seu filho. Quando o negócio de seu filho foi encerrou suas atividades, o banco procurou tomar posse da casa de Bundy. O senhor Bundy contestou a ação do banco alegando que o gerente do banco utilizou influência indevida para convencê-lo a firmar o acordo.

Julgado: O Tribunal julgou que, à luz dos fatos, existia uma relação fiduciária especial entre as partes que privou Bandy de seu livre-arbítrio. Consequentemente, o senhor Bundy não estava sujeito ao contrato que garantia o pagamento das dívidas de seu filho.

C. Quando a iniqüidade surge?

A iniqüidade é mais freqüentemente encontrada em circunstâncias onde uma das partes se encontra em uma posição de negociação superior sobre a outra e abusa dessa posição para impor condições de negócio extremamente injustas. A iniqüidade é geralmente encontrada em transações onde:

- O objeto do contrato é extremamente complexo e uma das partes não possui conhecimento especializado sobre a questão. Por exemplo, quando um banco introduz uma cláusula de isenção de responsabilidade em um contrato de investimento firmado com um consumidor;
- Um vendedor vende bens considerados necessários, como por exemplo, eletrodomésticos, através um contrato de adesão;
- Um vendedor aumenta consideravelmente o preço de produtos pelo uso de mecanismos tais como condições de crédito exorbitantes, o que faz com que a *vítima* pague um preço exorbitante pelos bens comprados.

PART 5 – ADVANCED READING

Fraudulent misrepresentation

A meeting of the minds is not considered to have occurred where one of the parties has misrepresented the truth in a pre-contractual statement leading up to the formation of the agreement. As we have seen, a representation is a statement of fact made by one party, inducing the other to enter the contract, but which is not sufficiently important to the subsequent agreement to be considered a term of the contract. Unlike cases of operable mistake, which will void a contract, agreements entered into pursuant to a misrepresentation are considered voidable at the option of the *misrepresentee*, i.e. the person to whom the misrepresentation was made. For a finding of fraudulent misrepresentation it is necessary to prove that X induced Y into a contract on the basis:

- of a misrepresentation of a fact made directly to the other party to the contract;
- that the misrepresentation was made knowingly with the intent to defraud; and that
- the other party relied on the misrepresentation and suffered injury as a result.

Difficulties can arise as to whether fraudulent misrepresentation has occurred if a party simultaneously tells the truth while at the same time also misrepresenting the truth. This can happen if X, while orally misrepresenting a material fact to Y, also by way of written documentation communicates the true facts of the situation to Y. In Redgrave v Hurd, Hurd contracted to buy Redgrave's house. The contract to buy the house was associated with another contract, whereby Hurd was buying an interest in Redgrave's legal practice. As regards the agreement to buy the house, Redgrave orally told Hurd that the revenue of the legal practice was £300 *per annum* (pa), and at this time also gave him documentation, which he claimed, was proof of this. In fact the documentation showed that Redgrave's legal practice was worth far less than £300 pa. However, Hurd did not read the papers and trusted Redgrave. When Hurd later discovered that the practice was worth less, he withdrew from the contract to buy the house. Redgrave applied to the Court for an order of specific performance, asking the Court to force Hurd to buy the house. Hurd claimed a right to rescind the contract on the grounds of Redgrave's fraudulent misrepresentation as to the value of the legal practice. Redgrave considered that, if Hurd had read the documentation given to him, he would have discovered that the practice was worth less and thus was prevented from claiming fraudulent misrepresentation. On appeal, reversing the first instance decision, the Court considered it to be irrelevant that Redgrave had given Hurd correct documentation or that Hurd had failed to read the documentation. Once Redgrave had orally misrepresented the value of the practice and Hurd relied on the misrepresentation, Hurd then had a right to rescind the contract on grounds of fraudulent misrepresentation. It is important to note that had Hurd sent the papers to be checked by an accountant, who then mistakenly advised him that the figures were correct, Hurd may not have succeeded in his action against Redgrave. For example, in *Attwood v Small*, Small orally misrepresented the earning capacity of a mine he sold to Attwood. However, at the time of the oral misrepresentation Small also had given documentation to Attwood contradicting his oral statement reflecting the truth as to the mine's production capacity. Attwood had an expert check the documentation against the oral representation and the expert negligently reported that the documentation corroborated the oral representation made by Small. It was held by the Court that Attwood had been induced into the contract, not by his reliance on Small's misrepresentation as to the earning capacity of the mine, but by his expert's negligent report on the content of the documentation that was supplied by Small to Attwood. Consequently, Attwood's action in fraudulent misrepresentation failed.

Chapter three

UNENFORCEABILITY, DISCHARGE AND REMEDIES FOR BREACH OF CONTRACT

PART 1 – TEXT 1 – INFORMATION

Classification of contracts

There are two main categories of contract in the common law world: simple contracts and **speciality contracts**. Speciality contracts, also referred to as **agreements under seal** or **deeds**[22], are a *special* form of contract that must be used for certain transactions; for example agreements for the transfer of land or agreements to guarantee the debts of another. Speciality contracts in order to be enforceable must be:

- *recorded in writing* Speciality contracts must be in writing. Formerly most common law countries required that they be **executed** under **seal**. Nowadays, although this is no longer the case, such contracts continue to be sometimes referred to as *contracts under seal*;
- *witnessed* The signature of the parties to the agreement must be witnessed, and even **notarized** in some common law jurisdictions; and finally
- *exchanged* Each party to the agreement must receive an original copy of the finalized contract document.

Only a limited number of transactions must be executed by speciality contract and in reality most business agreements in common law countries take the form of a simple contract. Unlike speciality contracts, simple contracts do not have to be in writing, witnessed, or exchanged between the parties. They can be entered into orally and only have to meet the requirements of offer and acceptance, consideration and an intention to create legal relations in order to be binding.

One of the advantages that attaches to a speciality contract is that the applicable **statute of limitations period** is twelve years instead of the six years applicable in the case of simple contracts. Moreover, unlike simple contracts, it is not necessary to show the existence of consideration in order to enforce a speciality contract. Finally, speciality contracts **rank in priority** above ordinary simple contracts and consequently **loan agreements** are often executed by way of speciality contract. It is for these reasons that a party may opt to negotiate a transaction by speciality contract, even if not legally required to do so.

---

[22] A speciality contract is referred to as a deed when it is a contract for the sale of land.

However, no matter the form of a contract, in order for it to be binding a fundamental requirement is that the parties to the agreement have the necessary **capacity** to contract.

What do we mean by capacity to contract?

As we have seen, a finding of incapacity may occur when one of the contracting parties is a **minor**, **insane** or intoxicated. Such contracts are said to be either void or **voidable**, depending on the circumstances. In the case of minors, a contract may be considered enforceable, notwithstanding the age of the parties, where the agreement concerns the supply of **necessities/necessaries** or where performance of the contract has already taken place and the minor has received good value.

In cases of insanity, the law is a little different. A person does not have to be **declared medically insane** in order for a contract to be void on grounds of insanity. Rather, the courts look to see if, at the time of entering in the contract, one of the parties was in a **mental condition** that **prevented** them from understanding what they were contracting to do. If this is established, the contract may be considered voidable or void, depending on the common law jurisdiction involved.

Where a party is intoxicated at the time of entering into a contract, it may be possible for that person to claim incapacity and repudiate the contract once they are **sober**. However, to succeed with such a claim, it is necessary to demonstrate that:

- the intoxicated party did not understand the nature of the contract; and
- their intoxication was **evident** to the other contracting party.

Discharge of contract

When both parties have performed the duties set out in a contract, the agreement is said to be **discharged**. A contract is normally discharged by the performance of the parties. However, at any time a contract may be discharged, despite the parties' **non-performance**, should the parties **so agree**. A contract will also be considered discharged if performance by the parties is **frustrated** by an outside event. Frustration occurs when an intervening event **renders** performance of the contract impossible, or illegal, or brings about so radical a change in the circumstances surrounding performance, that it essentially becomes something other than that which was originally agreed to by the parties.

Remedies for breach of contract

If either of the parties fails to exercise their duties under the contract, the other may either seek a remedy at common law or alternatively under the law of equity. The only common law remedy available is **damages**. Remedies available under equity include *inter alia* an:

- order of **specific performance, whereby** a party is required to perform its duties under the contract; or alternatively

- **injunction,** preventing a party from acting in such a way whereby they will be considered to **be in breach** of their contract.

Put simply, an order of specific performance is an order by the court requiring a party to behave in a certain way, while an injunction is an order to stop behaving in a certain way.

VOCABULARY

Specialty contract/agreement under seal – *contrato formal/convenção selada*
Deed – *escritura*
Seal – *selo*
Executed – *assinado*
To be witnessed – *sob o testemunho de*
To notarize – *ato de autenticação por um notário*
Statute of limitations period – *período de prescrição*
To rank in priority – *classificar como prioridade*
Loan agreement – *contrato de empréstimo*
Capacity – *capacidade*
Minor – *menor*
To be insane – *ser absolutamente incapaz devido à condição mental*
Voidable – *anulável*
Necessities – *necessidades*
To be declared medically insane – *ser declarado absolutamente incapaz devido à condição mental*
Mental condition – *condição mental*
To prevent – *prevenir, evitar*
Sober – *sóbrio*
To be evident – *ser evidente*
To discharge – *exonerar–se de um dever (ou, neste caso, extinção de um contrato)*
Non-performance – *não–execução (de um contrato)*
To so agree – *concordar em fazer isto*
Frustrated contract – *contrato não–executado*
To render – *tornar*
Damages – *danos*
Inter alia – *entre outros*
Specific performance – *ordem de execução em caso de não–execução de um contrato*
Whereby – *pelo qual, através do qual*
Injunction – *injunção*
To be in breach of a contract – *estar em situação de violação de contrato*

PART 1 – TEXT 1 – EXERCISES

1. Vocabulary test

Fill in the missing words using the vocabulary in Text 1

a)   Should one of the parties fail to perform his _____ under the contract, the other party to the contract may either seek an award of _____ or alternatively request a remedy in equity.

b)   In order to be bound by a contract it is necessary that the parties have the necessary _____ to contract, which will not be the case for minors, the mentally ill or _____ parties.

c)   The common law recognizes two types of contract: _____ contracts and _____ contracts. The latter are reserved to specific types of transactions, such as contracts for the sale of land.

d)   Where one of the parties to a _____ is a minor, the agreement will be categorized as _____.

e)   Speciality contracts must meet certain requirements; for example they must be _____ in writing and copies of the agreement must be _____ between the parties.

f)   Once the parties to an agreement have _____ their duties, the contract is said to have been _____.

g)   Any agreement entered into with a party who has been _____ medically insane is considered to be _____ and without effect.

h)   When an event occurs that _____ the performance of the agreement impossible, the contract may be considered _____.

2. Vocabulary test

Write sentences with the following pairs of words. Your sentence should demonstrate your knowledge of the relationship between the words

a)   Frustration/performance
b)   Injunction/remedy
c)   Statute of limitations/speciality contract
d)   Insane/capacity
e)   Agreement under seal/simple contracts
f)   Discharge/duties

3. Knowledge test

Each of the following statements is false; do you know why? Write a sentence stating why it is false

a)   Once a contract is signed its terms are binding, even if the conditions governing its performance have changed radically.

b)   Contracts in the common law world must meet the requirements of offer, acceptance, consideration and intention to create legal relations, if they are to be considered as creating a binding contract.

c)   The only remedy for breach of contract is damages.

d)   Speciality contracts have the same statute of limitations period as ordinary simple contracts.

e)   An injunction is an order by the court requiring a party to carry out their contractual duty.

PART 1 – TEXT 2 – MORE INFORMATION

Classification of contracts

There are two main categories of contract recognized by the common law:
- simple contracts; and
- **speciality contracts**.

Simple contracts make-up the vast majority of contracts and are valid whether they are entered into orally or in writing. For a simple contract to be considered enforceable, the four ingredients of offer, acceptance, consideration and intention to create legal relations must be present. Speciality contracts, also referred to as **agreements under seal** or **deeds**[23], are contracts that have to meet special requirements in order to be considered valid. To be enforceable, certain transactions must be entered into by way of a speciality contract, for example transactions involving the sale of land or an agreement guaranteeing the debts of another. The formula *signed, **sealed** and **delivered*** is often used in the **signing block** of speciality contracts in order to indicate that the transaction is being executed as a deed. What do formulae such as *signed, sealed and delivered* actually mean? This formula can be understood in the following way:
- *Signed* Signed clearly means that the parties must sign their names to the contract. This requirement in reality indicates that in order to be enforceable a speciality contract must be **recorded in writing**.
- *Sealed* Sealed is the requirement that the parties **affix** their seal on the contract. Most common law jurisdictions no longer impose this requirement.
- *Delivered* Delivered refers to the requirement that each party receives or has *delivered* to it (party) an original signed copy of the contract. In other words, original copies of the contract must be exchanged between the parties.

As the use of seals is no longer necessary in many common law countries, most **jurisdictions** now require that the actual signing of the agreement be either **witnessed** by at least one independent third party and/or that the contract be **notarized**. In place of signed sealed and delivered, a newer signing block formula, *signed as a deed*, is now often used by the parties.

One of the advantages that attaches to speciality contracts is that the **statute of limitation period** for such agreements is twelve years, double the six-year period applicable to simple contracts. Moreover, unlike simple contracts, it is not necessary to show the existence of consideration in order to enforce a

---

[23] A deed of title is the name given a deed when the transaction involves the transfer of title to land.

contract under seal. With such contracts, there is said to be an **irrebuttable** presumption as to the existence of consideration between the parties. Finally, speciality contracts are considered to **rank in priority** above ordinary simple contracts and consequently **loan agreements** often take this form, in an attempt to ensure that the lender in any such agreement has **priority** over other **creditors** in cases of **insolvency**.

Unenforceable contracts and the notion of incapacity

In order for an agreement to be binding, it is necessary that the parties have the necessary capacity to enter into the agreement. Incapacity to contract may occur when one of the contracting parties is a **minor**, **insane** or intoxicated.

1. Minors

It is a general principle of the common law that a contract entered into between an adult and a minor is unenforceable by the adult party but may be enforced by the minor. Such a contract is said to be **voidable**:

- *void* for the adult, insofar as an adult cannot enforce a contract against the wishes of the minor; but
- enforce*able* by the minor, should (s)he so choose, once advised as to the consequences of the contract by a suitably qualified adult.

There are however a number of exceptions to this, namely:

- contracts for **necessaries/necessities**; and
- contracts where performance has already taken place.

Contracts for necessaries The main exception to the rule that minors are not bound by their contractual obligations **occurs** in the case of contracts for necessaries. The United Kingdom's Sale of Goods Act, 1979 specifically provides that minors will be bound by the contracts they enter into, where they concern the purchase of necessaries, i.e. goods necessary for the life and wellbeing of the minor:

> *"Where necessaries are sold and delivered to a minor ... he must pay the reasonable price **therefore**. Necessaries **means** goods suitable to the condition of life of such a minor .... and to his actual **requirements** at the time of sale and **delivery"**[24].*

In *Chapple v Cooper* a young **widow**, who was a minor, **contracted** with an **undertaker** to carry out both the **burial** of her husband and the subsequent **erection of a memorial** over his grave. She later attempted to **repudiate** the contract on the basis that she was a minor. The Court considered the burial of the husband to be a necessary:

> *"if the law allows minors to marry, then it must also enforce contracts for the burial of those whom they marry".*

---

[24] The wording of the Act acknowledges that the notion of necessity may vary with the minor in question, i.e. what is necessary to the *condition of life* of one minor may not be considered necessary for the condition of life of another minor.

What is considered necessary is ultimately decided by reference to the **rule of reason** and an **objective consideration** of what is *necessary* for the minor in question. **Moreover**, even if the subject of the agreement is considered a *necessary* for the minor, the Sale of Goods Act provides that the minor may only be **obliged** to pay the normal **market rate** for **any such goods**.

Contracts where performance has already taken place The situation is a little different where performance of the contract has already **taken place**. Where property or goods are transferred to the minor **pursuant to** a contract and the minor has already paid for them, payment can normally only be **recovered** by the minor, if the minor demonstrates that the agreement was based on unfair contract terms. Moreover, although a person may repudiate a contract entered into as a minor before or upon their **attaining majority**, once that person has attained majority, any such repudiation must be carried out within a reasonable period of time; not taking action to repudiate the contract will be understood as an implied ratification of the contract.

2. Insanity

The law does not require that a person be actually **declared medically insane** in order for a contract to be considered void on grounds of insanity. Rather, the courts look to see if, at the time of entering in the contract, one of the parties was in a **mental condition** that **prevented** them from understanding what they were contracting to do.

Under traditional common law theory, there are two **categories** of contract with the insane:

- *contracts with the undeclared mentally ill* A party, even if suffering from a mental illness, will be bound by a contract if it can be shown that (s)he understood the nature of the obligation. However, if the mentally illness is such that a person can show that they were not capable of understanding the nature of the agreement and that the other party knew or should have known of their disability, the contract will normally be classified as voidable. Thus, the contract can subsequently be **either** approved or rejected by the mentally ill party. If a mental illness impairs a party's judgment but not their understanding of the contract, the contract will normally be considered enforceable, where the other party did not know they were ill;

- *contracts with those declared medically insane* A contract entered into with someone who has been declared medically insane is automatically void *ab initio*[25] and can never be considered **binding** on either of the parties, except in the case of a contract for necessaries. The necessaries exception also applies to *undeclared* mentally ill parties.

3. Intoxication

Where a party is intoxicated at the time of entering into a contract, it may be

---

[25]   Void from the moment it is entered into.

possible for them to claim incapacity and to repudiate the contract once they are **sober**. However, simply demonstrating intoxication is not sufficient to have the contract declared void, as the level of intoxication:

- **must be such** that the intoxicated person did not understand the nature of the contract they entered into; and
- should have been **evident** to the other non-intoxicated contracting party.

Discharge of contract

When both parties perform the duties set out in a contract, the obligations are considered discharged. Although the normal way to discharge a contract is for each of the parties to the contract to perform their respective duties, discharge of a contract can occur in a number of different ways:

- *discharge by performance* Where both parties perform or execute their **respective** duties under a contract, the contract is considered to have been discharged. For performance to amount to discharge, it is not necessary that the parties perform *all* the duties created by the contract. Instead, the law has recognized the notion of **substantial performance**. Thus, if some **minor** duties remain to be performed, the contract will **still** be regarded as discharged; although **damages** must be paid *in lieu of* the unperformed duties;
- *discharge resulting from the mutual agreement of the parties* The parties to a contract remain free at all times to bring their contract to an end by mutual agreement. However, a decision to **waive** performance will only be binding if the beneficiary of the **waiver** provides consideration in return for the waiver of the other party, i.e. if he pays for the waiver. If there is no consideration offered, the other party can in principle **renege** on his/her promise to waive performance. The waiver is considered to amount to a separate contract between the parties and thus must satisfy the requirements of offer, acceptance, *consideration* and intention to create legal relations in order to be binding;
- *discharge under the doctrine of frustration* **Frustration** is a doctrine developed by the common law courts and is not unlike the French civil law notion of *force majeure*. Under the doctrine of frustration, if an **event** occurs that **renders** performance of the contract impossible, illegal, or brings about so **radical** a change in the circumstances that the contract becomes essentially something different to what was originally intended by the parties, the contract will be considered to be frustrated and automatically discharged. There are different types of frustration.
  - *Frustration resulting from impossibility* Impossibility can occur for example where the subject of the contract is destroyed. In Taylor v Cadwell, the plaintiff agreed to hire a music hall from the defendant for the purpose of holding concerts on specified dates. However, **prior to** the first concert, a fire destroyed the

music hall. As a result, the purpose of the contract was held to be frustrated and the contract was discharged.

- *Frustration by subsequent illegality* Where the parties agree to do something that although legal at the time of the agreement is subsequently declared illegal, then the contract will be frustrated at the moment the illegality **attaches**. For example, an agreed **merger** that is subsequently ruled **anticompetitive** by the competition law authorities and prohibited. In a case like this the duties arising under the merger agreement will be considered automatically discharged, without either of the parties being liable for non-performance.

- *Frustration where there is a radical change in the circumstances of performance* In Krell v Henry the plaintiff agreed to rent an apartment to the defendant for a day. The defendant rented the apartment in order to be able to see the King's coronation procession; however, the rental contract did not make any mention of this. The coronation was cancelled and the defendant claimed that the contract had been frustrated. The plaintiff rejected this, saying that the defendant was still able to occupy the apartment at the agreed date and thus there had been no frustration of the agreement. The Court held that as a result of the cancellation of the coronation, the contract to rent the flat had been frustrated; it considered that the underlying purpose of the agreement was to view the coronation procession. Consequently the defendant was able to cancel the contract and did not have to pay for the apartment he had agreed to rent.

Remedies for breach of contract

If one of the parties fails to exercise their duties under a contract, a number of **remedies** are available. At common law the only available remedy is damages, i.e. financial compensation. Should a party not consider this remedy appropriate, (s)he may instead decide to ask the court for a remedy in equity. However, as we have already seen, equitable remedies are discretionary and will only be granted by the court if they believe an award of damages to be inappropriate as a remedy. Remedies available under equity include *inter alia* an:

- order of **specific performance**, **whereby** a party is required to specifically perform his/her duties under the contract; or alternatively
- **injunction**, preventing a party from acting in such a way whereby they will be in breach of their contract.

VOCABULARY

Specialty contract/agreement under seal – *contrato formal/convenção selada*
Deed – *escritura*
To execute an agreement – *executar um contrato (neste caso: aplicar)*
To be sealed – *ser selado*

To be delivered (exchanged) – *trocar uma cópia original assinada do contrato com as outras partes*

Signing block – *caso em que o contrato deve conter as assinaturas das partes*

To be evidenced or recorded in writing – *ser registrado por escrito*

To affix a seal on the contract – *fixar um selo em um contrato (contrato selado)*

LS (locus sigilli, i.e. the place of the seal) – *locus sigilli, local onde o selo foi fixado*

Jurisdiction – *jurisdição (to come within jurisdiction of the court – estar sob a competência do Tribunal)*

To witness a signature – *testemunhar a assinatura de um contrato*

To have a document notarized – *ter um ato certificado por um notário*

Statute of limitation period – *período de prescrição*

Irrebuttable – *irrefutável*

To rank in priority – *classificar como prioridade*

Loan agreement – *contrato de empréstimo*

Priority – *prioridade*

Creditor – *credor*

Insolvency – *insolvabilidade*

Minor (when referring to a person) – *menor*

Insane – *absolutamente incapaz devido à condição mental*

Voidable – *anulável*

Necessity – *necessidade (no caso de menores, alimentos)*

To occur – *acontecer, ocorrer*

Therefore – *portanto*

To mean – *significar*

Requirement – *obrigação, condição*

Delivery – *entrega*

Widow – *viúva*

To contract – *firmar contrato*

Undertaker – *agente funerário*

Burial – *enterro*

Erection of a memorial – *construção de um memorial*

To repudiate – *repudiar (neste caso: rejeitar o contrato)*

Rule of reason – *regra da razão*

Objective consideration – *avaliação objetiva*

Moreover – *ademais, além disso*

To be obliged to – *ser obrigado a*

Market rate – *valor de mercado*

Any such goods – *por esses tipos de bens*

To have taken place – *ocorrer*

Pursuant to – *segundo, de acordo com*

To recover something – *recuperar algo*

On attaining majority – *quando a maioria é alcançada*

To be declared medically insane – *ser declarado absolutamente incapaz devido à condição mental*

Mental condition – *condição mental*

To prevent – *prevenir, evitar*

Category – *categoria*

Either – *ou*
To declare – *declarar*
Binding – *obrigatório, compulsivo*
Sober – *sóbrio*
Must be such – *deve ser tal*
Evident – *evidente*
Duty – *dever*
To perform – *executar, quitar um dever*
Respective – *respectivo*
Substantial performance – *execução substancial*
Minor (non-important) – *pouco importante*
Still – *ainda*
Damage – *dano*
In lieu of – *no lugar de*
To waive – *renunciar a*
Waiver – *renúncia*
To renege on something – *renegar algo*
Frustration – *frustração*
Event – *evento*
To render – *tornar*
Radical – *radical*
Prior to – *anteriormente a*
To attach – *contituir (uma ilegalidade)*
Merger – *fusão*
Anticompetitive – *anticompetitivo*
To let (property) – *alugar (um imóvel)*
Remedy – *recurso*
Inter alia – *entre outros*
Specific performance – *ordem de execução em caso de não–execução de um contrato*
Whereby – *pelo qual, através do qual*
Injunction – *injunção*

PART 1 – TEXT 2 – EXERCISES

1. Definitions

Write a sentence defining each of the following terms – one sentence per term

- a) Rule of reason
- b) Capacity
- c) Waiver
- d) Frustration
- e) Specific performance
- f) Speciality contract
- g) Creditor
- h) Simple contract

2. Sentences

Write sentences with the following pairs of words demonstrating your knowledge of the relationship between them

 a) Damages/remedy
 b) Minor/voidable
 c) Equity/discretionary
 d) Mentally ill/void
 e) Injunction/specific performance
 f) Frustration/impossibility
 g) Simple contract/statute of limitations
 h) Substantial performance/damages
 i) Speciality contract/writing

3. Fill in the missing words

Using the vocabulary in Text 2, fill in the missing words

 a) Speciality contracts are contracts that must be _____ in writing, unlike simple contracts that can be entered into _____ .
 b) _____ are thought to be too young to have the necessary _____ to enter into a contract.
 c) Where there has been _____ performance by a party of his/her obligations under contract, the other party will only be able to sue for _____ , even though the contract has not been discharged.
 d) Pursuant to the doctrine of _____ the parties to a contract will not be _____ by their duties under their contract, where performance of the contract has changed radically.
 e) In the case of speciality contracts there is an _____ presumption of _____ .

4. Knowledge test

The following questions may be answered in writing or by way of discussion

 a) In your legal system, is there a distinction drawn between speciality contracts, (i.e. contracts that must meet certain formal requirements in order to be binding) and ordinary simple contracts?
 b) Do you think that it is appropriate that minors should be bound by contracts for necessaries?
 c) Should intoxicated people be allowed to escape their contractual responsibilities? After all, they have chosen to become intoxicated, why should they be protected?
 d) The doctrine of frustration allows for a contract to be considered no longer binding where the circumstances governing the performance of the contract have radically changed. Should the courts be providing relief for the parties in this way? Surely the parties are free to anticipate such change in their agreement if they wish. Should the fact that they choose not do so be respected by the courts?

PART 2 – QUICK LOOK GRAMMAR REVISION

Asking questions

1. Questions that can be answered using YES or NO ....

- *Do you know my partner Bob Hastings? Yes, I do, we go to the same health club.*
- *Are you studying English? Yes, I am studying legal English.*
- *Did Mohammed come to work this morning? No, he didn't, he went out to a party last night.*
- *Was Barbara in court this morning? No, she wasn't, she forgot to go.*

Note:

When answering a question in either the affirmative or the negative, it is just the auxiliary that is repeated.

Do you know John? Yes, I do.

The main verb can be reused if you wish to provide additional information:
Are you studying English? Yes, I am.
Are you studying English? Yes, I am studying legal English.

Note:

When answering a question in the negative it is possible to contract the auxiliary with the subject of the sentence in spoken English.

*Was Barbara in her office this morning? No, she **wasn't** =* CORRECT
*Was Barbara in her office this morning? No, she **was not** =* CORRECT

2. Information questions

Information questions are questions which use what is called an *information question word*, for example: **where, what, why, who, whom, which, whose, how** ......

Information questions are **normally** formed by combining the:

a) *information question word + b) auxiliary verb + c) subject + d) main verb*

Example: *a): Where b): does c): Bob d): work?*

However, when using WHO or WHAT as the subject of the sentence, the main verb is used as opposed to the auxiliary + main verb ......

Who came to the office yesterday? (Not "who did come...?")
What happened yesterday? (Not "what did happen...?")

3. Using *who, whom* **and** *what*

When do you use *who* and when do you use *whom*?

Who is the subject of the question, for example:

Who (subject) came to the office yesterday? Bob (subject) came to the office yesterday.

Whom is the object of the question, for example:

Whom (object) did you ring? I (subject) rang Jane (object).

What On the contrary, *what* is used whether it is the subject or the object of the sentence, for example:

What (subject) happened?
What (object) did you say?

> **Note:**
>
> In spoken English **WHO** is often used in place of **WHOM** ......
> BUT that still does not make it right ... "whom" is probably *more* correct!
>
> *Whom did you meet?* = correct
> *Who did you meet?* = not correct informal use

PART 2 – GRAMMAR EXERCISES

1. Ask a question .....

Write the question and answer in the negative on the basis of the statements below ......

Q. *Do you know my partner?*
A. No I don't. Statement: I don't know your partner.

a)	I go to court every day.
b)	I can't find a job.
c)	I met the client yesterday.
d)	I studied legal English.
e)	I won't be in court tomorrow.

2. Ask a question continued ......

Make a YES/NO question and an information question out of the following statements ......

> *Statement: I work there*
> YES/NO question: Do you work there?
> Information question: Where do you work?

    a)   She works there.
    b)   I'm working there.
    c)   He was working there.
    d)   They are going to work there.
    e)   Bob should work there.

3. More asking questions ......

Based on the statement, ask a question using what, who or whom ......

    a)   Bob went to court.
    b)   Mohammed saw Bob.
    c)   An accident happened.
    d)   Bob saw a client.
    e)   Bob saw a film.

PART 3 – AUDIO AND ORAL – LISTENING AND SPEAKING

Comprehension

Listen to the following conversation, make notes of all the relevant facts and then answer the questions below. If you have trouble understanding, follow the conversation while also reading the text.

Conversation between Bob Brewer and Mohammed Jones

Bob: "So, Mohammed, what's up?"
Mohammed: "I have a problem with a contract I entered into."
Bob: "Most problems have a solution Mohammed, why not give me the details?"
Mohammed: "Well this one is linked to my brother in law, Farrid, and I am not sure there is any solution for this guy."
Bob: "In-laws Mohammed ... tell me about it ...... so what has Farrid done?"
Mohammed: "Believe me, I don't have enough time to tell you everything he has done in his long-running attempt to ruin my business, but the reason I am here today is because he signed a contract committing my business, Luxe Car Imports into a five year contract."
Bob: "Five years!"
Mohammed: "Yup five long years, at a cost of over £150,000 a year."
Bob: "750 K in total ... *that's not nothing.*"
Mohammed: "No it's not, it will put me out of business, so you have to get me out of it."
Bob: "OK, tell me what happened and then we can see what the best approach is."

Mohammed: "Last week I left the office to go on a long weekend with my wife and children to Disneyland."

Bob: "Nice …"

Mohammed: "Well, it was meant to be; but Friday afternoon I got a text message on my phone from my nephew telling me I should ring the office *pronto*[1], as Farrid was in over his head[2] and about to sign an advertising agreement."

Bob: "So, what did you do?"

Mohammed: "What do you think I did? I immediately rang Farrid and asked him what he was doing."

Bob: "And he said?"

Mohammed: "He said I'm getting a great advertising deal Mohammed, you'll love it. So I immediately told him to stop it, but he said I did not understand just how good the deal was and that the advertising salesman opposite him, in his office, was telling him that if he did not sign now, the 30% reduction would be withdrawn."

Bob: "So what did you do?"

Mohammed: "I told him to pass the phone to the advertising salesman and once I got him on the phone I told him that I was not interested in signing the deal. Then I got Farrid back on the phone and told him not to sign anything and that I would have a look at it when I got back Monday. I even made an appointment with the advertising salesman for the following Monday, even though I had no intention of signing any advertising deal."

Bob: "So, what's the problem?"

Mohammed: "The problem is that when I turned up on Monday I found that Farrid, the idiot, had signed the contract despite what I'd said."

Bob: "Wow, some brother in law. So then I suspect you rang the advertising company to withdraw from the contract and they said no, that you had entered into a contract for a fixed term of five long expensive years."

Mohammed: "Yes exactly."

Bob: "OK Mohammed, here is the big question; does Farrid have the power to bind the company by contract?"

Mohammed: "No way man, he is only a car salesman; he likes to act the big executive around the showroom because he is my brother in law; but in reality, he is only employed to sell cars and he can't even do that! However, apparently the day that he signed the contract, he was sitting in my office and he told the advertising company salesman that he was a director and a family member!"

Bob: "When you were on the phone to the advertising salesman, did you tell him that Farrid did not have the power to bind the company under contract?"

Mohammed: "Yes of course I did, I told him he was only a car salesman, in fact I asked them both to get the hell out of my office."

Bob: "OK, so the salesman was informed that Farrid did not have the power to bind the company and you offered to meet with him the following Monday. It is looking pretty good Mohammed. The thing is that now we have to prove that you told the salesman that Farrid did not have the power to sign on behalf of the company."

---

[1] *Pronto* is slang for quickly.

[2] *To be in over your head*: to be doing something when you don't understand how it works.

Mohammed: "No problem, for the last three weeks I have been recording all the calls made."

Bob: "You what…?"

Mohammed: "Well someone, Farrid I think, has been ringing up "chat lines"[3] from different phones in the office, you know the type of thing ... To be honest I don't mind what he does … the thing is, it was costing a fortune."

Bob: "OK I'll write to the advertising company and ring them afterwards. For the moment we won't mention that we have a recording of the conversation because I don't know how legal that is. If they contact you … just tell them to get in touch with me and don't say anything else. Have you got a copy of the recorded conversation?"

Mohammed: "Yes, here in my pocket."

Bob: "OK good, you hold onto the original at home and give me the copy. I will write to these guys today. Oh and Mohammed … I think it is time that either you or your sister divorced Farrid!"

PART 3 – AUDIO COMPREHENSION – EXERCISES

1. Comprehension

From the notes you have taken, answer the following questions

a) What is the relationship between Mohammed and Farrid?
b) What kind of contract did Farrid enter into?
c) Why is Mohammed annoyed?
d) What is the final piece of advice Bob gives Mohammed?
e) How can Mohammed prove that he talked to the advertising salesman?
f) For how long has Mohammed been recording telephone conversations?

2. Speaking practice

In the following series of conversation couplets, develop suitable responses to the questions asked

a) Bob: "So Mohammed, why do you want to see me?"
   Mohammed: "_____"
b) Bob: "What is your relationship with Farrid?"
   Mohammed: "_____."
c) Bob: "So Mohammed, what did Farrid do exactly?
   Mohammed: "_____"
d) Bob: "How much does the advertising contract cost?"
   Mohammed: "_____."
e) Bob "How can we prove that you talked to the advertising salesman?"
   Bob: "_____."
f) Bob: "So where were you when Farrid entered into the contract?"
   Bob: "_____."
g) Mohammed: "What does Farrid do for you Mohammed?"
   Bob: "_____."

---

[3] Chat lines are lines often used by pornography retailers.

3. Speaking practice continued ......

Create five other conversation couplets using in each couplet at least one word from the vocabulary found in Part 1, Text 1 or Text 2

4. Speaking practice continued ......

Listen to the suggested replies and repeat

a)   Bob: "So Mohammed, why do you want to see me?"
     Mohammed: "Because one of my employees entered into an advertising contract without my permission."

b)   Bob: "What is your relationship with Farrid?"
     Mohammed: "He is my sister's husband, so he is my brother in law."

c)   Bob: "So Mohammed, what did Farrid do exactly?"
     Mohammed: "Against my express instructions he entered into an advertising contract."

d)   Bob: "How much does the advertising contract cost?"
     Mohammed: "£750,000 over five years."

e)   Bob: "How can you prove that you talked to the advertising salesman?"
     Bob: "I recorded the telephone conversation."

f)   Bob: "So where were you when Farrid entered into the contract?"
     Bob: "I was on a long weekend at Disneyland with my family."

g)   Bob: "What exactly does Farrid do for you Mohammed?"
     Mohammed: "He works as a car salesman."

5. Associated questions

Discuss the following questions

a)   Would Mohammed be bound by the contract entered into by his employee, Farrid in your country?

b)   Is it possible to enter into a binding agreement orally in your country or does it have to be in writing?

c)   In your jurisdiction is there a distinction made between simple contracts and speciality contracts?

d)   Can X ever be bound by a contract entered into by another? For example, can a party ever presume that another is acting as an agent for X and thus has the power to bind X in contract?

PART 4 – TRANSLATION EXERCISES

When carrying out the translations it is not necessary to translate directly word for word; rather the emphasis should be on translating the sense of the text. Language is not directly interchangeable and so direct translations do not always convey the meaning in the text.

Translate the following texts from English to Portuguese

A. Negligent misrepresentation – Hedley Byrne Co. Ltd. v. Heller Partners, 1967

Facts: Hedley Byrne (HB) were advertising agents. A customer, Easipower Ltd, put in a large order with HB and as a result HB decided to check Easipower's financial position. They asked Easipower's bank, Heller & Partners Ltd., if the business was solvent and the bank replied that Easipower could be *considered good for its ordinary business engagements*. Their letter was headed with the disclaimer *"without responsibility on the part of this bank"*. Easipower subsequently went into liquidation and HB lost £17,000. HB sued the bank for negligent misrepresentation.

Held: The Court found that Heller & Partners was guilty of *negligent misrepresentation*.

B. What do the courts understand by the term "necessaries"? – Nash v Inman, 1908

Facts: Inman was an undergraduate student at Cambridge University. He was quite a spendthrift and considered it necessary to buy twelve fancy waistcoats from Mr. Nash, a tailor. However, prior to the actual delivery of the waistcoats, he attempted to repudiate the contract on the basis that he was a minor and thus was not bound by the contract. Nash claimed that the fashionable waistcoats were a *necessity* for the minor and that the contract was thus a contract for necessaries and consequently enforceable.

Held: In the opinion of the court Inman was not liable to pay for the waistcoats, as according to evidence given by his father, the young man was already amply supplied with clothing.

C. Limits placed by the courts concerning the notion of necessities – Valentini v Canali – 1889

Facts: Valentini, a minor, bought furniture for his apartment. After using it for a number of months, he sought to return it on the basis that he had entered into the contract as a minor. Canali resisted Valentini's claims, considering that Valentini had paid the normal market price for the furniture and thus had not been exploited, even if he was a minor at the moment of entering into the contract.

Held: It would be unfair if Valentini, after using the furniture for a number of months, was suddenly able to return it to Canali and receive a refund of the purchase price. Especially important for the Court was the fact that Valentini as a minor had not been exploited by Canali and had paid the normal market rate for the furniture.

Translate the following texts from Portuguese to English

A. Como os tribunais interpretam o conceito de violação antecipada?–Hochster contra De la Tour, 1853

Julgado: Uma violação antecipada ocorre quando uma das partes de um contrato informa a outra parte que não irá mais cumprir com seus deveres estabelecidos pelo acordo antes da data de execução do contrato. No caso de Hochster contra de la Tour, o senhor de la Tour aceitou de empregar Hochster como mensageiro a partir do dia 1º de junho. Entretanto, no dia 11 de maio, de la Tour informou Hochster que ele não precisaria mais de seus serviços e não iria mais empregá-lo de acordo com o que havia sido combinado. Hochster imediatamente perpetra uma ação judicial de perdas e danos; entretanto, de la Tour argumentou que ele não poderia cumprir o contrato antes do dia 1º de junho.

Julgado: Hochster podia impetrar uma ação à partir do dia que de la Tour o informou que ele não iria mais cumprir suas obrigações contratuais e não precisava esperar a data prevista para a execução do contrato.

B. Quitação por renúncia

Em qualquer momento após a assinatura de um contrato, as partes podem posteriormente concordam em anular o contrato antes de sua execução do dever contratual por uma das partes. Neste caso, diz-se que eles renunciam à necessidade de execução. Entretanto, é importante notar que qualquer acordo de renúncia de execução constitui novo contrato e, portanto, para vincular juridicamente, ele deve satisfazer as quatro condições básicas do contrato: oferta, aceitação, contrapartida e intenção de criar uma relação jurídica. Se estas condições não forem atendidas, o acordo de uma das partes de renunciar à execução não obriga.

C. Remédios em eqüidade: ordem de execução e injunções

Como o único remédio disponível no Common Law é a ação por perdas e danos, caso uma das partes desejar que a outra execute o contrato, o recurso ao tribunal é necessário para a expedição de uma ordem de execução em eqüidade. Uma ordem de execução é uma ordem que exige que uma das partes cumpra seu dever contratual conforme determinado em contrato. Entretanto, a eqüidade é um remédio discricionário: o tribunal só irá determinar uma solução em eqüidade se for demonstrado que os danos não são justos. Um outro remédio em eqüidade é a injunção. Uma injunção é uma ordem do tribunal que exige que umas das partes se abstenha de fazer algo.

PART 5 – ADVANCED READING

Discharge under the doctrine of frustration

As we have seen, contracts may be discharged through the operation of the law under the doctrine of frustration. If during the operation of the agreement an event occurs that renders performance:

- impossible;
- illegal; or
- brings about so radical a change in the circumstances that the contract becomes essentially something different to what was originally intended;

the contract will be considered as being frustrated. However, for frustration to apply it is necessary to show that the:

- event was not provided for in the contract;
- frustration was not self-induced;
- event destroys the very root or essence of the contract.

In **Tsakiroglou Co. v Noblee Thorl. GmbH**, the fact that the Suez Canal was blocked, forcing a ship to go around the Cape of Good Hope, was not held to frustrate a contract to carry goods by ship from Port Sudan to Hamburg, despite the fact that the contract was significantly more expensive to perform. In the opinion of the Court, for the event to lead to a finding of frustration, it would have been necessary to demonstrate that transport of the goods via the Suez Canal was within both party's contemplation at the time of entering into the contract and formed part of their agreement. In **Blackburn Bobbin v Allen**, the defendant agreed to supply the plaintiff with Finnish pine wood. Unknown to the plaintiff, the defendant did not actually have the wood in stock but had to order it from Finland. However, before it could be ordered, war broke out, cutting off the supply. The Court did not accept that the contract had been frustrated, as the method of supply was not mentioned in the contract and was thus irrelevant to the plaintiff who had contracted for wood, not for its manner of delivery.

Consequently, frustration differs from the notion of *force majeure* developed by the civil law:

- *frustration* is operable as performance becomes too onerous, impractical or impossible either objectively or from the parties' subjective point of view;
- *force majeure* is operable because performance is objectively no longer possible.

Thus, force majeure is centered solely on the event and on whether it renders performance impossible, while frustration is measured by reference to the parties' appreciation of the event and thus is not limited to the event itself. As a result frustration can potentially have a wider scope of application, as it is not limited to an objective evaluation of whether performance is possible or not. Frustration includes impossibility but also extends to situations where performance, although possible, has changed radically. Thus, a severe change in prices from the moment of signing the agreement to the moment of actual performance may be considered a frustrating event. This would not normally be an operable event under force majeure. Moreover, frustration, when operable, terminates the agreement. On the contrary, an event of force majeure may either terminate or suspend the agreement, depending on the facts of the case. Finally the fact that an event has already occurred in the past will not necessarily prevent it from being considered a frustrating event. However, under the doctrine of force majeure an event has to be unforeseeable if it is to amount to *force majeure*.

Chapter four

TORT LAW

PART 1 – TEXT 1 – INFORMATION

Classification of torts

A tort is a wrong resulting from a breach of civil duty. The common law courts created **tort law** in order to provide **redress** for **civil wrongs arising out of** situations not necessarily covered by other areas of law such as contract law.

There are three principal types of tort:
- *non-intentional torts* In the case of non-intentional torts, the civil wrong or **harm** is not intended by the **tortfeasor** and liability results from the negligent manner in which the unintended act is carried out;
- *intentional torts* To be liable under the heading of intentional torts, the tortfeasor must intend to violate the plaintiff's rights, i.e. to do the tortious act. It is normally not necessary to show an intention to harm the plaintiff or that (s)he necessarily suffered **loss**, as a result of the tortfeasor **committing** the act in question;
- *strict liability torts* **Strict liability torts** concern loss caused by an **inherently** dangerous object for which the owner is liable, **regardless of whether** (s)he intended the harm or was negligent in the manner in which (s)he acted.

Non-intentional torts – negligence

Negligence is said to involve any kind of **behavior** whereby one party non-intentionally causes loss to another by acting without **reasonable care** for that person's safety.

In order to succeed in a negligence action, it is necessary to **meet** four basic conditions.
- *The existence of a duty of care* The plaintiff must **prove** that the defendant **owed** him/her a **duty of care**. A duty of care is said to exist if the defendant should have **foreseen** the risk of causing injury to the plaintiff. For example, the driver of a bus should foresee that if (s)he drives too quickly, (s)he might cause injury to his/her passengers; (s)he therefore owes a duty of care to those passengers.
- *Breach of the duty of care* **Thereafter**, the courts look to see whether the duty of care that the defendant owed the plaintiff has been **breached** by the behavior in question, i.e. if the bus driver drove the bus dangerously or too quickly. Whether the bus was driven

dangerously or not is decided by reference to the opinion of the reasonable man, taking all the circumstances of the case into account.

- *Loss* Once the existence of a duty of care and the breach of the duty have been established, it is then necessary to show that an injury or loss resulted **therefrom**, i.e. that the plaintiff suffered damage.
- *The existence of a causal link* Finally, it is necessary for the plaintiff to show the existence of a **causal link** between the loss suffered and the defendant's *unreasonable* behavior. Moreover, even if a causal link is established, it must not be too **remote**, i.e. that the link between the behavior and the harm caused must be sufficiently direct.

Normally the **burden of proof** is on the party **alleging** negligence, i.e. the victim of the behavior must show that the other party was negligent. However, under the doctrine of *res ipsa loquitur*, where the duty of care owed by one party to another is self evident, it falls on the defendant and not the claimant to demonstrate that the accident did not result from negligence. In this way, the **burden of proof** is **shifted** from the **claimant** to the defendant.

Even if the accident is said to result from the defendant's negligence, the defendant will not be considered **liable** for *all* the loss suffered by the claimant, if it is established that the plaintiff also contributed to the accident through his/her own negligence. Here we are referring to the notion of **contributory negligence**. For example, failure by the plaintiff to wear a safety belt in a car driven by the defendant will probably result in the plaintiff being considered as having contributed to any damage (s)he suffered in the event of a car **crash**. As proof of contributory negligence originally worked as a bar to the recovery of damages, an alternative doctrine referred to as comparative negligence was developed. Under the doctrine of comparative negligence, the amount of the injured party's compensation is based on a *comparison* between the negligent conduct of the defendant and that of the plaintiff.

Although traditionally the courts developed the area of tort law, the legislative branch has taken an increasing interest in the field over the last few decades. Consequently, in the United Kingdom and other common law countries, statutes have been adopted defining the negligence in certain defined circumstances. Generally, this law is referred to as statutory torts and, in the area of negligence, statutory negligence. For example, in the United Kingdom manufacturers of products intended for public use are strictly liable for any defects in their products. This is referred to as the law on **product liability**, and United Kingdom legislation in this area results from a European Union **directive**. One difference between statutory torts and common law torts is that actions brought under a statutory tort may benefit from a **statute of limitations period** longer than the three years normally applicable in the case of common law negligence actions.

VOCABULARY

Tort law – *normas de responsabilidade civil*

Redress – *reparação*
Civil wrong – *delito civil*
To arise out of – *decorrer de*
Harm – *dano*
Tortfeasor – *autor do delito civil*
Loss – *perda, dano*
To commit – *cometer*
Strict liability tort – *responsabilidade objetiva*
Inherently – *inerente*
Regardless of whether – *independentemente de*
Behavior – *comportamento*
Reasonable care – *cuidado razoável*
In order to – *afim de*
To meet (a condition) – *preencher (uma condição)/to meet a person – conhecer alguém*
To prove – *provar*
To owe – *dever (algo)*
Duty of care – *dever de cuidado*
To foresee – *prever*
Thereafter – *posteriormente*
To breach – *violar*
Therefrom – *assim, deste modo*
Causal link – *nexo de causalidade*
Remote – *remoto*
Burden of proof – *ônus da prova*
To allege – *alegar*
Res ipsa loquitur – *do latim "a coisa fala por si própria"*
Train track – *via férrea*
To shift the burden of proof – *inverter o ônus da prova*
Claimant – *requerente*
Liable – *responsável*
Contributory negligence – *negligência da vítima (ser parcialmente responsável)*
Crash – *acidente (de carro)*
Product liability – *responsabilidade sobre um produto defeituoso*
European Union directive – *diretiva da União Européia*
Statute of limitations period – *prazo de prescrição*

PART 1 – TEXT 1 – EXERCISES

1. Vocabulary test

Fill in the missing words using the vocabulary in Text 1

a) Pursuant to the doctrine of _____, the burden of proof is on the defendant where the cause of the accident appears _____.

b) There are three types of tort: _____ torts, intentional torts and _____ torts.

c) Once the plaintiff has established the existence of a duty of care, _____ of the duty of care and loss, he must then establish the existence of a_____ between the loss suffered and the defendant's behavior.

d) Even where the defendant is responsible for the accident, the _____ may be held partly liable for the damage he suffered under the heading of _____ negligence.

e) Although the area of tort law was above all developed by the common law courts, parliament has also created _____ torts in areas such as _____ liability.

f) In the area of intentional torts, it is necessary to show that the _____ responsible for the act, _____ the consequences of his act.

g) The function of tort law is to provide _____ for civil _____.

h) In the area of _____ torts, the defendant is considered liable for the damage caused, even if he did not intend it or was not _____ in the manner of his behavior.

2. Vocabulary test

Write sentences with the following pairs of words. Your sentence should demonstrate your knowledge of the relationship between the words

a) Behavior/loss
b) Burden of proof/defendant
c) Causal link/ remote
d) Statutory tort/case law
e) Tortfeasor/negligent
f) Duty of care/breach

3. Knowledge test

Each of the following statements is false; do you know why? Write a sentence stating why it is false

a) Whether the plaintiff contributed to the loss suffered is irrelevant, once the negligence of the defendant is established.

b) The area of negligence is made up entirely of the case law created by the common law courts.

c) Under the doctrine of *res ipsa loquitur* the plaintiff must establish that the defendant was negligent.

d) The causal connection between the plaintiff's action and the defendant's injury does not have to be direct and may even be remote.

e) As long as the defendant can show that (s)he was not negligent and did not intend to harm the plaintiff, (s)he will not be liable, even under the heading of strict liability torts.

PART 1 – TEXT 2 – MORE INFORMATION

Classification of torts

A tort is a wrong resulting from a breach of civil duty. Early in the development of the common law, the common law system **drew a distinction between** two types of **wrong**:

- wrongs of a general kind that were in fact crimes against society or the King. This law developed into the area of criminal law, the object of which is to **punish** an **offender**; and
- personal wrongs that were **left** to be **resolved** by the parties themselves. This second area, now known as civil law, includes areas of law such as contract law and tort law. Unlike criminal law, the **primary object** of **actions** in civil law is to **compensate** the **injured party** and not to punish the defendant.

Tort law was created by the common law courts to provide **redress** for civil wrongs **arising out of** situations not necessarily covered by contract. Under tort law, a person who has **committed** a civil wrong may be **sued** by any person who has **suffered damage** or **loss** as a result of their *tortious* act. The damage may be caused to either a person or to their property.

The common law recognizes three main types of tort:

- *non-intentional torts* In the case of **non-intentional torts** it is not necessary to **prove** that the defendant actually intended to cause the **harm** suffered by the plaintiff (also referred to as the claimant or complainant). It is only necessary to show that the plaintiff's act was negligent and that a reasonable person would have been **aware** or foreseen that his/her act might cause loss to the plaintiff in the circumstances;
- *intentional torts* In the case of intentional torts, it is necessary that the **tortfeasor** actually *intended* to do the tortious act. It is not necessary to show an intention to harm the plaintiff or that (s)he intended the plaintiff to suffer loss;
- *strict liability torts* **Strict liability torts** concern **inherently** dangerous objects or activities. For example, owning a factory that makes bombs or keeping a **vicious** dog on one's property. In such cases, the owner may be held **strictly liable** for all harm resulting from such activities, independent of whether (s)he was negligent or intended the consequences.

Non-intentional torts – negligence

Negligence is said to **involve** any kind of **behavior whereby** one party non-intentionally **causes** loss to another, by acting without reasonable care for their **safety**. Negligence applies to any type of negligent behavior, for example a person driving a car too quickly, or a shop owner who washes the floor of his shop and leaves the floor wet, causing a customer to **slip** and suffer injury.

The courts in the celebrated case of Donoghue v Stevenson developed the law of negligence.

Case study: Donoghue v Stevenson – 1932

Facts: The plaintiff was in a pub with a friend. The plaintiff's friend bought the plaintiff a **fizzy drink**. The drink came in an **opaque** brown glass bottle and consequently the plaintiff was unable to see the actual contents of the bottle. The plaintiff drank the ginger ale and found a **decomposed snail** at the bottom of the drink, after which she became ill. The plaintiff could not sue the bar owner or the **manufacturer** of the drink in contract law, as she had not actually bought the drink; it had been given to her by her friend and consequently she had no **privity of contract**. As a result, she sued the manufacturer in tort, asking the court to recognize a new area of tort law, based on the negligence of the manufacturer.

Held: In an important decision, the Court considered that manufacturers owe a duty of care to all people that they could or should **reasonably foresee** as coming into contact with their products. As a result, the Court held that although the plaintiff had no actual contractual relationship with the manufacturer, the latter nonetheless was held to owe her a **duty of care** and, since he had failed in that duty by allowing a decomposed snail into the plaintiff's drink, the plaintiff had a right to damages for any loss **occasioned** by this negligence.

According to the Court commenting on the general scope of the duty of care principle:

> *"You must take reasonable care to avoid acts or omissions which you can reasonably foresee would be likely to injure your neighbor. Who then is my neighbor? The answer seems to be – persons who are so closely and directly affected by my act that I ought reasonably to have them in contemplation as being so affected when I am directing my mind to the acts or omissions which are called into question."*

Thus, in order to succeed in a negligence action, it is necessary for the plaintiff to prove a number of things, namely the:
- *existence of a duty of care* The first thing that must be **demonstrated** when bringing an action in negligence is that there is an actual duty of care owed by the **alleged** negligent party to the victim. As we can see from the above case, under the tort of negligence every person is required to take reasonable care to avoid acts or omissions that they should reasonably foresee would be likely to injure another. This is referred to as the **neighbor principle**;
- *breach of the duty of care* Once it is established that there is an actual duty of care between the parties, the question of whether the duty of care has been **breached** is decided by reference to the **test** of the reasonable man. **Pursuant to** this test, if X is to be considered liable to Y for a negligent act:
  - it is necessary that *a reasonable man would consider that X should have foreseen, at the time of performing the act, that Y could have been injured by his/her behavior;* and that consequently
  - *X should have **altered** his/her behavior to **avoid** this **outcome**.*

The **scope** of the duty of care owed to the plaintiff **depends on** the circumstances of each case. For example, will X, the driver of a car travelling at 180 km/h who injures Y, a pedestrian standing at the side of the road, be liable for Y's injuries under the law of negligence? First, is there a duty of care between the parties? Yes, because all **motorists owe** a duty of care to other road users not to act in a way that will cause them injury. Second, was this duty breached? Normally yes, as a speed of 180 km/h is generally considered unreasonably fast. However, this **analysis** would **differ** if X was a **racing driver** and Y a **spectator** at a **racetrack**. In this case, although X always owes Y a duty to take care, the actual scope of the duty differs. In the context of a car race, X is no longer driving unreasonably fast and Y will probably be considered as having accepted a certain risk when deciding to attend the race. Indeed it is normally because of the speed that people go to watch car races. For this type of situation, the common law courts have created the rule: *volenti non fit injuria*, which can be translated to mean that *to the willing, no injury is done*. The rule applies where the claimant either expressly or implicitly consents to the risk of loss or damage. Thus, Y should have reasonably foreseen that an accident was possible and consequently (s)he and the other spectators are assumed to accept that risk of injury when going to see the car race. In other words, the scope of the duty of care can only be decided by reference to the facts of each case;

- *actual damage suffered* Once Y has established the existence of a duty of care and that this duty was breached by X, it is necessary that Y show that actual injury or loss resulted from X's behavior. In tort law, a person will only be compensated for loss actually suffered. If X drives too quickly but causes no actual loss or injury to Y, then Y has no case in negligence law against X;

- *causation and remoteness* Finally, it is necessary to show a sufficient **causal link** between the loss and X's behavior and that this link is not too remote. For example, X drives too quickly and has an accident in which Y breaks his/her leg. X will normally be liable to Y in negligence for the injury resulting from the negligent driving. However, what if, as a result of the accident, Y's leg is chronically **weakened** and five years later Y falls down a staircase and breaks his/her other leg? Is X also liable for the second injury to Y's other leg? Probably not, because the injury will be considered too remote. X will only ever be liable for the injuries that could have been **reasonably foreseen** by X at the time of driving the car too quickly. The negligent act has to be the proximate or primary cause of the injury. This requirement is sometimes referred to as legal causation.

The burden of proof and the notion of res ipsa loquitur

Where the duty owed by one party to another is self-evident and cannot be denied, the rule *res ipsa loquitur*[4] is considered to apply. As we have seen, the burden of proof is on the claimant to prove that the defendant owed the plaintiff a duty of care. However, under the *res ipsa loquitur* rule, where the:

---

[4]   Res ipsa loquitur can be translated as *the thing speaks for itself*, i.e. it is obvious.

- *element* causing the damage is shown to be under the control of the defendant; and
- accident is something that does not normally occur, if those who have control of the *element* take proper care;

it is for the defendant and not the claimant to demonstrate that the accident did not result from his/her negligence.

In this way the burden of proof is **shifted** from the **claimant** to the defendant, who must demonstrate that (s)he was not responsible for the loss suffered by the plaintiff. For example, a person is walking by a **warehouse** when a box falls out of a window and hits the person on the head. Normally the victim will be unable to prove that the box fell from the window because of negligence on the part of the owner of the building. After all, (s)he will not know why the box fell from the window. Thus, under normal negligence rules the victim would be unable to prove negligence, as (s)he will have no direct proof of an actual breach of the duty of care by the owner of the warehouse. However, under the doctrine of *res ipsa loquitur* the burden of proof will be reversed. Pursuant to this doctrine, given that:

- the box was under the control of the owner of the building;
- a box will not normally fall out of a window in the absence of negligence on the part of the owner of the building;
- the victim did nothing to cause the actual accident,

it will be for the owner of the building to prove that (s)he was not negligent, and not for the victim to establish the owner's negligence.

What do we mean by the notion of contributory negligence?

If it can be **shown** that the loss or harm would have been less serious if the claimant had not contributed to it by his/her own negligence, the **liability** of the defendant to the plaintiff may be **reduced**. This is referred to as the notion of **contributory negligence** or **comparative** negligence. For example, Y accepts a lift from X in his car. Upon entering the car, Y **refuses** to **comply** with X's suggestion that (s)he attach his/her safety belt and thereafter X, who drives negligently, has an accident **resulting** in Y suffering injury. Y may have a cause of action in negligence against X; however, the amount of damages Y will receive could be reduced **in proportion** to the contribution (s)he made to the loss, as a result of his/her refusal to wear a safety belt. Originally proof of contributory negligence worked as an absolute bar to the recovery of damages and continues to do so in some common law states. However, other common law jurisdictions have adopted a *modified* system of contributory negligence, whereby the plaintiff's negligence only acts as a bar to recovery of loss, if (s) he contributed to over 50% of the damage. Alternatively, some common law jurisdictions apply a system of comparative negligence, whereby the amount of the injured party's compensation is based on a *comparison* between the negligent conduct of the defendant and that of the plaintiff, one set off against the other. The formula for making this comparative calculation can be quite complicated.

Statutory torts

Although the area of non-intentional torts is dominated by the case law of the common law courts, the legislative power in most common law countries has also created **statutory torts** concerning areas such as **product liability**, **occupiers' liability** or employers' liability. In this way, manufacturers of products intended for public use are considered strictly liable for any defects in their products. In the same way, occupiers of land owe a clearly defined duty of care to people who come onto their land and employers are normally considered **vicariously liable** for damages caused by their employees. The law on product liability results from an **EU directive** in this area, **implemented** into UK national law. Indeed, tort law is a good example of how the United Kingdom's common law system, as a result of its membership of the European Union, is taking on characteristics normally associated with the civil law, i.e. an increasing emphasis is being placed on written law, necessarily leading to a reduction in the role of judge-made law.

Vocabulary

To draw a distinction between – *fazer distinção entre*
Wrong – *delito, dano*
To punish – *punir, sancionar*
Offender – *pessoa que violou a lei*
To leave something to be resolved – *deixar algo para ser resolvido*
Primary object – *objeto primário*
Action (in law) – *ação (jurídica)*
To compensate – *compensar*
Injured party – *parte lesada*
Redress – *reparação*
To arise out of – *decorrer de*
To commit – *cometer*
To sue – *processar*
To suffer damage – *sofrer um dano*
Loss – *perda, dano*
Non-intentional tort – *delito não intencional*
To prove – *provar*
Harm – *dano*
To be aware of – *estar consciente de*
Tortfeasor – *autor do delito civil*
Strict liability tort – *responsabilidade objetiva*
To suffer – *sofrer*
Inherently – *inerente*
Vicious – *perverso, mau*
Strictly liable – *objetivamente responsável*
To involve – *implicar*
Behavior – *comportamento*
Whereby – *pelo qual, através do qual*
To cause – *causar*

Safety – *segurança*
To slip – *escorregar*
Celebrated case – *caso judicial célebre*
Fizzy drink – *bebida espumante*
Opaque – *opaco*
To be ill – *estar doente*
Decomposed snail – *caracol em decomposição*
Manufacturer – *fabricante*
Privity of contract – *eficácia do contrato*
To reasonably foresee – *prever de forma razoável*
Duty of care – *obrigação de cuidado*
To be occasion by (to be caused) – *ser ocasionado por, ser causado por*
To demonstrate – *demonstrar*
Alleged – *alegado*
Neighbor principle – *princípio do próximo*
To breach – *violar*
Test – *teste*
Pursuant to – *segundo, de acordo com*
To alter – *alterar*
To avoid – *evitar*
Outcome – *resultado, consequência*
Scope – *escopo, alcance*
To depend on – *depender de*
Motorist – *motorista*
To owe – *dever (algo)*
Analysis – *análise*
To differ – *discordar*
Racing driver – *piloto de corrida*
Spectator – *espectador*
Race track – *circuito de corrida*
Causation – *causalidade*
Remoteness – *distanciamento*
Causal link – *nexo de causalidade*
To be weakened – *ser enfraquecido*
Burden of proof – *ônus da prova*
Res ipsa loquitur – *do latim "a coisa fala por si própria"*
To shift – *inverter, mudar de lugar*
Claimant – *requerente*
Warehouse – *armazém*
To be shown – *ser mostrado*
Liability – *responsabilidade*
To be reduced – *ser reduzido*
Contributory negligence – *negligência da vítima (ser parcialmente responsável)*
To refuse – *recusar*
To comply – *obedecer, preencher (uma condição)*
To result – *resultar*
To be in proportion – *estar em proporção a*
Statutory tort – *regime de responsabilidade civil de origem legislativa*

Product liability – *responsabilidade sobre um produto defeituoso*
Occupiers' liability – *responsabidade dos ocupantes uma propriedade sobre terceiros que entrarem na propriedade*
Vicarious liability – *responsabilidade de um superior hierárquico sobre as ações de seus subordinados*
EU directive – *diretiva da União Européia*
To implement a directive – *aplicar uma diretiva*

PART 1 – TEXT 2 – EXERCISES

1. Definitions

Write a sentence defining each of the following terms – one sentence per term

a)   Neighbor principle
b)   Res ipsa loquitur
c)   Remoteness
d)   Statutory tort
e)   Reasonable foreseeability
f)   Liability
g)   Causal link
h)   Tortfeasor

2. Sentences

Write sentences with the following pairs of words demonstrating your knowledge of the relationship between them

a)   Causality/loss
b)   Tortfeasor/Liable
c)   Vicarious liability/employee
d)   Strict liability/intentional tort
e)   Redress/harm
f)   Loss/remoteness
g)   Negligence/neighbor principle
h)   Duty of care/foresee
i)   Res ipsa loquitur/burden of proof

3. Fill in the missing words

Using the vocabulary in Text 2, fill in the missing words

a)   Under the law of negligence, each person owes his/her neighbors a _____ of care not to do any act which they should reasonably _____ will harm them.
b)   Tort law seeks to compensate victims of a civil _____, where they have suffered _____ as a result of the acts of another.
c)   Under the doctrine of _____ the burden of proof in a negligence action will be shifted from the plaintiff to the _____.
d)   The function of civil law is to _____ injured parties, whilst the role of criminal law is to _____.

e)   In cases involving _____ liability, an employer will be considered responsible for the acts of his/her _____, as they are considered to be under his/her control.

4. Knowledge test

The following questions may be answered in writing or by way of discussion

a)   In your legal system, is there a distinction drawn between different types of torts?

b)   Is there a case law-orientated system of negligence in your system or is it dealt with under the heading of statutory law?

c)   Should intoxicated people be allowed to escape their responsibility under tort law? How are the intoxicated treated under common law tort law?

d)   How is the issue of strict liability dealt with in your legal system?

PART 2 – QUICK LOOK GRAMMAR REVISION

Asking questions continued ......

1. Using WHAT + DO = asking questions about types of activity

WHAT + DO is used to ask questions about a specific activity:
- **What does** Jane **do** every morning? She goes to work.
- **What is** Jane **doing**? She is working.
- **What did** Jane **do** yesterday? She went to work.
- **What is** Jane going to **do** tomorrow? She is going to go to work.
- **What will** Jane **do** tomorrow? She will go to work.
- **What would** Jane like to **do** tomorrow? She would like to go to work.
- **What does** Jane want to **do** this evening? She wants to work.
- **What should** Jane **do** about her career? She should work harder.

2. Using WHICH = offering a choice

WHICH is used when the person asking the question wants the party to whom they are addressing the question to make a choice between the alternatives that are being offered:
Frank: Can I borrow your car?
Jane: I have two cars, **which car** do you want? **Which one** do you want? **Which** do you want?[5]
Frank: The black one.

Which is used not only with singular nouns but also with plural nouns:
Jane: I love those earrings ......
Frank: **Which** earrings do you want me to buy? **Which** ones do you want me to buy? **Which** are you going to buy?
Jane: None, I already bought them ......

---

[5]   Which car do you want? /Which one do you want?/Which do you want? – each of these three sentences means the same thing.

3. Using WHAT KIND OF = asking for specific information

WHAT KIND OF asks for precision concerning something specific that is found within a general category:

What kind of cooking do you like?

I like French cooking/ Italian cooking/Chinese cooking/Spanish cooking ......

The general category is cooking and the question seeks specific information as regards what specific category of cooking is liked:

French, Italian, Chinese and Spanish are all specific types of cooking and thus are suitable responses to the question ......

Note:

WHAT KIND OF may be followed by a singular noun, a plural or a noun that can be either:

What kind of flower is that?
What kind of flowers are those?
What kind of fruit is that?
What kind of sheep is that?

PART 2 – GRAMMAR EXERCISES

1. Using WHAT + DO ......

Make sentences using WHAT + DO (appropriate tense) to ask a question in the context of the answer to the question......

What are you doing right now?
I am drafting a contract.

a) _____ last night?
I worked.

b) _____ tomorrow?
I am going to be in court.

c) _____ tomorrow?
I want to go to visit a client in prison.

d) _____ tomorrow?
I need to work on my presentation to the court.

e) _____ tomorrow?
I would like to take a day's holiday.

f) _____ to improve my English.
You should spend a year working in London.

2. Using WHICH ......

Complete the sentence using WHICH or WHAT in the context of the answer ......

a) I have two cases, _____.
I want that one.

b) _____.
I bought a car last Saturday.

c) _____.
Barbara borrowed that file.

d) Tell me _____.
I want that one.

e) _____.
London was the city I liked the most when I visited Europe.

3. Using WHAT KIND OF......

Answer the questions in complete sentences ......

a) What kind of law do you like the best?
b) What kind of music do you like?
c) What kind of books do you like to read?
d) What kind of law firm would you like to work in?
e) What kind of car would you like to drive?

PART 3 – AUDIO AND ORAL – LISTENING AND SPEAKING

Comprehension

Listen to the following conversation, make notes of all the relevant facts and then answer the questions below. If you have trouble understanding, follow the conversation while also reading the text.

Conversation between James, a solicitor and Frank, his client

James: "Hello Frank, you look as if you have had an accident."
Frank: "Yes I did."
James: "What happened, were you run over by a bus?"
Frank: "Yes, well it was a car actually."
James: "Why don't you tell me all about it?"
Frank: "Well, it was last Friday."
James: "Night or day?"
Frank: "Pardon?"
James: "Did the accident happen during the night or the day?"
Frank: "The night, well late evening, at around 7:30 ... 8:00pm."
James: "What happened exactly?"
Frank: "Well it was after work on the building site, as usual on a Friday myself and some mates went for a couple of drinks."
James: "A couple?"
Frank: "Well three or four."
James: "Three or four?"
Frank: "Well five actually."
James: "So you went for a drink after work and had five pints of beer, correct?"
Frank: "Yeah five pints and a whisky as well."
James: "OK six drinks; over what amount of time?"
Frank: "What?"

James: "Over what amount of time did you consume the six drinks? I want to find out how drunk you were."

Frank: "I wasn't drunk at all … it was the other guy's fault."

James: "OK, tell me about the other guy."

Frank: "So as I said I went for a few drinks after work, at around 7:30 – 8:00pm I decided it was about time to go home to the missus."

James: "Your wife?"

Frank: "Yeah my wife, well my girlfriend really but we've been together for about four years now off and on."

James: "So you left the pub to go home to your girlfriend; what happened next?"

Frank: "Yeah I left the bar, went out of the main door, slipped on the footpath, fell off the footpath onto the road and was run over by a car."

James: "And what do you want me to do?"

Frank: "What! Take an action for negligent driving against the owner of the car; look at the condition I am in."

James: "Was the other guy driving particularly fast?"

Frank: "I don't know, to be honest I don't remember so well."

James: "OK so … you fell on the road and had an accident. Sorry to tell you Frank but I can't do anything for you. It is true that people owe each other a duty of care not to harm each other under the law of negligence. But you my friend were completely drunk; you fell over and caused an accident. You'd better hope that the other guy does not bring an action against you!"

Frank: "Some solicitor you are…."

James: "Just telling it as it is Frank, the best advice I can give you is to cut down on the booze after work!"

PART 3 – AUDIO COMPREHENSION – EXERCISES

1. Comprehension

From the notes you have taken, answer the following questions

    a)   What happened to Frank when he left the bar?

    b)   Is Frank married?

    c)   Was the driver of the car driving too quickly?

    d)   How many drinks in total did Frank have?

    e)   What was Frank doing before he went for a drink?

    f)   What does Frank want James to do?

2. Speaking practice

In the following series of conversation couplets, develop suitable responses to the questions asked

    a)   James: "So Frank, what happened to you?"
            Frank: "_____"

    b)   James: "How many drinks did you have?"
            Frank: "_____."

    c)   James: "Frank are you married?
            Frank: "_____"

d) James: What happened to you when you left the bar?"
   Frank: "_____."
e) James: "What time was it when you left the bar?"
   James: "_____."
f) James: "On what day did the accident happen?"
   James: "_____."
g) Frank: "So James, do you think I can bring an action against the driver of the car?"
   James: "_____."
h) Frank: "What do you advise me to do James?"
   James: "_____."

3. Speaking practice continued ......

Create five other conversation using in each couplet at least one word from the vocabulary found in Part I, Text 1 or Text 2

4. Speaking practice continued ......

Listen to the suggested replies and repeat

a) James: "So Frank what happened to you?"
   Frank: "I was run over by a car."
b) James: "How many drinks did you have?"
   Frank: "Well let me see, I had about five beers and a whisky."
c) James: "Frank are you married?
   Frank: "No, but my girlfriend and I have been together for three to four years."
d) James: "What happened to you when you left the bar?"
   Frank: "After I left the bar I slipped on the footpath and was run over."
e) James: "What time was it when you left the bar?"
   Frank: "I guess it was around 7:30 – 8:00 pm."
f) James: "On what day did the accident happen?"
   Frank: "The accident occurred on a Friday."
g) Frank: "So do you think I can bring an action against the driver of the car?"
   James: "I'm afraid you have no right of action against the driver of the car."
h) Frank: "What do you advise me to do?"
   James: "My advice to you Frank is to cut down on the booze!"

5. Associated questions

Discuss the following questions

a) In your country, would Frank have a solution in law?
b) What is the law on civil responsibility and negligence in your jurisdiction?
c) Do you think that the common law system encourages litigation by imposing a general duty of care at all levels of society?

d) Does case law play too great a role in the area of negligence? In your opinion, should this area be the subject of more statutory interference?

PART 4 – TRANSLATION EXERCISES

When carrying out the translations it is not necessary to translate directly word for word; rather the emphasis should be on translating the sense of the text. Language is not directly interchangeable and so direct translations do not always convey the meaning in the text.

Translate the following texts from English to Portuguese

A. What is the scope of the duty of care? – Smolden v White, 1997

Facts: Smolden was a rugby player. While participating in a game of rugby he was injured. Smolden alleged that the referee, Mr. White, had failed in his duty to referee the match correctly and it was as a result of this that he was injured. Consequently he sued White in negligence seeking compensation for the damage he had suffered.

Held: In the Court's opinion, every referee owes a duty of care to the players in the games he referees to ensure that the rules of the game are applied correctly. In failing in this duty, White was responsible to Smolden for the damage he suffered during the game.

B. When does an intervening event break the chain of causation? – Regina v. Blaue, 1975

The defendant stabbed an 18 year-old woman and punctured her lung. At the hospital, the victim was told she would need a blood transfusion to save her life, but refused this as contrary to her religious beliefs. As a direct result of her decision, she died the next day.

Held: In the opinion of the Court, those who use violence against other people must take their victims as they find them. This principle applies to the mental as well as the physical characteristics of the victim. The Court considered that the defendant was guilty of murder, even though the victim died as a direct result of her decision to refuse a blood transfusion; a decision linked to her extreme religious beliefs.

Translate the following texts from Portuguese to English

A. A noção de dever de cuidado se estende a um choque nervoso? McLouglin contra O'Brian, 1983

Fatos: Um dos filhos da autora da ação foi assassinado e seu marido e segundo filho ficaram feridos em um acidente causado pela negligência do réu (O'Brian). A autora não foi testemunha do acidente e estava em sua casa quando foi informada que sua família se envolveu em um acidente. Ela se dirigiu imediatamente ao hospital e sofreu um choque nervoso quando soube que sua filha estava morta. Ela processou o réu por negligência e exigiu compensação pelos danos sofridos devido ao choque nervoso que sofreu.

Julgado: Na opinião do Tribunal o réu poderia ter razoavelmente previsto que os resultados provocados pela sua negligência provocariam um choque nervoso na autora, e que portanto ele era responsável pelo dano que ela sofreu.

B. Os direitos de uma vítima de um delito persistem mesmo após a sua morte?

Uma das regras fundamentais do Common Law é a regra de que uma ação pessoal morre junto com a morte da vítima de um delito. Portanto, se X morrer devido à negligência de Y, o direito de perpetrar uma ação pelos danos sofridos cessa com a sua morte. Entretanto, o poder legislativo tomou certas medidas para evitar os efeitos negativos desta regra. De acordo com a lei dos acidentes fatais de 1976, os parentes próximos da pessoa morta podem processar Y no nome de X caso consigam provar que eles sofreram perda pecuniária devido ao acidente. Entretanto, se Y também morrer no acidente, nenhuma ação contra o seu patrimônio é possível.

C. Como devemos compreender a noção de responsabilidade pelos atos de terceiros?

Se X, empregado de Y, ferir Z ao exercer seu trabalho de forma negligente, Z pode perpetrar uma ação tanto contra X que contra Y. Y é responsável por Z pelos atos de X. Entretanto, é importante que se compreenda duas situações:
* Quando X é um empregado de Y; e
* Quando X é empregado por como prestador de serviço independente.

A regra geral é que o empregador é responsável por todos os atos de seus empregados no exercício de seus trabalhos. No caso do prestador de serviço independente, o empregador só será responsável pelos atos que ele expressamente ou implicitamente o ordenou a fazer.

PART 5 – ADVANCED READING

Donoghue v Stevenson

Donoghue v Stevenson is one of the most important cases in the common law, as it established the modern common law concept of negligence.

Facts

Mrs. Donoghue and her friend went to a local cafe in Scotland. Mrs. Donoghue's friend ordered and paid for a drink. After both had consumed some of the drink, which came in an opaque brown glass bottle, they poured the remainder of the bottle into their glasses and discovered the remains of a decomposed snail. Mrs. Donoghue subsequently claimed to suffer from gastroenteritis and to be in a state of shock. She decided to bring an action against the manufacturer of the drink, Mr. Stevenson; however, not having bought the drink, she had no relationship with him in contract, i.e. she had no privity of contract, and so had to bring her action under a different area of law. She consequently sued the manufacturer under the tort law of negligence, claiming that he had breached the duty of care he owed her. The concept of *duty of care* existed in tort law at the time Mrs. Donoghue was bringing her case. However, it was limited to cases where there was a special relationship between the parties or where the product causing the damage was particularly dangerous. Thus, in order to win her case, Mrs. Donoghue had to convince the courts to expand the notion of duty of care to ordinary consumers. Her lawyer argued that any manufacturer placing a product for human consumption onto the market should be liable for any damage caused, where it is established that (s)he failed to exercise reasonable care to ensure it was fit for human consumption. This, her lawyer argued, was especially true if the product was packaged in such a way that the consumer was unable to see the contents.

Decision of the House of Lords

The Court based its decision on a *negative* application of the Christian principle of *do unto others as you would have them do unto you*[6], what the Court referred to as the *neighbor principle*. Applying this principle to the area of negligence, the Court considered that each person in society must take reasonable care to avoid acts or omissions which, they might reasonably foresee, would be likely to injure their neighbor. As to who is *a neighbor*, the Court said it is any person directly affected by the act of another, where such person should be within the reasonable contemplation of the person committing the act in question. Finally, as to when a person should be in the reasonable contemplation of another, the Court said the question should be decided by reference to the opinion of the reasonable man.

The effect of this decision was to provide protection for people affected by the careless acts of others. Such protection was becoming increasingly necessary in an industrialized consumer society with increased interaction between people. Moreover, this right was deemed to exist in circumstances where there is no contractual relationship between the parties.

To succeed in a negligence action, it is necessary that the plaintiff demonstrate that: a) there is a duty of care between the parties; b) the duty of care was breached; c) the plaintiff suffered damage; and d) there is a sufficient causal link between the act of the defendant and the loss suffered by the plaintiff.

---

[6] Matthew 7 :12, the Bible.

Chapter five

INTENTIONAL AND STRICT LIABILITY TORTS

Intentional torts and the notion of strict liability

Intentional torts arise when the victim can show that the defendant actually intended to **commit** the tort in question. On the contrary, liability under the heading of **strict liability torts** arises not from the defendant's **tortious act** but rather from the **harm** resulting from the defendant's decision to keep in his/her **possession** or use an inherently dangerous *thing*. It is the possession of this element, rather than the defendant's actions concerning same that is deemed to create the liability. Consequently, the defendant is considered strictly liable even where (s)he has done nothing wrong and intended no harm to occur.

Intentional torts

There are many different types of intentional tort.
- *Trespass to the person* Examples of **trespass to the person** include **assault** and **battery**. Assault is the tort of intentionally putting someone **in fear of** being attacked, without physically touching him/her. Battery is the tort of deliberately **hurting** another person physically, i.e. actually touching them. Another intentional tort to the person is **false imprisonment**, which involves **confining** a **victim** in a place, which they are **prevented** from leaving.
- *Trespass to land* **Trespass to land** involves entering and/or placing products on the land of another. **Dumping rubbish** in a neighbor's garden is an example of trespass to land.
- *Trespass to goods* **Trespass to goods** involves the intentional interference with the goods or possessions of another. In order to establish trespass to goods, one must show that the **tortfeasor** interfered with goods owned by another and that he intended to do so.
- *Nuisance* Nuisance can be divided into **public nuisance** and **private nuisance**. Public nuisance is an **unlawful act** or **omission interfering** with the **safety** or comfort of the general public. An example of public nuisance is a **factory** that **emits nasty odors**. Private nuisance involves private **acts**, such as a man allowing his dog to enter his **neighbor**'s property, **causing damage** to his garden.
- *Defamation* Defamation is the tort of making **untrue statements** about others. The tort of defamation only offers **redress** for the actual damage caused by an untrue statement and does not **seek** to

compensate the plaintiff for the actual making of the statement in itself. In an action for defamation, damages can be awarded for loss of earnings, impairment of reputation and also for emotional suffering linked to the making of the statement.

Strict liability torts

In the case of strict liability torts, a person will be held strictly responsible for any harm caused by inherently dangerous elements under their control. The notion of strict liability is only applied to things or activities that are **inherently** dangerous, such as **storing explosives** or using **hazardous materials**. Interestingly, it is not necessary to prove that the defendant was negligent or intended to cause harm in order to succeed in a claim under the **heading** of strict liability.

However, to establish **liability** it is necessary to demonstrate that the dangerous *thing* that caused the harm:
- is inherently dangerous; and that
- the defendant brought the element onto his property.

Defenses to actions in tort

Defenses regarding intentional and non-intentional torts include the defense of necessity or of self-defense. Necessity is said to occur when the tortfeasor had no choice but to act in the way (s)he did because of the circumstances surrounding his/her act; for example, trespassing on the land of another in order to avoid a dangerous animal. Liability can also be avoided if the party committing the **alleged tort** can show that (s)he had been given permission by law to act in the way (s)he did or that (s)he was requested or allowed by the plaintiff to act in the way (s)he did.

There is no real **defense** to strict liability torts except to show that the damage resulted from an **Act of God** or that the damage resulted from the act of a stranger **over whom** the owner had no **control**.

Vocabulary

To commit – *cometer*
Strict liability tort – *responsabilidade objetiva*
Tortious act – *ato ilícito*
Possession – *posse*
Harm – *dano*
Trespass to the person – *delito contra a pessoa*
Assault – *tentativa de agressão*
Battery – *violência física*
In fear of – *ter medo de*
To hurt – *ferir*
False imprisonment – *sequestro, cárcere privado*
To confine someone – *confinar alguém*

Victim – *vítima*
To prevent – *prevenir, impedir*
Trespass to land – *invasão de imóvel*
To dump rubbish – *jogar lixo fora*
Trespass to goods – *provocar danos a bens móveis de terceiros*
Tortfeasor – *autor do delito civil*
Public nuisance – *perturbação da ordem pública*
Private nuisance – *perturbação a terceiros*
Unlawful act – *ato ilegal*
Omission – *omissão*
To interfere – *incomodar*
Safety – *segurança*
Factory – *fábrica*
To emit – *emitir*
Nasty odor – *odor nauseabundo*
Act – *ato*
Neighbor – *vizinho*
To cause – *causar*
Damage – *dano*
Untrue statement – *declaração falsa*
Redress – *reparação*
To seek – *procurar*
Inherently – *inerentemente*
Heading – *a título de*
To be liable – *ser responsável*
To store explosives – *estocar explosivos*
Hazardous material – *produtos perigosos*
Defense – *defesa*
Act of God – *força maior*
Over whom – *sobre quem*
Control – *controle*
To request – *pedir*
To perform – *executar, quitar um dever*
Alleged tort – *pretenso delito*

PART 1 – TEXT 1 – EXERCISES

1. Vocabulary test

Fill in the missing words using the vocabulary in Text 1

a) The tort of _____ provides compensation in cases where untrue statements are made and seeks to offer _____ for the damage caused by the statement.

b) Tort law recognizes three types of trespass: trespass to _____ , trespass to the_____ and trespass to goods.

c) The area of strict _____ torts applies to activities that are _____ dangerous.

d) A person will be considered liable for their _____ acts, if it can be shown that they intended to _____ a tort.

e) _____ nuisance differs from private nuisance, as it is necessary to demonstrate that the acts of the defendant had a negative effect on the general public. On the contrary, to establish _____nuisance, it is necessary to show _____ resulting from a private act.

f) To prove _____ under the heading of strict liability torts it is necessary to show that the _____ in question was under the control of the defendant.

g) Trespass to the _____ can involve either _____ or actual battery.

h) _____ a person in a place and preventing them from freely leaving that place gives rise to liability for _____.

2. Vocabulary test

Write sentences with the following pairs of words. Your sentence should demonstrate your knowledge of the relationship between the words

a) Trespass to the person/battery
b) Nuisance/damage
c) Defamation/statement
d) Hazardous/control
e) Assault/victim
f) Tortfeasor/liable

3. Knowledge test

Each of the following statements is false; do you know why? Write a sentence stating why it is false

a) The tort of assault involves one party hitting another person.

b) Liability arises under strict liability torts, once it has been proved that the element that caused the damage is dangerous, even if it was not under the defendant's control.

c) Even if a statement is true, if it harms another person an action under the heading of defamation may possibly exist.

d) Even if the damage results from an Act of God or from the act of a stranger, a party will be considered strictly liability, if the damage resulted from a dangerous element.

e) Even if the tortious act was necessary, a defendant cannot escape liability under the tort of trespass to land.

PART 1 – TEXT 2 – MORE INFORMATION

Intentional torts and notion of strict liability

If a **victim** can **show** that the defendant actually **intended** to **commit** a tort, **instead of bringing an action** in negligence, the plaintiff's claim can be **pursued** as an intentional tort. Thus, unlike with negligence, intent must be shown. **Alternatively**, if the victim is unable to establish either an intention or negligence as regards the act of the defendant, in certain limited circumstances an action may be brought under the heading of **strict liability**. To succeed in an action under this **heading**, it is necessary to show that the **harm** resulted from the defendant possessing an *element* so dangerous that (s)he is responsible for any resulting damage, **despite** the **lack** of intention or negligence on his/her part.

Intentional torts

A **plaintiff** wishing to **prove** that the defendant committed an intentional tort must demonstrate:

- *intent* That the **tortfeasor** intended to commit the tortious act in question. It is not always necessary to show that the defendant *intended* the actual consequence;
- *causation* Unlike the tort of negligence, remoteness and causation play a far less important role in the case of intentional torts. Normally, it is only necessary for the plaintiff to show that *but for the tortious act* the injury would not have occurred, i.e. the injury would not have occurred if the defendant had not acted in the way (s)he did. It is not necessary to show proximate cause as in the case of negligence, i.e. that the act was the primary *cause* of the loss suffered.

There are a number of different *common law* intentional torts.

- ***Trespass to the person*** Trespass to the person can take a number of different forms:
  - *assault* Assault is the tort of intentionally **causing apprehension** of immediate harmful or offensive contact as regards another, but where *no physical contact* occurs. For example, **wielding** a knife in front of a person, putting them in fear for their safety but not actually hitting or stabbing them, will be **construed** as assault;
  - *battery* Battery is the tort of intentionally hitting or causing offensive *contact* with a person or something closely related to them, for example, knocking their hat of their head. Unlike assault, battery involves actual physical contact with the other party. Obviously, both assault and battery are also offences under criminal law and often an action based on one follows the other;
  - *false imprisonment* False imprisonment involves **confining** the victim to a place which they are **prevented** from leaving. In some common law jurisdictions, for example in the United States, there is an exception to the false imprisonment rule under what is known as the *"shopkeeper's privilege"*. Under this exception, a shopkeeper is allowed to **detain** a suspected **shoplifter** on **store property** for a reasonable period of time, in order to **investigate** whether they have stolen goods;
  - *intentional infliction of emotional distress* (IIED) The tort of IIED was created to complement the tort of assault. IIED will occur where a person intentionally causes another emotional distress, provoking **nervous shock** as a result. This is not the easiest of torts to prove, as the courts are suspicious of trying

to measure mental suffering in financial terms. Thus in order to **succeed** in a claim for IIED, the behavior complained of must be truly **outrageous**. For example, **maliciously** ringing a person to inform them that their **spouse** has died in a road accident.

- Trespass to land
  Trespass to land involves entering and/or **placing** products on the land of another. For example, **dumping** rubbish in a neighbor's **garden** is an example of trespass to land. As volition to commit the tortious act must be present, no liability will attach in cases of **sleepwalking**.

- Trespass to **goods/chattels**
  Trespass to goods involves the intentional interference with the goods of another. In order to establish liability under the heading of trespass to goods, it is first necessary for the plaintiff to demonstrate ownership of the goods in question. **Thereafter**, the plaintiff must show that the tortfeasor interfered with the goods. The area of trespass to goods is governed in the United Kingdom by the *Torts (Interference with Goods) Act, 1977*. Where trespass to the goods results in the goods being kept and used by another, the defendant will instead be the subject of an action in **conversion**. A classic example of conversion occurs when a person finds the lost property of another and decides to keep it, rather than returning it to its owner. In such a case, one is clearly doing more than simply interfering with ownership, as is the case with trespass to goods. Conversion is also a crime under criminal law (criminal conversion), i.e. the defendant will be liable under both criminal and civil law. Criminal conversion can be distinguished from theft, as there is no need to show intent to deprive the owner of possession of the good in question.

- Nuisance
  Nuisance involves interference with a person's land or **servitudes**[7]. Unlike trespass, which is **actionable per se**, in the case of nuisance it is necessary to prove actual loss resulting from the nuisance, in order to receive compensation. Nuisance can be divided into **public nuisance** and **private nuisance**:
  - public nuisance is an unlawful act or **omission interfering** with the safety or comfort of the general public. An example of public nuisance is a factory that **emits nasty poisonous odors**. Public nuisance may be prosecuted by the state as a crime, **whilst** members of the public may also **sue** the owner of the nuisance in tort;
  - private nuisance involves an act, the **scope of which** has only limited effect. For example, a man allowing his dog to enter his neighbor's property, leading to the garden being damaged. In such a case, it is possible for the owner of the property to sue the owner of the dog. However, normally it is necessary to prove that the event has happened on a number of occasions before it becomes **actionable**. Also, it should be **emphasized** that the

---

[7] A servitude is an obligation that runs with land, i.e. a right over land.

courts consider that, in modern life, the applicable principle should be *live and let live* and thus **overly** sensitive people are not protected under this tort.

- Defamation

  Defamation is the general term used to describe the act of making untrue statements about others. Other terms exist to describe specific types of defamation, for example: **calumny, libel,** and **slander.** Calumny and slander are used for spoken, transient words and libel for written, permanent words. The **tort of false light** also exists and involves the making of a statement, which although true, creates a false impression and was intentionally made with this purpose in mind. As regards actions in defamation, if the defendant can show that the statement was true, then the action will not be successful. Above all, defamation seeks to offer redress for the damage to reputation caused by an untrue statement, and not to compensate for the actual making of the statement. In an action for defamation, damages can be awarded for loss of earnings, impairment of reputation and also for emotional suffering linked to the making of the statement. An action in false light exists to compensate people for damage to their feelings, emotional well-being or dignity as opposed to their reputation.

Strict liability torts and the rule in Rylands v Fletcher

In the case of strict liability torts, a person is held strictly responsible for what occurs, **regardless of whether** they have been negligent or intended the harm. To establish liability under this heading, it is necessary to demonstrate that the:
- *element* was inherently dangerous; and
- defendant brought the element onto his property.

In such circumstances, the defendant is deemed to keep the element at his/her own risk, for example a loaded gun, and is considered strictly liable for any harm that results **therefrom**. Once these criteria are satisfied, the victim does not need to prove that the tortfeasor acted with intent or that (s)he was negligent. Neither does it matter if the defendant took precautions regarding the dangerous element, or indeed that (s)he had good faith. The defendant is considered strictly liable for any harm that results. As we have seen, strict liability is only applied to things or activities that are inherently dangerous, such as storing **explosives,** using **hazardous materials** or keeping a vicious dog on one's property.

The courts, in the case of Rylands v Fletcher developed the notion of strict liability torts for the first time.

Case study: Rylands v Fletcher, 1868

Facts: In this case Mr. Rylands employed an **independent contractor** to construct a reservoir on his land. Rylands carried out the works in order to have sufficient water to be able to **power a mill** that he owned. The construction of the reservoir made use of an old **mine shaft** on Rylands' property. Unknown to Rylands the mineshaft was linked to his neighbor's mine, owned by a Mr. Fletcher. Fletcher's mine was still producing **ore**.

When Rylands filled the newly constructed reservoir, the water travelled through the old mine shaft located on Ryland's property and **flooded** Fletcher's mine. Fletcher sued Rylands for the damage caused to his mine. *Held*: Despite the fact that the damage was not considered to result from any negligence on the part of Rylands or that he clearly did not intend the harm that was caused, the **latter** (Rylands) was nonetheless liable for the damage to Fletcher's mine. The liability was held to result from the inherently dangerous character of storing large quantities of water by Rylands on his land. In the opinion of the court:

"a person who for his own purposes brings onto his land anything likely to cause damage if it escapes, must keep it at his own peril and is liable for any and all damage that is a natural consequence of its escape and which damage is foreseeable by the land owner."

Defenses to actions in tort

As regards the torts of negligence and intentional torts, a number of different defenses exist.

- *Agreement* Perhaps the best defense to an **allegation** of **tortious conduct** is to demonstrate that the person indicated that they were in agreement with the behavior in question. This defense is often referred to as *volenti non fit injuria*, i.e. no injury can be done to a **willing person**. Under this heading come injuries that occur in the context of playing a sport. For example, an injured boxer would not be able to claim for injuries (s)he suffered, unless his/her opponent acted outside the rules of the sport and hit him/her with a chair for example. In the same way, as we have already seen, a spectator at a **car rally** would normally be considered as having accepted the danger resulting from being close to cars driven at high speeds.
- *Necessity* If the defendant can show that the behavior complained of was necessary or unavoidable, then the complainant's action will not succeed. For example, if a prisoner on **hunger strike** is **force fed** against their **will**, (s)he will be unable to bring an action in tort on the grounds of trespass to the person. The prison authorities will be able to successfully argue that in order to save the prisoner's life it was necessary to act as they did.
- *Mistake* Although as a general rule mistake is not considered a defense in law, where the mistake in question is reasonable, the courts may be willing to accept a defendant's **plea** on these grounds. For example, if a trespasser to land reasonably believed that the land in question belonged to him/her, the actual owner of the land would not be able to successfully sue the defendant **on grounds of** trespass to land.
- *Self-defense* At all times, a person is entitled to use *reasonable* force to defend themselves against **unwarranted attacks**, whether intentional or non-intentional. However, it is required that the party acting in self-defense act in proportion to the attack to which (s)he is subjected.
- *Statutory authority* Frequently, statutes may **authorize** either a **government agency** or a private party/company to **carry out works**

for the benefit of society in general; for example the building of a public road. Normally, the authority granted in these circumstances is conditional on the work being carried out in such a way as to ensure that third parties experience only reasonable loss.

There is no real defense to strict liability torts, except to show that the damage resulted from an act of God or the act of a stranger over whom the owner had no control. Of course, as with intentional and non-intentional torts, if it can be shown that the complainant had previously agreed to the conduct in question, the defendant will not be considered liable.

VOCABULARY

Victim – *vítima*
To show – *mostrar*
To intend – *ter a intenção de*
To commit – *cometer*
Instead of – *ao invés de*
To bring an action – *propor uma ação judicial*
To pursue a claim – *prosseguir com uma ação ou pedido judicial*
Alternatively – *alternativamente*
Strict liability – *responsabilidade absoluta*
Heading – *a título de*
Harm – *dano*
Element – *elemento*
Despite – *apesar de*
Lack – *ausência, falta*
Plaintiff – *demandante, requerente*
To prove – *provar*
Tortfeasor – *autor do delito*
To inflict – *infligir*
Trespass to the person – *delito contra a pessoa*
Assault – *tentativa de agressão*
To cause – *causar*
Apprehension – *apreensão*
To wield – *empunhar*
To be construed as – *ser interpretado como*
Battery – *violência física*
False imprisonment – *sequestro, cárcere privado*
To confine someone – *confinar alguém*
To prevent – *prevenir, impedir*
Shopkeeper's privilege – *privilégio do comerciante*
To detain – *deter*
Shoplifter – *ladrão de loja*
Store property – *depenências da loja*
To investigate – *investigar*
Stolen – *furtado*

Intentional infliction of emotional distress – *imposição intencional de dano ou sofrimento emocional*
Nervous stress – *estresse nervoso*
To succeed – *obter êxito*
Outrageous – *ultrajante, revoltante*
Maliciously – *maliciosamente*
Spouse – *esposa, esposo*
Trespass to land – *invasão de imóvel*
To place – *colocar*
To dump – *jogar fora, descarregar*
Garden – *jardim*
Sleepwalking – *sonambulismo*
Goods, chattels – *bens*
Thereafter – *posteriormente*
Conversion – *malversação, dilapidação*
Nuisance – *perturbação*
Servitude – *servidão*
To be actionable per se – *ser passível de ser processado judicialmente*
Public nuisance – *perturbação da ordem pública*
Private nuisance – *perturbação a terceiros*
Omission – *omissão*
To interfere – *incomodar*
To emit – *emitir*
Nasty odor – *odor nauseabundo*
Poisonous – *tóxico, venenoso*
Whilst – *enquanto, ao passo que*
To sue – *processar*
Scope – *escopo, alcance*
Of which – *do qual*
Actionable – *contestável*
To emphasize – *enfatizar*
Overly – *excessivamente*
Calumny – *calúnia*
Libel – *difamação (por escrito)*
Slander – *difamação (oral)*
Tort of false light – *delito que consiste em criar intencionalmente uma falta impressão sobre uma pessoa*
Regardless of whether – *independentemente de*
Therefrom – *daí*
Explosive – *explosivo*
Hazardous material – *produtos perigosos*
Independent contractor – *prestador de serviço independente*
To power a mill – *alimentar um moinho*
Mineshaft – *mina*
Ore – *minério*
To flood – *inundar*
The latter – *este último*
Allegation – *alegação*

Tortious conduct – *comportamento delituoso*
Willing person – *pessoa que consente*
Car rally – *corrida de rally*
Hunger strike – *greve de fome*
To be force fed – *ser alimentado à força*
Will – *vontade*
Plea – *pleito*
On grounds of – *sob o argumento de*
Unwarranted attack – *ataque não provocado*
Statutory authority – *autoridade legislativa*
To authorize – *autorizar*
Government agency – *autoridade pública*
To carry out works – *realizar obras*
So empowered – *desta forma habilitado*

PART 1 – TEXT 2 – EXERCISES

1. Definitions

Write a sentence defining each of the following terms – one sentence per term

- a) Tortfeasor
- b) Slander
- c) Servitude
- d) Nuisance
- e) Trespass
- f) Libel
- g) Tortious behavior
- h) Conversion

2. Sentences

Write sentences with the following pairs of words demonstrating your knowledge of the relationship between them

- a) Trespass/battery
- b) Shopkeeper's privilege/false imprisonment
- c) Chattels/conversion
- d) Hazardous/liability
- e) Tortious/defendant
- f) Libel/untrue
- g) Statutory tort/common law tort[8]
- h) Nuisance/public
- i) Necessity/defense

---

[8]   A statutory tort is a tort created by law adopted by the legislature; common law tort is a tort created by the common law courts.

3. Fill in the missing words

Using the vocabulary in Text 2, fill in the missing words

a) The tort of _____ imprisonment involves _____ a person in a place against their _____.

b) The tort of trespass to _____ is established when it can be shown that the defendant entered onto the property of another without _____.

c) A plaintiff may bring an action in _____, where the defendant has _____ him/her by speaking in an untrue way.

d) Public _____ involves acting in a way that causes disturbance to the public in general, whilst _____ nuisance occurs where only an individual is disturbed by the behavior.

e) The tort of false _____ involves making a statement that gives a false impression but which is nonetheless _____.

4. Knowledge test

The following questions may be answered in writing or by way of discussion

a) Is the area of tort law developed primarily by the courts or by statute law in your jurisdiction?

b) Does the notion of strict liability exist in your country?

c) Is it practical to try and compensate people for emotional suffering? Is it not too personal and too random to be capable of consistent measurement in financial terms?

d) How is the problem of defamation dealt with in your jurisdiction?

PART 2 – QUICK LOOK GRAMMAR REVISION

Asking questions continued ......

1. Using WHOSE

Whose is used to ask about possession:
- **Whose** notes are those? They are Jane's notes.
- **Whose** pen is this? It is Frank's pen.
- **Whose** book did you borrow? I borrowed John's book.

Note:

Who's and *Whose* have the same pronunciation:
   Who's is a contraction of WHO IS
   Whose enquires as to who is in possession

Note:

When using **whose** the person asking the question may omit to mention the noun if its meaning is clear:
   That is a lovely book. **Whose** is it?

2. *Using HOW, HOW OFTEN, HOW FAR, HOW LONG*

HOW

HOW is used when enquiring as to the manner in which something was done, or with an adjective/adverb to define the extent of the situation described by that adjective/adverb:

To describe the manner in which something was done (with a verb):
- **How** did you become a lawyer specialized in litigation?
- **How** did you get to work this morning?
- **How** do you have so many clients?

More general uses of how:
- **How** do you spell miscellaneous?
- **How** do you do?
- **How** is it going?

Used with an adjective or adverb:
- **How tall** are you?
- **How old** is your wife?
- **How long** will it take?
- **How quickly** can you draft the contract?

HOW OFTEN

HOW OFTEN poses a question from the point of view of frequency:
- **How often** do you go on holiday?
- **How often** do you see your client?

Note:

How often can be replaced by the words *how many times*
How many times is often qualified by using the words a day/a week/a month/a year:
Example: How many times a week do you go to the gym?

Note:

Normally when responding to a question asking **how often** or **how many times**, the answer involves use of a frequency expression such as:
Question: **How often/many times** do you go to the gym?
Answer: **Every** day, **every other** day[9], **once** a day, **twice** a week, **three times** a week, **a lot, occasionally, hardly ever, not very often, never, almost never, too often**

HOW FAR

How far is used to ask questions about distance:
- **How far** is it from London to New York?
- **How far** is it to London?

---

[9]   Every other day means every second day.

- **How far** do you live from your office?

Note:

How far can be replaced by the questions such as *how many + a measurement of distance:*
   How many kilometers to New York from London?

Note:

When replying to a question using how far or how many kilometers/miles, the sentence will often be structured as follows:
   It is (distance = 3,500 miles) **from** London **to** New York.

HOW LONG
HOW LONG asks for information concerning length of time:
- **How long** does it take to travel to London from here?
- **How long** does it take you to get to your office in the morning?
- **How long** was your trip?

Note:

How long can be replaced by the questions such as *how many + a measurement of time:*
   How many hours does it take to travel from London to New York?

PART 2 – GRAMMAR EXERCISES

1. Using WHOSE ......

Make sentences using WHOSE to ask a question in the context of the answer to the question......

   <u>*Whose* book *is* this</u>?
   It is Angela's book.

a) _____ these?
   They are Jack's files.
b) _____ that?
   It's Jenny's file.
c) _____ those?
   They are John's notes.
d) _____ this?
   It is Frank's briefcase.
e) _____ car ____?
   Tom's, I borrowed it last night.

2. Using HOW ......

Make sentences using HOW to ask a question in the context of the answer to the question............

a) _____?
I take the bus to get to work.

b) _____?
I speak English very well.

c) _____?
I walked to the office today.

d) _____?
I usually drive at 55 miles an hour.

e) _____?
To become a lawyer I studied law at university and then sat the bar exam.

3. Using HOW OFTEN......

Make sentences using HOW OFTEN to ask a question in the context of the answer to the question............

a) _____?
I go to the movies once a week.

b) _____?
I read the newspaper every day.

c) _____?
I go swimming every morning.

d) _____?
I go out to eat every Friday evening.

e) _____?
I am never late for work.

4. Using HOW FAR......

Make sentences using HOW FAR to ask a question in the context of the answer to the question............

a) _____?
It is 30 miles from Manchester to Liverpool.

b) _____?
New York is very far away.

c) _____?
The nearest bank is five blocks away[10].

d) _____?
I live about four miles from the University.

e) _____?
I go jogging for five miles every day.

---

10   A block is a measurement of urban planning and refers to a block of buildings in a city built on a grid system.

5. Using HOW LONG ......

Make sentences using HOW LONG to ask a question in the context of the answer to the question.............

a) _____?

It takes me twenty minutes to walk to my office.

b) _____?

It took John two days to draft the contract.

c) _____?

The meeting should last for three hours.

d) _____?

I should be finished in court by 17:00 hrs.

e) _____?

It took me eight hours to fly to New York.

PART 3 – AUDIO AND ORAL – LISTENING AND SPEAKING

Comprehension

Listen to the following conversation, make notes of all the relevant facts and then answer the questions below. If you have trouble understanding, follow the conversation while also reading the text.

Conversation between solicitor John Swift and his client David Thompson

John: "Hello David, so what brings you here?"

David: "Hello John, I'm being sued by one of my neighbors and need your help."

John: "That's what we are here for David; so tell me what happened?"

David: "Mmmn it is a little bit embarrassing."

John: "What have you done now David?"

David: "You see I'm being accused of trespass to land."

John: "Well did you?"

David: "Did I what?"

John: "Trespass on someone else's land or not?"

David: "Well yes and no."

John: "Yes and no; there should be only one answer to that question David; either yes or no, not yes AND no!"

David: "OK the answer is yes; but I did not know I was doing it."

John: "Ah I see, you did not know it was your neighbor's land, is that it?"

David: "I didn't even know I was there, if the truth be told."

John: "What do you mean you did not even know you were there? This is becoming a little weird David."

David: "Well, it is a little weird because she is also threatening to sue me for assault."

John: "Oh no David what have you done? At what time of the day did this happen?"

David: "Apparently it was three o' clock in the morning but to be frank I don't remember anything."

John: "Oh David, were you by any chance drinking?"

David: "No, I was asleep."

John: "What do you mean you were asleep?"

David: "The reason I don't remember anything is because I was asleep. I went to bed that night at around 10pm as I do every night. The next thing I know I am in my neighbor's living room half dressed and she is screaming at me to get out."

John: "And did you?"

David: "Of course, I ran out of there if you must know, ran back into my own bed and actually fell back to sleep immediately. The next thing I know the doorbell is ringing and the police are at the door. They asked me what happened and I explained. That was over a week ago, I just heard from them yesterday and apparently they have decided not to bring any criminal proceedings against me, as they believe I was sleepwalking."

John: "But your neighbor does not, is that it?"

David: "Well, I don't know what she believes, but I met her this morning and she just said that she was going to make me pay by bringing an action in tort law for trespass. Trespass to what I asked her and she said trespass to land and she might also bring an action for assault. Frankly, she is very scary!"

John: "OK David I understand. The first thing to do is to do nothing until you hear formally from her solicitor. It sounds to me as if she is just trying to scare you. But just so that you know, trespass is an intentional tort. That means that to be liable for trespass you have to actually intend to trespass. Obviously if you were asleep, this is not the case. So as long as we can show that you were sleepwalking, there will be no case against you. Did the police believe you were sleepwalking? It seems that they did."

David: "Yes they did. I gave them a report from my doctor. You see I have a history of sleepwalking and have been treated for it in the past."

John: "OK so David. It looks like you have nothing to worry about. Why not go home, forget about it and try to get a good night's sleep!"

PART 3 – AUDIO COMPREHENSION – EXERCISES

1. Comprehension

From the notes you have taken, answer the following questions

- a) What has David's neighbor threatened to do?
- b) What was the opinion of the police?
- c) When did David go to his neighbor's house?
- d) What proof has David that he was sleepwalking?
- e) What is the opinion of David's solicitor John?
- f) What advice does John give David at the end of their meeting?

2. Speaking practice

In the following series of conversation couplets develop suitable responses to the questions asked

- a) John: "Hello David, so what did you do?"
     David: "_____"
- b) John: "At what time did it happen David?"

David: "_____."
c) John: "What do the police think?"
    David: "_____"
d) John: "What is your neighbor suing you for exactly?"
    David: "_____."
e) John: "Were you awake when you entered your neighbor's property?"
    David: "_____."
f) John: "Have you a medical record concerning your problem with sleepwalking?"
    David: "_____."
g) John: "Were you drinking that evening?"
    David: "_____."

3. Speaking practice continued ......

Create five other conversation couplets using in each couplet at least one word from the vocabulary found in Part I, Text 1 or Text 2

4. Speaking practice continued ......

Listen to the suggested replies and repeat

a) John: "Hello David, so what did you do?"
    David: "Well I don't really remember, but my neighbor says I sleepwalked onto her property."
b) John: "What time did it happen at David?"
    David: "Apparently it was three o'clock in the morning."
c) John: "What do the police think?
    David: "They think I was sleepwalking and have decided not to bring proceedings against me."
d) John: "What is your neighbor suing you for exactly?"
    David: "Trespass to land and she may also sue me for assault."
e) John: "Were you awake when you entered your neighbor's property?"
    David: "No, I was sleepwalking."
f) John: "Have you a medical record concerning your problem with sleepwalking?"
    David: "Yes, I have a medical report from my doctor confirming that I sometimes sleepwalk."
g) John: "Were you drinking that evening?"
    David: "No, I was not drinking; in fact I went to bed early, at around 10pm."

5. Associated questions

Discuss the following questions

a) Would David be guilty of trespass to property in your country?
b) What is the law on trespass to property and trespass to the person in your jurisdiction?
c) Is there such a thing as strict liability torts in your country?

d)   What would be your advice to David, applying the law of your country?

PART 4 – TRANSLATION EXERCISES

When carrying out the translations it is not necessary to translate directly word for word; rather the emphasis should be on translating the sense of the text. Language is not directly interchangeable and so direct translations do not always convey the meaning in the text.

Translate the following texts from English to Portuguese

A. The difference between nuisance and trespass to land

The torts of nuisance and trespass to land are similar and it is sometimes difficult to distinguish between the two. Nonetheless fundamental differences exist between them. First, trespass to land is actionable *per se*, i.e. there is no need to prove actual damage or loss. In contrast, to succeed in an action of nuisance, it is necessary to demonstrate that actual loss resulted from the act deemed to be a nuisance. Trespass involves actual entry onto the land of another, whilst nuisance does not necessarily involve any actual physical trespass on the land of another. Indeed, the nuisance can be and often is created on the defendant's land, but its negative effect then travels to the plaintiff's land. For example, if a neighbor plays very loud music at night. Finally, trespass only needs to occur once to be actionable. On the contrary, in the case of nuisance it is normally necessary to demonstrate that the nuisance has a repetitive character, if one is to succeed.

B. Limits on the volenti non fit injuria defense (to a willing person, injury is not done) – Bowater v Rowley Regis Corporation, 1945

Facts: The plaintiff, a city employee, was ordered by his foreman to use a horse which had been dangerous in the past. The employee protested at the request but the manager insisted. Some weeks later the horse bolted and the plaintiff suffered personal injuries. The city council claimed that the employee should fail in his action for damages, on the basis that he had agreed to use the horse.

Held: With regard to the doctrine *volenti non fit injuria*, a man cannot be said to be truly *willing* unless he is in a position to choose freely, and freedom of choice requires the absence of any feeling of constraint. Such freedom of choice is not normally found to exist in an employer/employee relationship.

C. The notion of "shopkeeper's privilege"

Many common law jurisdictions recognize the notion of *shopkeeper's privilege*. Under this rule, a shopkeeper may detain a suspected shoplifter on store property for a reasonable period of time. However, a shopkeeper may only do so, where he can show reasonable cause that the person detained has in fact committed or attempted to commit theft of store goods. Moreover, shopkeepers who have detained innocent shoppers under this heading have been sued under the heading of false imprisonment. Consequently, this right cannot be compared to the right of police officers to detain suspected criminals.

Translate the following texts from Portuguese to English

A. *A provocação de sofrimento emocional*

A provocação de sofrimento emocional é um delito controverso, seja ele causado por negligência ou intencionalmente. Entretanto, a provocação de sofrimento emocional por negligência é a mais controversa das duas. Como situação passível de provocar ação judicial, o sofrimento emocional existe na maioria dos países do common law, mas é interpretado de forma restritiva. O conceito subjacente deste tipo de ação é o de que todos nós possuímos o dever legal de agir com um cuidado razoável para evitar danos emocionais a terceiros. Este delito deve ser contrastado com o delito de provocação intencional de sofrimento emocional, na medida em que não há necessidade de provar a real intenção de provocar sofrimento.

B. *Difamação e defesas*

Nos países do common law, para que haja sucesso na ação de difamação, deve ser comprovado que a suposta declaração difamatória é falsa. Conseqüentemente, provar que a declaração contestada é verdadeira é geralmente a melhor defesa contra uma ação por difamação. Declarações feitas de boa-fé e sob a razoável crença de que são verdadeiras são geralmente tratadas da mesma forma que as declarações verdadeiras; entretanto, o tribunal pode colocar em dúvida o caráter razoável da convicção ou crença em questão. A noção de imunidade, tal como a imunidade parlamentar, permite a exclusão de todo o tipo de ação por difamação na maioria dos países do common law. Ademais, regras especiais são aplicadas no caso de pessoas públicas. Na maior parte dos sistemas jurídicos, para que uma pessoa pública ganhe uma ação por difamação, a declaração deve ter sido publicada sob circunstâncias que indicam que o autor sabia da falsidade da declaração e que foi imprudente com relação a verificação de sua veracidade.

C. *Ameaça e agressão – quando é que são autorizados?*

Para que alguém não seja condenado por ameaça ou por agressão, o réu deve demonstrar que possui um privilégio, ou seja, que ele possui o direito de ameaçar ou de "tocar" o requerente, como, por exemplo, para se proteger. O privilégio será considerado como existente para oficiais de justiça a partir do momento que for demonstrado que a força física usada foi necessária para a realização de uma prisão legal. A grande maioria das jurisdições do common law autorizam o recurso a um certo nível de coação física ou de violência para proteção de bens contra roubo ou dano. Na realidade, algumas jurisdições dos Estados Unidos possuem leis extraordinariamente amplas que permitem o uso significativo ou até mortal de força para prevenir o furto de bens. Por fim, em diversos países do common law os pais são legalmente autorizados a aplicar força física razoável para disciplinar seus filhos.

PART 5 – ADVANCED READING

The relationship between contract law and tort law

As we have seen, the common law is divided into two main areas: civil law and criminal law; contract law and tort law make up part of civil law. Although both are part of the same category of law, there are a number of differences between tort law and contract law. The primary difference is the fact that tort law imposes what can be considered public duties, whilst contract law is concerned with private duties. By this is meant that if one does not expressly or impliedly enter into a contract, no contractual rights or duties will exist; i.e. contractual rights and duties result from party choice, i.e. a deliberate choice of a party. In tort law, rights and duties arise not from personal choice but are imposed by the state and result from a person's being a member of a society.

Tort law is said to protect *in rem* whilst contract law protects *in personam*. By *in rem* rights we mean rights that people enjoy generally, and which are incumbent or imposed on others generally. On the contrary, *in personam* rights are rights that are only enjoyed individually. For example, in the area of negligence, the duty imposed is based on the general standards of society, underwritten by the requirement of foreseeability. Under the neighbor principle, every person is expected to behave in a reasonable manner and not to act in a way that they can reasonably foresee may harm another. It is for this reason that the role of damages in the law of negligence is different from that in contract law. In negligence, a person is required to pay damages to another as a result of breaching the standard of care defined in the context of foreseeable harm; damages are only payable for foreseeable loss. As a result, no liability will result from negligence, if:

- the loss is not foreseeable, i.e. *fault* is defined by foreseeability; and further
- there is no actual loss inflicted as a result of the violation of the right in negligence.

Thus, in negligence the *fault* or *violation* must first be foreseeable to be actionable, and the subsequent extent of liability is also measured by foreseeability; foreseeability consequently plays a dual role. On the contrary, in contract law foreseeability is not required to establish fault. The doctrine of frustration provides a limited exception in cases of non-foreseeable fault, but foreseeability is not an integral element in establishing fault under contract law. Indeed, it was for this reason that it took the common law so long to establish the doctrine of frustration and why its application is *subjective* rather than *objective* in character based on the notion that the contract, because of the frustrating event, is no longer what the parties envisaged.

Further, damages in contract law are not as extensive as in tort law. In contract law they are limited to restoring the person to the position they would have been in, had the contract been performed. This is because liability in contract law is not based on the notion of a public duty and thus has no real basis in morality. Consequently, a party is only owed what they are due under the terms of their contract, as the contract defines the extent of their rights and the parties are free to deal with the issue of non-performance in the contract document. Under the law of negligence, a party may attempt to exclude liability through warning the other party of existing dangers, but is only allowed to exempt responsibility subject to overriding public interest needs. Finally, the parties in contract law are required to mitigate their loss, whilst no such duty exists under the law of negligence. As we have seen, contributory or comparative negligence doctrines do exist, but these are aimed more at the moment the breach occurs rather than at the post-breach stage, which is the case with mitigation in contract law.

Chapter six

CRIMINAL LAW IN COMMON LAW COUNTRIES

Common law criminal procedure

In the common law world, criminal law procedure operates by way of an **adversarial system**. Consequently, there is competition rather than cooperation between the State, referred to as the prosecution, and the defense, referred to as the **accused/defendant**.

The criminal process will be discussed under a number of different **headings**, namely:
- police powers and the rights of the **suspect** after **arrest**;
- **charging** the suspect;
- the subsequent prosecution before the courts.

The police and rights of the suspect after arrest

As in most countries, the police represent the first step in common law criminal procedure. In common law jurisdictions, the police may arrest a suspect when there is a **reasonable suspicion** that (s)he has **committed a crime**. Clearly, the police are not required to have enough **evidence** to secure a **conviction** when making an arrest, but they should have some evidence justifying the arrest. Arrest normally occurs after the issuing of an **arrest warrant**[11] by the courts; however, the police are obviously free to arrest any person who is actually committing a crime in front of them without such a warrant. Once in police **custody**, the suspect or **detainee** is interviewed by the police. In some common law countries such as the United Kingdom all **interviews** at detention stage must be **recorded** and, **prior to** and during **any such** interview, the suspect is entitled to receive free legal advice.

Charging the accused

If the police consider that they have sufficient evidence against someone, they will formally charge him/her with an **offence**. From the moment the suspect is formally charged, (s)he is referred to as the accused or the defendant, depending on the jurisdiction. Offences in the common law system are classified as:
- *minor offences, summary offences, non-indictable offences,*

---

[11] Sometimes also referred to as a *bench warrant*. However, a bench warrant is a specific type of arrest warrant, usually issued after an accused has failed to appear in court.

      misdemeanors These four different terms are effectively interchangeable and refer to offences of limited seriousness such as drunkenness, speeding offences etc. They are referred to as minor offences to signify their *minor* character. One uses the descriptive of **summary** offences, referring to the fact that such crimes are tried by a judge/magistrate sitting alone without a jury, i.e. they are tried **summarily**; and finally they are called non-indictable offences because such offences do not benefit from a pre-trial preliminary hearing, referred to as an **indictment** hearing[12];

- *felonies/indictable offences* These are more serious offences such as **murder**, **manslaughter**, **rape** or **armed robbery** and in most common law jurisdictions benefit from a preliminary hearing prior to the actual trial;

- *triable either way offences* This is a classification relied on in the UK, which refers to offences that fall somewhere in between the above two categories. Such offences can be tried as either non-indictable offences or indictable offences depending on the choice of the parties.

The prosecution

In the United Kingdom, once the defendant is charged, the police will send the file to the **Crown Prosecution Service** (CPS). It is the CPS and not the police that decide **whether** to prosecute the accused or not. Should the CPS decide not to bring a prosecution, private individuals may **exceptionally** bring a prosecution in their place. This is a relatively rare event and is to a certain extent **frowned upon** by the authorities. To successfully bring a private prosecution, it is necessary to **demonstrate** to the courts that the CPS was clearly incorrect in coming to its decision not to prosecute the accused.

The courts

For criminal matters there are two main **courts of original criminal jurisdiction** in the United Kingdom: the Magistrates' Court and the Crown Court. The Magistrates' Court deals with minor or summary offences. More serious offences, referred to as indictable offences, are heard before the Crown Court. As we have seen, there exists a third category of offence, referred to as triable either way offences, which are hybrid offences somewhere in between minor offences and indictable offences as regards their seriousness, for example **theft**. Triable either way offences may be tried summarily in the Magistrates' Court or by judge and jury in the Crown Court. Although the accused has an automatic right to have such an offence tried by judge and jury in the Crown Court, if (s) he wishes to have the matter tried summarily before the Magistrates' Court, the latter Court has to confirm its willingness to take the case. **Appeal lies** from the Magistrates' Court to the Crown Court or where the appeal concerns a question of law, to the High Court. Appeals from the Crown Court lie to the Criminal

---

[12] An indictment hearing occurs in the case of serious offences requiring the state to establish that it has sufficient evidence against the accused (referred to as a prima facie case) to justify bringing the accused for trial.

Court of Appeal. There is a time limit of twenty-one days to **file** or **lodge** an application for appeal.

VOCABULARY

Adversarial system – *sistema acusatório (principal procedimento do common law, baseado no princípio da confrontação entre as partes)*
Accused – *acusado*
Heading – *título, cabeçalho*
Suspect – *suspeito*
To arrest – *prender*
To charge – *acusar*
Reasonable suspicion – *suspeita razoável (ocorre quando um certo número de provas e indícios justificam a consideração de alguém como suspeito)*
To commit a crime – *cometer um crime*
Evidence – *evidência, prova*
Conviction – *condenação (sentence – pena)*
Arrest warrant – *mandado de prisão*
Custody – *custódia*
Detainee – *detento*
Interview – *interrogatório*
To record – *gravar*
Prior to – *anteriormente a*
Any such interview – *este tipo de interrogatório*
Offence – *infração*
Accused – *acusado*
Minor/summary/non-indictable offence – *delito de menor potencial ofensivo*
Summary – *sumário*
Summarily – *sumariamente*
Indictment hearing – *audiência preliminar para estabelecer a existência ou não de elementos suficientes que justifiquem o início de uma ação judicial*
Indictable offence/felony – *crime grave*
Murder – *assassinato, homocídio doloso*
Manslaughter – *homocídio preterdoloso*
Rape – *estupro*
Armed robbery – *assalto à mão armada*
Theft – *furto (petty theft – pequenos furtos)*
Triable - either-way offence – *crimes que podem ser julgados tanto pelo Magistrates Courts quanto pela Crown Court*
Crown Prosecution Service – *promotor, Ministério Público*
Whether – *se*
Exceptionally – *excepcionalmente*
To frown upon – *desaprovar*
To demonstrate – *demonstrar*
Court of original criminal jurisdiction – *tribunal de primeira instância em material penal*

An appeal lies from the Magistrates Court to the Crown Court – *uma decisão do Magistrates Court pode ser objeto de um recurso perante o Crown Court*
To file/lodge an appeal – *interpor um recurso*
To lodge a complaint against someone – *prestar queixa contra alguém*

PART 1 – TEXT 1 – EXERCISES

1. Vocabulary test

Fill in the missing words using the vocabulary in Text 1

a) The decision to bring a prosecution is brought by the _____ in the United Kingdom and by the office of the _____ in the United States.
b) Crimes such as murder are considered to be _____ and are brought to trial before the _____.
c) In cases involving felonies, the _____ in the US has the right to a trial by _____ made up of twelve non-interested parties.
d) In the case of a _____ offence, the accused can either opt for trial before the Crown Court or a _____ hearing before the Magistrates' Court.
e) Appeal _____ from the Magistrates' Court to the Crown Court and from the Crown court to the _____.
f) Before they arrest a suspect, the police must have _____ that (s)he committed the _____ they are investigating.
g) When in detention, the _____ has the right to see a _____.
h) When _____ the accused, the police must record the _____.
i) The _____ that the police collected, clearly proved that the accused _____ the crime.
j) After interviewing the suspect the police decided to formally _____ him with the offence.

2. Vocabulary test

Write sentences with the following pairs of words. Your sentence should demonstrate your knowledge of the relationship between the words

a) Common law/adversarial system
b) Detention/solicitor
c) Suspect/defendant
d) Triable either way offence/Crown Court
e) Charge/accused
f) Murder/Magistrates' Court

3. Knowledge test

Each of the following statements is false; do you know why? Write a sentence stating why it is false

a) After interviewing the accused, the police will decide whether to prosecute him or not.

b)   Offences such as speeding are triable either way offences and may be tried either in the Magistrates' Court or the Crown Court.

c)   Appeal lies from the Magistrates' Court to the Court of Criminal Appeal.

d)   The police may arrest a suspect at any time but must have a reasonable suspicion that (s)he committed the offence if they are to charge him/her.

e)   There is a six-month time limit for filing appeals from the Crown Court to the Court of Criminal Appeal.

f)   Only the CPS can prosecute someone accused of a crime.

PART 1 – TEXT 2 – MORE INFORMATION

Common law criminal procedure

Criminal law in the common law system differs fundamentally from criminal law in civil law jurisdictions. In common law countries, unlike in some civil law countries, there is no **investigating judge** representing the interests of all the parties involved. Instead, in the common law there is a clear contest between the **prosecution**, i.e. the state, and the **accused**. As the system is **adversarial**, there is little or no cooperation between the prosecution and the defense, with some **discovery of documentation** occurring **prior to** the trial.

The criminal process can be discussed under a number of different **headings,** namely the:
- police and the rights of the **suspect** after **arrest**;
- **charging** of the suspect;
- rights of the accused or **defendant** after being **charged**;
- prosecution; and
- courts.

The police and rights of the suspect after arrest

The police represent the first step in common law criminal procedure. In the United Kingdom, the police force is divided into different independent local police forces. In the United States, different police forces are found at **local, state** and **federal level**. Criminal procedure is similar in most common law countries and for the purposes of the present discussion it is proposed to limit our study to the system in place in the United Kingdom.

In the United Kingdom, the police may arrest a suspect when they have **reasonable suspicion** against him/her. The police are not required to have sufficient **evidence** to secure a **conviction** when making an arrest, but they must have some evidence establishing the possible guilt of the accused, i.e. a reasonable suspicion. Arrests are normally carried out **on foot of an arrest warrant** issued by a magistrate. Once arrested, the suspect or **detainee** is interviewed by the police and at this stage (s)he is said to be **in detention** or in police **custody**. The suspect **has not as yet** been charged with an offence by the police. **Interviews** at detention stage must be recorded and, prior to and during any such interview, the suspect is entitled to receive free legal advice from a lawyer, without the police being present. In the United Kingdom, this advice is given by a solicitor. If required to participate in an **identification parade**, also referred to as a **line-up**, the suspect is also allowed to have his/her solicitor present to ensure that the proper procedure is followed.

As well as having the right to a lawyer, the suspect is also **entitled** to contact a friend or a family member to inform them of his/her arrest. However, this right may be refused during the initial 36 hours following arrest, where the offence involved is a serious one, such as murder or rape, and where there is a **legitimate fear** that communication with the outside world may lead to interference with the **investigation**. Once the first six hours of detention have come to an end, any further detention must be **authorized** by a **senior police officer**. For most **offences**, there is a 24-hour limit to detention, which may be extended by another 12 hours in exceptional cases, if the offence is a serious one. Even more exceptionally, it is possible for the police to apply to the courts for a further 96-hour extension; otherwise the suspect must be either released or charged with a specific offence. In many common law countries, if the accused is suspected of terrorism, even longer detention periods are possible.

Charging the accused

If the police consider that they have sufficient evidence against someone, they will formally charge him/her with an offence. When charging a suspect, the police must **fill out** a **charge sheet** which lists the offences the accused is thought to have committed. Once charged, the suspect or detainee becomes known as the accused or the defendant (different common law jurisdictions use different terms; England & Wales speak of the *defendant*, in Scotland the term used is *accused* or *the panel*). If the offence is a minor matter such as a road traffic offence, known as a **minor, non-indictable or summary offence**, the police, instead of arresting and charging the accused, will instead **serve** the accused with a **summons** through the post. The summons is a legal document requiring the accused to appear or to go before the Magistrates' Court on a certain date.

The rights of the accused after being charged

When in detention, there is a universal right to free legal aid. However, once the suspect is charged, access to free legal aid is **means tested**. When a suspect **relies on** free legal aid at detention stage, the solicitor chosen for him/her comes from a list of local solicitors **drawn up** under the **duty solicitors' scheme, made up of** solicitors who have indicated their availability for this type of work. Such solicitors are called *duty solicitors* and their inclusion on the duty solicitor's list is no indication of their ability in the area of criminal law. Consequently, if the accused is not satisfied with his/her duty solicitor when in detention, (s)he may request another solicitor, once (s)he has been formally charged.

Once charged, the defendant has a right to **bail**. Under established **case law**, bail may only be refused if the prosecution establishes that there are **substantial grounds** for believing that the accused may either:

- not appear for trial;
- **commit** further **offences** when out on bail; or
- interfere with witnesses if given bail.

Bail, if granted, may be **unconditional**, i.e., the granting of the bail is not subject to the accused fulfilling any conditions. Alternatively, it may be made conditi|onal on the accused providing the court with either a:
- **surety**, i.e. a promise or guarantee by a reputable third party to pay a fixed amount of money to the court, if the defendant does not appear for trial; or
- **security, whereby** the defendant actually pays a fixed amount of money to the court, which money is returned to him/her once the bail period comes to an end and (s)he has respected the conditions attached to granting the bail.

At the time of arrest and of being charged, the accused will have no contact with a barrister. All legal advice is given by solicitors. Moreover, should the crime be a minor offence, tried before the Magistrates' Court, a solicitor will probably also represent the accused in court. Normally, it is only where the offence involved is a serious crime, referred to as an **indictable offence**, that the services of a barrister will be considered necessary. In this event, the solicitor will collect all the evidence, including police and medical reports, charge sheet, witness statements etc. together in a file, referred to as a **brief**, and then **instructs** or **briefs** the barrister selected to represent the client in court.

The prosecution

Once the defendant is charged, the police will send the file to the **Crown Prosecution Service** (CPS). It is the CPS, and not the police, who will decide on the basis of the evidence whether to prosecute the accused or not. At this **stage**, the CPS may alter the charges made by the police against the accused, frequently reducing them to make the securing of a conviction more probable. If they decide to proceed with the case, the CPS will, in the case of an indictable offence, **appoint** a barrister to represent the state; however, if the matter concerns a minor offence, they will normally use a lawyer working for the CPS to represent them. **Increasingly**, the police will **liaise with** the CPS to take advice as to whether they should charge the accused. Should the CPS decide not to bring a prosecution, private individuals may decide to bring a prosecution in their place. This is a relatively rare event and is to a certain extent **frowned upon** by the authorities. To successfully bring a private prosecution, it is necessary to demonstrate to the court that the CPS is incorrect in coming to their decision not to prosecute the accused.

The courts

For criminal matters there are two main **courts of original criminal jurisdiction**, namely the Magistrates' Court and the Crown Court. The Magistrates' Court deals with what are referred to as minor, summary or non-indictable offences (referred to as a misdemeanor in the US). These different terms are interchangeable and

refer to offences of limited seriousness such as drunkenness, speeding offences etc. They are referred to as *minor offences* to signify the *minor* character of the offence. One uses the descriptive *summary offences* to refer to the fact that such crimes are tried without a jury, i.e. the offence is tried **summarily**. Finally, they are called *non-indictable offences* because, unlike indictable offences, they do not benefit from a pre-trial hearing referred to, depending on the common law jurisdiction concerned, as an examining trial, committal hearing, preliminary hearing, **indictment** hearing or **grand jury hearing**. In the case of minor offences, sentences are normally limited to six months' imprisonment, although for certain acts this may be extended to twelve months. If the court wishes to impose a **harsher** sentence, then the case must be sent to the Crown Court for sentencing, which process is referred to as a **committal for sentence**. The Magistrates' Court can **sit** as either:
- *three magistrates* In such a case, the sitting magistrates will not have legal qualifications and are known as **lay magistrates**. In this event, the magistrates work with a qualified law **clerk** to help them with the legal issues that may be raised during the trial; or
- *a single **district judge*** The district judge is a qualified lawyer.

More serious offences, referred to as indictable offences, are heard before the Crown Court. Coming under the heading of serious offences are crimes such as **murder, manslaughter, rape** or **armed robbery**. Prior to the actual trial of indictable offences before the Crown Court, there is a **pre-hearing**, which also takes place in the Crown Court, to officially record the **plea** of the accused. In many common law jurisdictions, but no longer in the UK, the pre-hearing also exists to establish whether there is a *prima facie* case against the accused justifying the subsequent trial. After the pre-hearing, the subsequent trial in the Crown Court is by judge and **jury**. At the end of the trial, the jury of twelve citizens decides upon the guilt or innocence of the defendant. Thereafter, the sentence is imposed by the judge in a subsequent sentencing hearing.

However, only 5% of criminal cases actually end up before the Crown Court, as there also is another type of offence, referred to as a **triable either way offence**. A triable either way offence is a hybrid offence that may be tried summarily by the Magistrates' Court or before the Crown Court as an indictable offence. Only less serious indictable offences such as **theft** and assault are defined as triable either way offences. With triable either way offences the accused may, after the Magistrates' Court has sanctioned his/her choice, choose to have a summary trial before the Magistrates' Court instead of before the Crown Court. However, the accused can insist that the matter be tried by judge and jury before the Crown Court. Frequently, the accused prefers to have a summary hearing in the Magistrates' Court, as (s)he is likely to receive a shorter sentence. Moreover, the procedure is faster and less expensive.

If the matter concerns an indictable offence and the accused is found guilty before the Crown Court, the case will normally be adjourned, so as to allow both parties the time to prepare for the sentencing hearing. It is only at this time that the previous **record** of the accused is revealed to the court. The court is also informed of any **mitigating factors** that might help to reduce the sentence of the accused.

Sometimes prior to the end of the trial and often at the time the accused is being charged, the prosecution will offer the defendant a **deal**, whereby (s)he is promised a reduced sentence in return for pleading guilty. This is referred to as **plea bargaining** and has been introduced as a means of encouraging guilty pleas, thereby reducing the number of full trials before the courts. Plea bargaining has been criticized from the point of view that it can encourage innocent people to plead guilty; it does however, have the benefit of making the system more efficient.

In the case of minor offences, **appeal lies** from the Magistrates' Court either to the Crown Court or exceptionally to the Queen's Bench Division of the High Court, where the appeal regards the interpretation of a point of law. Appeal from the Crown Court lies to the Criminal Court of Appeal. Appeals from the Criminal Division of the Court of Appeal on questions of law are heard before the Supreme Court. There is a time limit of twenty one days for the **filing** of an application for appeal. **Leave to appeal** is not always **granted** and many requests fail, as it must be established that the conviction, the subject of the appeal, was **unsafe**, i.e., that there was a substantial error in the proceedings **at first instance**.

VOCABULARY

Investigating judge – *juiz de instrução*
Prosecution – *promotor, Ministério Público*
Accused – *acusado*
Adversarial system – *sistema acusatório*
Discovery of documentation – *apresentação de documentos*
Prior to – *anteriormente a*
Headings – *título, cabeçalho, motivos*
Suspect – *suspeito*
To arrest – *prender*
To charge – *acusar*
Defendant – *réu*
To be charged with an offence – *ser acusado de um crime*
Local police – *polícia local*
State police – *polícia do Estado*
Federal police – *polícia federal*
Reasonable suspicion – *suspeita razoável*
Evidence – *evidência, prova*
Conviction – *condenação*
On foot of – *sob o fundamento de*
Arrest warrant – *mandado de prisão*
Detainee – *detento*
To be in detention – *estar em detenção*

Custody – *custódia*
Has not as yet – *não foi ainda*
Police interview – *interrogatório de polícia*
Identification parade, line-up – *sessão de identificação de suspeitos*
To be entitled to – *para ter direito a*
Legitimate fear – *medo legítimo*
Investigation – *investigação*
To authorize – *autorizar*
Senior police officer – *policial de cargo superior, como, por exemplo police inspector – inspetor de polícia, police commissioner – comissário de polícia, police headquarters – quartel general de polícia, police station – delegacia*
To fill out – *preencher*
Charge sheet – *boletim de ocorrência*
Minor, summary, non-indictable offence – *delito de menor potencial ofensivo*
Summons – *citação*
To be means tested – *ser objeto de controle dos recursos pessoais*
To rely on – *contar com, depender de*
Drawn-up – *lavrado*
Duty solicitors' scheme – *programa de ajuda jurisdicional através do qual o acusado pode se beneficiar de um advogado à título gratuito*
Made up of – *constituído de*
Bail – *caução*
Case law – *jurisprudência*
Substantial ground – *motivo sério e real*
To commit – *cometer*
Offence (offense) – *infração, delito, crime*
Unconditional – *incondicional*
Surety – *caução (neste caso: garantia dada por um fiador)*
Security – *caução (neste caso: pagamento efetivo de uma caução)*
Whereby – *pelo qual, através do qual*
Felony – *crime*
Indictable offence – *infracão (crime ou delito)*
Brief – *petição*
To instruct, brief – *dar instrução, transmitir, confiar uma petição (ao barrister)*
Crown Prosecution Service – *promotor, Ministério Público*
Stage – *etapa*
To appoint – *nomear, designar*
Increasingly – *de forma crescente, cada vez mais*
To liaise with – *manter ligação com*
To frown upon – *desaprovar*
Court of original criminal jurisdiction – *tribunal de primeira instância em matéria penal*
Summarily – *sumariamente (summary trial – julgamento sumário)*
Indictment – *acusação formal*
Magistrate – *juiz do Magistrates Court (também chamado de District Judge, juge profissional do Magistrates Court)*
Harsh – *severo*
Committal for sentence – *apresentação de sentença*

Lay magistrate – *juiz não profissional*
Magistrates sit – *o Magistrates compõe–se*
Clerk – *escriturário*
District judge – *juiz do distrito*
Murder – *assassinato, homicídio doloso*
Manslaughter – *homicídio preterdoloso*
Rape – *estupro*
Armed robbery – *assalto à mão armada*
Pre-hearing, indictment – *audiência preliminar para estabelecer a existência ou não de elementos suficientes que justifiquem o início de uma ação judicial*
To enter a plea – *alegar ser culpado ou inocente*
Prima facie case – *existência de elementos suficientes para justificar a abertura de processo judicial*
Grand jury hearing – *audiência preliminar do júri de acusação nos EUA*
Jury – *júri*
Triable - either-way offence – *crimes que podem ser julgados tanto pelo Magistrates Courts quanto pela Crown Court*
To be sanctioned – *(neste caso) aprovar*
Theft – *furto (petty theft – pequenos furtos; grand theft – furto de bens cujo valor os torna submetidos à lei federal dos Estados Unidos)*
(Criminal) record – *antecedentes criminais*
Mitigating factor – *circunstâncias antenuantes*
Deal – *acordo*
Plea bargaining – *declarar–se culpado (negociação da pena entre a defesa e a acusação se o acusado declarar–se culpado)*
An appeal lies from the Magistrates Court to the Crown Court – *uma decisão do Magistrates Court pode ser objeto de um recurso perante o Crown Court*
Leave to appeal – *permissão para interpor recurso*
To grant – *conceder*
Unsafe decision – *decisão mal fundamentada*
At first instance – *na primeira instância*

PART 1 – TEXT 2 – EXERCISES

1. Definitions

Write a sentence defining each of the following terms – one sentence per term

   a)   Detention
   b)   Identification parade
   c)   Charge sheet
   d)   Legal aid
   e)   Arrest
   f)   Bail
   g)   Preliminary hearing
   h)   Plea bargaining

2. Sentences

Write sentences with the following pairs of words demonstrating your knowledge of the relationship between them

- a) Minor offence/indictable offence
- b) Manslaughter/triable either way offence
- c) Appeal/time limit
- d) Arrest/detention
- e) Police interview/lawyer
- f) Jury/summary offence
- g) Free legal aid/Duty Solicitors' Scheme
- h) Reasonable suspicion/arrest
- i) Magistrate/District Judge

3. Fill in the missing words

Using the vocabulary in Text 2, fill in the missing words

- a) An offence classified as a _____ gives the accused a choice between a _____ trial before the Magistrates' Court or a trial by judge and _____ before the _____ Court.
- b) Under the _____ Scheme, anyone in police _____ has the right to consult a lawyer free of charge.
- c) When in police custody, the _____ can be held for a period of six hours, after which further detention must be authorized by a _____. The accused is also _____ to contact a family member or friend.
- d) An application for _____ may be made during the preliminary hearing before the Magistrates' Court. Normally, such an application is granted, although the _____ may require the accused to provide a surety or a _____, to ensure that the accused will turn up at his/her trial. Bail may be refused if it is demonstrated that the accused may interfere with _____.
- e) Once the police have _____ the accused, his/her file is sent to the _____, which decides whether to prosecute him/her or not. The accused may be offered the possibility of a _____, whereby (s)he agrees to plead guilty in return for being charged with a lesser _____.

4. Knowledge test

The following questions may be answered in writing or by way of discussion

- a) Compare the rights of the accused under the UK criminal system with the rights enjoyed by the accused under your criminal system.
- b) The adversarial nature of the common law system in criminal law is fundamentally unfair as, instead of having an investigating judge, as is the case in the civil law system, it places the accused in a position of direct competition with the State, which has much greater resources. Discuss.
- c) As the large majority of defendants in criminal matters are guilty, less

money should be spent on protecting their rights and more money on preventing the causes of crime in the first place. Discuss.

d)   Prisons are meant to fulfil three fundamental purposes: deterrence, retribution and rehabilitation. Do you believe they are achieving these aims?

PART 2 – QUICK LOOK GRAMMAR REVISION

Auxiliary verbs

1. Using *but* and *and* with auxiliary verbs

Frequently after *but* and *and* the main verb is not repeated and in its place an auxiliary verb is used:

- **I do not work** a lot in my office **but** fortunately my partners **do**.
- **I like pleading** before the courts **but** my partners **do not**.
- **I have** already **seen** the client **but** John **has not**.
- **I do not like** family law **and** John **does not** either.
- **I have** already **seen** that film **and** John **has** too.
- Mr. Smith **is not** here **and** Mr. Roberts **isn't** either.

Note:

The auxiliary acts as a substitute for the main verb, and after *but* or *and* **normally** takes the same tense or modal as the main verb.
Example:
I *had* already seen the client but John *had* not.

2. Auxiliary verbs – tag questions (questions found at the end of a sentence)

Tag questions are normally used when speaking and frequently seek to confirm the earlier statement, for example:

- You will take the case, **won't you**?
- Frank knows the other lawyer, **doesn't he**?
- You don't like me, **do you**?
- You won't forget, **will you**?

Tag questions are also used to ask a question in a very polite way, for example:

- You wouldn't know where the court house is, **would you**?

Note:

The general rule is that if the first part of the statement is in the affirmative, then the second part is in the negative; and if the first part of the statement is in the negative, then the tag question is in the positive.
Example:
You like working here, **don't** you?
You don't like working here, **do** you?

However, this is only a general rule and there are exceptions.
Example:
> **Let's** go, **shall we**?

Note:

The intonation used by the speaker will frequently indicate if the tag question is meant to confirm the earlier preceding statement or if it is meant as a real question.

If the entire sentence is spoken using the same intonation (or the tag question is spoken with a falling intonation), then the tag question is being used to convey a confirmation of the statement to which it is attached.

However, if the tag question is spoken using a higher intonation than that used in the preceding statement, then it is meant as a question.
Example:
> You know Frank, don't you – statement (intonation the same or falling)
> You know Frank, **don't you**[13] – question (intonation rising)

Note:

When answering a tag question, the answer is independent of the actual form of the question contained in the tag and instead addresses the actual subject of the question. In the example below, the answer is the same despite the form of the question, because both answers address the underlying question of the sun's color.
Example:
> The sun is blue, isn't it? No **it isn't**.
> The sun isn't blue, is it? No **it isn't**.

Note:

Tag questions are sometimes added to the end of an order to make it friendlier BUT it is still an order.
Example:
> Come in to my office, **will you/won't you**?

Note:

Tag questions in negative statements normally indicate a certain amount of hostility and are often used to confirm a point.
Example:
> So you don't want to come to the meeting, **do you**?

---

[13] Bold indicates use of a higher intonation.

PART 2 – GRAMMAR EXERCISES

1. Using auxiliary verbs with *but* and *and* ......

Finish the sentence......

> The winning lawyer prepared his case but the losing lawyer......
> **did not.**

a)   Frank does not come to the office everyday but John ......
b)   Jim was in court yesterday but Albert ......
c)   Helen will not be at the meeting this afternoon but Angela ......
d)   I will be at the meeting and Tom ...... too.
e)   I have an important meeting tomorrow, I should go back to the hotel and you ...... too.
f)   George has already prepared the brief but Anthony ......
g)   Harold hasn't seen the client yet, and Martha ...... either.

2. Using auxiliary verbs with *but* and *and* continued......

Finish the sentence......

a)   Frank isn't in the office today, Frank ...... either.
b)   Bob hasn't finished pleading, but James ......
c)   I have to stay in the office tonight, but Laura ......
d)   Eric would like a cup of tea and a biscuit and Emma ...... too.
e)   Aurore has two weeks of holidays left, but Elizabeth ......
f)   You don't have to be at the meeting, but John ......
g)   James has worked with our Firm for two years, and I ...... too.

3. Using tag questions......

Add appropriate tag questions to the following statements......

> You worked for that client ...... **didn't you?**

a)   Bob works with a good law firm _____?
b)   Bob is in court _____?
c)   George will be in the office tomorrow _____?
d)   John speaks English _____?
e)   John can speak English _____?

PART 3 – AUDIO AND ORAL – LISTENING AND SPEAKING

Comprehension

Listen to the following conversation, make notes of all the relevant facts and then answer the questions below. If you have trouble understanding, follow the conversation while also reading the text.

Conversation between Mike Jenkins, a solicitor, and Fred Fry, who has been charged with theft by the police

Mike: "Hello, Mr. Fry, I am the solicitor who has been appointed to you under the free legal aid scheme."

Fred: "Thank you for coming to see me so quickly; it is not very nice in here and I want to get out on bail as soon as possible. Can you help me?"

Mike: "Of course, but first we will have to go over the facts of your case and see what exactly you want to do."

Fred: "OK, tell me what you wish to know."

Mike: "Well, I have a copy of your charge sheet here and according to the police you were caught breaking into a supermarket in Liverpool. At the time they arrested you, you were putting a TV in your car."

Fred: "Well in fact there has been a bit of a mix-up."

Mike: "Please Mr. Fry, let me finish and then you can say whatever it is you have to say."

Fred: "Sorry for interrupting, please continue."

Mike: "You have been charged with theft and your hearing will take place later this afternoon. How do you want to plead?"

Fred: "Guilty, no actually I want to plead innocent as I wouldn't have robbed the TV if they had taken back the faulty TV they sold me last month; in fact it is they who are the real thieves."

Mike: "Well, Mr. Fry that is a separate matter but I suppose we might try to use it as a mitigating factor later on during the trial. At the moment, let's just try to concentrate on what we will do during the hearing. "

Fred: "But if they had taken back the broken TV they sold me and replaced it with a new one, I would never have robbed…"

Mike: "Please Mr. Fry, I have asked you not to interrupt me. You are due in court this afternoon and we really don't have much time. "

Fred: "Sorry."

Mike: "So as I was saying, this afternoon you will also have to decide the court you want to be tried before. You see, as theft is a triable either way offence, you will have to decide if you want a summary hearing in the Magistrates' Court or a jury trial in the Crown Court."

Fred: "What's the difference?"

Mike: "Good question. Well first of all sentencing is lower in the Magistrates' Court and it is cheaper, but you won't have the benefit of a jury trial".

Fred: "I don't know, what do you think?"

Mike: "If you persist in pleading innocent before the Crown Court even though you were caught red-handed by the police, you may benefit from a sympathetic jury. However, don't expect any mercy from the court if you are found guilty, as you will have wasted a lot of their time and put the State to the expense of a jury trial and the courts will not appreciate that."

Fred: "So you are saying that I should plead guilty and throw myself on the mercy of the Magistrates' Court?"

Mike: "I'm not here to tell you what to do, that must be your decision; but if it was my choice, I would plead guilty in the Magistrates' Court."

Fred: "OK, I'll do as you say."

Mike: "Good, after you have entered a guilty plea and indicated to the court that we are opting for a summary trial, I will apply to the court for bail and seeing as you don't have any previous convictions, bail should be granted and you'll be out by this afternoon. Then in a few weeks there will be the sentencing hearing. OK goodbye Mr. Fry, I will see you this afternoon at the hearing."

Fred: "Yes, goodbye, see you this afternoon."

PART 3 – AUDIO COMPREHENSION – EXERCISES

1. Comprehension

From the notes you have taken, answer the following questions

a) How does Fred initially want to plead, innocent or guilty?
b) Why does Fred think he is not guilty?
c) What is the name of the hearing Fred will have to attend in the afternoon?
d) According to Mike what is a triable either way offence?
e) Why should Fred be granted bail automatically?
f) What is the benefit of choosing to be tried summarily before the Magistrates' Court?

2. Speaking practice

In the following series of conversation couplets develop suitable responses to the questions asked

a) Mike: "Hello Mr. Fry, I hope they are treating you properly in jail."
   Fred: "_____."
b) Mike: "Do you want to tell me how you ended up in jail?"
   Fred: "_____."
c) Mike: "So how do you think you want to plead?"
   Fred: "_____"
d) Mike: "Theft is a triable either way offence, do you understand what this means?"
   Fred: "_____."
e) Mike: "Would you prefer to have a jury trial?"
   Fred: "_____."
f) Mike: "Do you want to make an application for bail and if you do, have you anything to offer the court as surety?"
   Fred: "_____."
g) Mike: "Are there any mitigating factors that might help the court to understand why you committed this crime?"

Fred: "_____."

h)   Mike: "Do you understand the function of the preliminary hearing?"
     Fred: "_____."

i)   Mike: "Do you have anyone who would be willing to appear as a character witness on your behalf?"
     Fred: "_____."

j)   Mike: "Why do you want to be tried summarily in the Magistrates' Court?"
     Fred: "_____."

3. Speaking practice continued ......

Create five other conversation couplets using in each couplet at least one word from the vocabulary found in Part I

4. Speaking practice continued ......

Listen to the suggested replies and repeat

a)   Mike: "Hello Mr. Fry, I hope they are treating you properly in jail."
     Fred: "Yes fine I guess; it is prison after all."

b)   Mike: "Do you want to tell me how you ended up in jail?"
     Fred: "Well, they say I stole a TV but I was only taking the TV because the shop refused to give me a new one, after the one they sold me did not work."

c)   Mike: "So how do you think you want to plead?"
     Fred: "I don't think I did anything wrong, so I want to plead innocent."

d)   Mike: "Theft is a triable either way offence, do you understand what this means?"
     Fred: "From what you explained, it means I can either choose to be tried summarily before the Magistrates' Court or alternatively opt for trial by jury before the Crown Court."

e)   Mike: "Would you prefer to have a jury trial?"
     Fred: "Yes, because I think they might be more sympathetic to my case."

f)   Mike: "Do you want to make an application for bail and if you do, have you anything to offer the court as surety?"
     Fred: "Yes I want to apply for bail. I could put my house up as surety."

g)   Mike: "Are there any mitigating factors that might help the court understand why you committed this crime?"
     Fred: "Yes, they sold me a faulty TV and refused to replace it when I brought it back to them."

h)   Mike: "Do you understand the function of the preliminary hearing?"
     Fred: "Basically it is there to record whether I am pleading innocent or guilty to the crime with which I am charged."

i)   Mike: "Do you have anyone who would be willing to appear as a character witness on your behalf?"
     Fred: "Not really, maybe my wife or my Mother!"

j)   Mike: "Why do you want to be tried summarily in the Magistrates' Court?"
Fred: "Because, I will probably get a lower sentence."

5. Associated questions

Discuss the following questions

a)   How would Fred's case be dealt with in your country?
b)   Would Fred be released on bail in your jurisdiction? In your answer discuss the conditions governing bail or its equivalent in your country.
c)   Is there any equivalent to a triable either way offence in your country? Would Fred have the right to a trial by jury?
d)   Would you like to work in the area of criminal law? Explain your answer.

PART 4 – TRANSLATION EXERCISES

When carrying out the translations it is not necessary to translate directly word for word; rather the emphasis should be on translating the sense of the text. Language is not directly interchangeable and so direct translations do not always convey the meaning in the text.

Translate the following texts from English to Portuguese

A. Plea bargaining

A plea bargain, also called a plea agreement, a plea deal or *copping a plea[1]*, involves the prosecutor offering the defendant the opportunity to plead guilty to a lesser charge in return for a lighter sentence. For example, a criminal defendant charged with a felony may be offered the opportunity to plead guilty to a summary offence, which may not carry jail time. The prosecution will agree to this in order to secure a conviction and to avoid the costs associated with a felony trial. However, plea bargaining can present the accused with a dilemma; even if (s)he is not guilty (s)he may be tempted to plead guilty to a lesser charge, in order to avoid a lengthy jail sentence.

B. What is mens rea?

Mens rea must be established if someone is to be successfully convicted of a criminal offense. Mens rea requires that the accused had, at the time of committing the offense, a guilty intention or a "guilty mind". The common law test of criminal liability is summed up by the phrase *actus non facit reum nisi mens sit rea* i.e. *the act does not make a person guilty unless the mind is also guilty*. Thus the accused must have intended the offense. Mens rea is presumed to exist in many cases and in reality it will often be for the accused to establish the lack of mens rea, if (s)he is to avoid being convicted.

---

[1]   This is street speak and is not an official term.

C. Is ignorance of a law a defense?

It is a general rule of the common law that ignorance of the law is no defense to criminal prosecution. However, the courts have sometimes found that if a law is particularly complex, ignorance may be relied on as a mitigating factor, and even as a defense if the misunderstanding is in good faith and where the law is excessively complex. Indeed, the ever growing number of statutes and regulations has sometimes made it next to impossible for the average citizen to be fully aware of all the obligations established by law. Moreover, reasonable reliance by an accused on an official government statement as to the scope of a particular law, which statement is afterwards determined to be incorrect, will normally allow the accused either to avoid conviction or to receive a reduced fine or sentence.

Translate the following texts from Portuguese to English

A. O que é imprudência?

A imprudência ocorre quando há uma evidência clara de que o acusado previu ou deveria ter previsto o resultado de suas ações, mesmo se ele não desejava que o resultado ocorresse. Ao decidir continuar com seu comportamento, o acusado assumiu o risco de causar perda ou dano, e por isso considera-se que ele foi imprudente. O acusado, ao conhecer a imprudência de seus atos, teve que escolher continuar ou não continuar com seu comportamento. De acordo com a doutrina do common law, o acusado manifesta a intenção de expor a vítima ao perigo quando decide prosseguir com seu comportamento. Desta forma, quanto maior a probabilidade de dano à vítima, maior será o grau de imprudência e, conseqüentemente, maior será a pena imputada ao réu.

B. Qual é a importância do motivo para o direito penal?

Uma das questões mais importantes dos procedimentos criminais é a questão do motivo. Se for comprovado que o acusado teve um motivo consistente com o que de fato ocorreu, isto aumentará a possibilidade de que o crime foi cometido pelo acusado e tornará a posição do promotor em processar o acusado mais credível. Ao contrário, se houver uma evidência clara que de que o acusado não possuía qualquer motivo ou de que possuía motivos para não cometer o crime, isto normalmente será fatal do ponto de vista do promotor. Entretanto, uma suposta falta de motivo não pode ser utilizada como defesa; ela será utilizada de forma geral ou circunstancial para desacreditar a acusação feita pelo promotor.

C. O motivo não pode ser confundido com a noção de mens rea: Regina contra Yip Chung, 1995

Fatos: Yip Chung foi condenado por contrabando de heroína e apresentou recurso da sentença. Sua apelação baseou-se no fato de que ele havia alegado que o juiz de primeira instância não considerou a ausência de *mens rea*. Chung alegou que se ele agiu como contrabandista ao importar heroína para o Reino Unido, ele o fez para tentar entregar à Justiça a gangue criminosa responsável pelo tráfico de drogas e não para realmente trazer drogas ao país.

Julgado: A apelação de Chung foi rejeitada pela Câmara dos Lordes. Segundo o julgamento do tribunal, ele confessou no próprio recurso a intenção de cometer o crime. Para o tribunal, o motivo que o levou a cometer o crime, ou seja, a vontade de capturar outros criminosos, era irrelevante e não poderia ser utilizado como defesa.

PART 5 – ADVANCED READING

The actors in the criminal process and the burden of proof in criminal law

In the UK, the main actors in the criminal process are the police and the Crown Prosecution Service (CPS). Both are independent of each other but work in close cooperation. The police investigate and decide whether or not to charge the defendant. Thereafter, the CPS decides whether to prosecute the defendant before the courts. There is also an option for private individuals to prosecute an individual if it is felt the CPS took an incorrect decision not to prosecute. Unlike in some civil law jurisdictions, the accused has a right to bail before trial unless there is a *reasonable* belief, as opposed to *apprehension*, that the detainee will:

- abscond;
- commit further offences whilst on bail;
- intimidate witnesses; or
- be the victim of reprisals.

There are two main forms of bail in the UK:

- *police bail* In the case of police bail, the defendant is free to leave the police station but must return to sign in at certain times, for example daily or weekly. While on bail the defendant may be required to wear a monitor, whereby his/her movements can be tracked;
- *court bail* In the case of court bail, the accused is free but is expected to appear in court on the day of his/her trial. Failure to attend at court is an offence for which the maximum sentence is either three months in the case of the Magistrates' Court or 12 months in the Crown Court.

To convict a criminal defendant, the state must prove that the defendant is guilty beyond all reasonable doubt. The defendant is presumed innocent until proven guilty. This presumption of innocence means not only that the prosecutor must convince the jury of the defendant's guilt, but also that the defendant need not say or do anything in his/her own defense. Indeed, prior to the defendant having to defend him/herself, the prosecution has to first prove its case. Once the prosecution has presented its evidence, the accused may and usually does ask the court to decide that there is no case to answer, i.e. that the state has failed to discharge the evidentiary burden of proof necessary to overcome the presumption of innocence. Even if the state proves that the defendant committed the act, the defendant can rely on defenses such as:

- *insanity* The defense of insanity is based on the principle that the defendant can only be found guilty if (s)he is capable of controlling his/her behavior and understanding that what (s)he has done is wrong.

Insanity, for the purposes of criminal law is generally defined as *the inability to distinguish right from wrong*;

- *self-defense* Self-defense is a defense frequently relied on by those charged with violent offences. Under this defense, the defendant accepts that (s)he committed the crime but claims that the act was justified on grounds of self-preservation;
- *intoxication* As in contract law, defendants who act under the influence of drugs or alcohol may be able to argue that their mental functioning was so impaired that they cannot be held accountable for their actions. Generally, however, voluntary intoxication does not excuse criminal conduct and indeed, depending on the circumstances, the fact of being intoxicated may itself be a crime or an aggravating circumstance.

In some common law jurisdictions the right to silence has been partly removed in the case of certain crimes insofar as a negative inference may be drawn from its exercise.

Chapter seven

COMPANY LAW

PART 1 – TEXT 1 – INFORMATION

Businesses in the common law world

A **company** is a general name for a collection of natural or legal persons sharing a common purpose often operating in the area of business. The following are the most popular forms of company in the common law world.

- *Corporations* A **corporation** is a **legal entity** not unlike a natural person for the purposes of the law. Instead of corporation, the term company is often used in the UK to describe such entities. On the contrary, in the United States, the term corporation is sometimes used as a broad term and refers to many different types of businesses, including but not limited to separate legal corporate entities. A corporation **enjoys** legal independence from its **shareholders** and consequently, if a corporation **fails**, shareholders enjoy what is referred to as limited liability, i.e. they will only lose the money they actually invested in the company and, beyond this, they will not be held responsible for its **debts**. So that members of the public will be **aware** that they are **dealing with** a business that is a legal entity separate from its representatives, corporations are normally identified through the use of **abbreviations** such as *Ltd.* (**limited liability**), *PLC* (**public limited corporation/company**), *Inc.* (**Incorporated**) and *Corp.* (corporation) after their name[2]. Corporations are subject to a **double taxation burden** insofar as the corporation first pays corporate tax on its profits and then its shareholders are required to pay income tax, if company profits are **distributed** to them **by way of dividend**. Corporations can be publicly or privately owned. Publicly owned corporations are called publicly **listed** corporations and privately owned companies are called **private limited companies** (private company limited by shares).
- *Limited liability companies (LLCs)/limited liability partnerships (LLPs)* Created in the United States under US state legislation, an LLC offers its members[3] limited liability but is treated as a **pass through entity** for tax purposes. Consequently an LLC is not subject to a double taxation burden. The UK equivalent to an LLC is a **limited**

---

[2]   PLC can also stand for *publicly listed company*. Both PLC and Inc. corporations are open to members of the public while Ltd. companies usually have a limited number of owners. There is no real difference between Corp. and Inc., except that one stands for *incorporated* and the other for *corporation*.

[3]   Investors in an LLC are called *members* and not shareholders as in the case of PLCs.

liability partnership. An LLP is, despite its name, a body corporate in which the members/partners enjoy limited liability in the same way as investors in a corporation. However, like LLCs, LLPs are considered to be pass through business entities and members are taxed only once on earnings. Thus, partners in an LLP enjoy the best of both worlds: limited liability, and a reduced tax burden. It is also possible in common law jurisdictions to form unlimited liability companies but they are relatively rare because of the obvious risks attached to unlimited liability.

* *Non-profit organizations* **Non-profit organizations** (NPOs) are normally charitable organizations taking the form of a corporation. In many common law countries, NPOs are given favorable tax treatment because of their charitable activities.

* *General partnerships* A **general partnership** is a pass through business in which the **partners**, who are also the business's owners, share directly in its profits and losses. From a tax **point of view** partnerships are more advantageous than corporations, **insofar as** the partners are only taxed once on the **profits** of the partnership. However, a negative aspect of a general partnership is that the partners, unlike the owners of a corporation, do not enjoy limited liability and thus are **exposed** financially, should the business begin to lose money. Moreover, the partners are **jointly and severally liable** for the actions of other partners, and thus the potential financial liability created by a general partnership is significant when compared with a corporation. It is for this reason that law firms prefer to take the form of an LLC or LLP, as opposed to the more traditional general partnership structure.

* *Sole proprietorships* A **sole proprietorship/trader** is a business that has no legal existence separate from its owner. For tax purposes, it is considered to be a pass through business. **Accordingly**, the sole proprietor or sole trader enjoys no limited liability as regards the debts of his/her business and is considered *solely* responsible for the same. The advantage that sole proprietorships have over more complicated business structures is that they are easy to establish, incur next to no maintenance/running costs and are mostly **unregulated** in common law jurisdictions.

Winding up/liquidation of companies

Winding up describes the process pursuant to which a company **ceases to trade** and the **assets** and property of the business are redistributed **amongst** the company's investors and/or **creditors**. The winding up can be entered into on a voluntary basis by the company or may be forced on the company if **unpaid creditors** apply to the court for a **liquidation order**. At this time the company is said to go into liquidation.

Vocabulary

Company – *empresa*
Corporation – *corporação, sociedade em comandita por ações (ou mais comumente, sociedade anônima)*
Legal entity – *pessoa jurídica*
To enjoy – *beneficiar*
Shareholder – *acionista*
To fail – *sofrer falência*
Debt – *dívida*
To be aware – *estar consciente de*
To deal with something – *lidar com algo*
Abbreviation – *abreviação*
Limited (liability) – *responsabilidade limitada*
Public Limited Corporation/Company – *sociedade anônima (S/A)*
Incorporated – *sociedade anônima (verbo: to incorporate – estabelecer uma empresa que possui personalidade jurídica)*
Double taxation burden – *dupla tributação*
To distribute – *distribuir*
By way of – *através de*
Dividend – *dividendos*
Listed – *cotado na bolsa de valores*
Private limited (liability) company – *sociedade limitada*
Non-profit organization – *organização sem fins lucrativos*
General partnership – *sociedade em nome coletivo*
Pass through business – *empresa que permite a tributação direta aos seus associados e que desta forma evita uma dupla tributação*
Partner – *sócio*
Point of view – *ponto de vista*
Insofar as – *na medida em que*
Profit – *lucro*
To be exposed to – *ser exposto a*
Joint and severally liable – *responsabilidade solidária*
Limited liability partnership – *sociedade limitada*
Sole proprietorship/trader – *empresa em nome individual*
Accordingly – *conseqüentemente*
Unregulated – *não regulado*
To wind-up – *liqüidar*
Liquidation – *liqüidação*
To cease – *cessar*
To trade – *negociar*
Asset – *bens, ativos*
Amongst/among – *entre*
Creditor – *credores*
Unpaid creditor – *credor não pago*
Liquidation order (liquidation by court order, winding-up of a company under court supervision) – *liqüidação em juízo*

PART 1 – TEXT 1 – EXERCISES

1. Vocabulary test

Fill in the missing words using the vocabulary in Text 1

a) Corporations are said to have a _____ burden, insofar as the corporation and shareholders both have to pay _____.

b) Corporations are said to be separate _____ independent of their _____.

c) In a limited liability partnership the _____ benefit from _____.

d) For tax purposes a sole _____ is said to be a _____ business, insofar as it is the owner and not the business that is considered liable for taxes.

e) In a general partnership, the partners are said to be _____ liable for the acts of the other _____.

f) _____ have different abbreviations after their names such as Ltd., Plc., _____ or _____.

g) When a company is _____ up it ceases to _____ and creditors are paid out of the remaining _____.

h) There are two types of partnership: _____ and _____; the latter do not enjoy limited liability as regards debts.

2. Vocabulary test

Write sentences with the following pairs of words. Your sentence should demonstrate your knowledge of the relationship between the words

a) Debt/liable

b) Tax/sole proprietorship

c) Pass through business/partnership

d) Dividend/shareholder

e) Creditor/assets

f) Double taxation burden/corporation

3. Knowledge test

Each of the following statements is false; do you know why? Write a sentence stating why it is false

a) Corporations are pass-through businesses.

b) Corporations are never open to members of the public.

c) Partnership structures always impose joint and several liability on their members.

d) Creditors of wound-up corporations have no right to be reimbursed.

e) NPO's are taxed like all companies.

f) The members of an LLP enjoy limited liability but are subject to a double taxation burden.

PART 1 – TEXT 2 – MORE INFORMATION

Businesses in the common law world

Businesses differ in size and activity, from the simple **sole trader** operating on the **high street** to large global **multinationals**, often taking the form of **public limited corporations**. In legal terms, a business can generally be referred to as an **undertaking**, or more specifically a **company**, and the law **regulating** such entities is simply known as **company law**. The word company is a general legal **term** describing a collection of legal or natural persons coming together for an express purpose that can take different legal forms. In the UK, the word **corporation** is used to describe a specific type of company recognized in law as having a **separate legal personality**. The word company is used generally to describe corporations and can also be used to describe other types of business formations. However, businesses such as partnerships are not referred to as corporations or companies and instead words such as *firm* are often used to describe them. On the contrary, in the US, the word corporation has wider meaning and can apply to business entities such as **partnerships** and separate legal entities. As there is some confusion as to the use of the term *corporation*, in this text the term will be used in the sense of a separate legal entity or body corporate.

One way to classify a business is as either a:
- *pass-through company* A **pass-through company** is one in which the **profits** and losses of the business pass directly through to its **owners**; or
- *separate business entity corporation* A **separate business entity corporation** is one in which the profits and losses of the business are **attributable** to the corporation itself and not to its actual owners.

However, within these two basic **categories**, there are many different types of company recognized by the common law.

Different types of companies and business structures

The best-known type of company in the Anglo-American world is a corporation, although other forms of business formation also exist, **such as** partnerships or **sole proprietorships**.

Corporations

In common law **jurisdictions**, separate legal entity corporations **share** certain common **characteristics**, namely:
- a separate legal personality;
- **limited liability**;
- **shares**, normally **transferable**, representing their underlying value or **worth**;
- a centralized **management** governed by a **board of directors**.

Thus, a corporation is a **legal entity** having its own existence, not unlike a natural person, for the purposes of the law. As a corporation has a separate legal identity, it will continue to exist **indefinitely** until the moment it is **wound up** by its members or is **liquidated** by its **creditors**, in the event that it is unable to pay its debts. The defining characteristic of a corporation is that it **enjoys** legal independence from its **shareholders**. Consequently, if a corporation **fails**, shareholders enjoy what is referred to as limited liability, i.e. they will only lose the money they actually invested in the company and they will not be held responsible for its **debts**. So that members of the public will be **aware** that they are **dealing with** a business that is a legal entity separate from its investors, corporations are normally identified through use of **abbreviations** such as *Ltd.* (**Limited**), *PLC* (public limited corporation)[4], *Inc.* (**Incorporated**) and *Corp.* (Corporation) after their name.

One of the major negative features of a corporation is that it effectively imposes a **double taxation burden** on its owners. Thus, the corporation is taxed directly on its **profits**, through the imposition of **corporation tax**, and **thereafter** the corporation's investors or shareholders are taxed again on this profit, if and when it is **distributed** to them **by way of dividend**.

As a corporation has a separate legal identity, enjoying its own **legal capacity** and legal **rights**, it can sue and also be sued, i.e. bring actions against third parties in its own name. Consequently, state authorities **investigating** a company, for example the **competition** or the **tax authorities**, must respect the corporation's **human rights** and allow it a **fair hearing**, etc. Failure to do so will allow the company to successfully **invalidate** the investigation and **avoid** any **fine** that may have been **imposed** on it.

A Corporation **interacts** with four main **groups** of people: its management, its **employees**, its owners (also referred to as shareholders or **investors**) and finally its **customers**. The role of company law is to regulate the interaction between the corporation and these four groups[5]. A corporation is usually set up by **registering** or **filing** the company's **articles of incorporation** (also referred to as the **articles of association/articles of organization**) and **memorandum of association** (MoA) with the **Companies Office** of the jurisdiction in which it is establishing[6]. These two documents together form the **constitution** or rulebook of the company and are sometimes referred to as the corporate *by laws* in the US. **Briefly** they set out the company's **purpose/object**, how it is to be

---

[4] PLC can also stand for *publicly listed company*. *Listed* means that the shares of the company are listed on a stock market, such as the New York Stock Exchange, and may be bought and sold by members of the public.

[5] Although the area of labor law also obviously governs the relationship between corporations and their employees.

[6] In the United States each state has the right to create a company and thereafter the company is subject to that State's company law regime. There is no such thing as a company created under federal law. This has led to competition between the fifty different states as regards their company law regulatory model, as each state competes to attract businesses. This competition is sometimes referred to as the *Delaware effect*, *negative competition* or the *race to the bottom*. See the discussion in the text above.

managed by its **directors**, the rules to be respected at its **board meetings** and how shares are to be **issued** etc. Once the relevant Companies Office approves these documents, a company may **carry out** business in the state in which it has been incorporated, **respecting** at all times the **regulatory rules** applicable in that state. In the United Kingdom, the Companies Acts of 2006 and 2010 have reduced the importance of MoAs. It is now a much shorter document, with much of the information it once contained instead set out in the articles of association.

The reform in the UK is aimed at making it easier for companies to do business. Indeed, if a state or jurisdiction has placed an **emphasis** on developing regulatory laws that are favorable to companies, for example simplified legal rules, low corporate taxes, **restricted** protection for **workers**, restricted liability for company officers etc., companies will probably choose to establish in that state (sometimes referred to as the **host state**), in preference to a state that **favors employee rights**, complex company law procedures and high corporate taxes. Such host states/jurisdictions **in turn** receive valuable tax **revenue** and jobs from the companies that choose to incorporate on their territory. Thus, the application of a **reduced tax rate** can conversely lead to an increase in the **tax base** and consequently to an increase in **tax returns** for the state. Moreover, reduced protection for workers can lead to more employment. This is clearly a politically sensitive issue and in an increasingly globalized world it has created a situation where jurisdictions are sometimes said to **compete** by way of their regulatory models to attract companies. In other words, states develop a **regulatory regime**, not just to control or regulate companies but also to attract companies to their jurisdiction. The process of regulatory competition between states is a phenomenon known as the **Delaware effect**, named after the State of Delaware in the United States. In the United States, the State of Delaware is the state in which most US companies choose to incorporate because of its corporation friendly legislation. Such pro-business legislation is sometimes referred to as **enabling legislation**, as it *enables* business to be carried out easily.

Corporations can be publicly or privately owned companies. Publicly owned corporations are called publicly listed companies or public liability corporations (PLCs) and privately owned companies are called **private limited companies**. If they are publicly owned, this means that their shares are **traded** publicly "**over the counter**" (OTC) on a **stock exchange**, for example the New York Stock Exchange. Shares in such companies may be sold to any member of the public that chooses to **purchase** them. This allows a public corporation to **raise funds** directly from members of the public. If a corporation is privately owned, its shares are not publicly traded and ownership is restricted to a limited number of private investors in accordance with the company's articles of association. For this reason, private companies are also referred to as **closed corporations**.

It is also possible in some common law jurisdictions such as the United Kingdom to form unlimited liability companies, but they are relatively rare as shareholders are considered to have unlimited joint and several liability; however such companies do have the advantage of not having to make their financial statements public, i.e. they do not have to file their annual accounts with the Companies Office. This offers greater secrecy to investors and is a major advantage.

Limited liability companies (LLCs) and Limited liability partnerships (LLPs)

An LLC is a hybrid business formation created by the different US states over the last twenty years. LLCs are attractive because they allow their members to enjoy the limited liability features of a corporation but are treated as **pass-through entities** for tax purposes. In other words, they are said to be tax transparent. Each state has its own LLC legislation, and some states have developed specific LLC structures, whereby the limited liability of its members is restricted to certain types of legal action, or where the structure is required to pay limited tax along with its members' taxes. However, the standard LLC in the US offers members the benefits associated with corporations and partnerships, namely:

- limited liability (corporations);
- the non-imposition of a double taxation burden (partnership).

Unlike corporations, LLCs have a limited lifespan depending on the legislation in the US state in which they are created[7]. The UK equivalent to an LLC is a **limited liability partnership** (LLP). An LLP is a body corporate and thus the members enjoy limited liability. Moreover, like LLCs, LLPs are treated as pass-through entities and consequently members are only taxed once on earnings. Unlike LLCs, there is no limit placed on the lifespan of an LLP. Both LLPs and LLCs are much loved by law firms and accountancy firms, as they allow them to develop global strategies without incurring unmanageable risk.

It is also possible to form limited partnerships (LP) in most common law jurisdictions. An LP creates two types of partners, one of which enjoys limited liability and the other of which does not. Investing partners benefit from limited liability[8] but unlimited liability is imposed on the general partner(s) responsible for the day-to-day running of the partnership. LPs have to some extent been eclipsed by the appearance of LLCs and LLPs.

Non-profit corporations

Non-profit organizations (NPOs) are organizations that, in place of distributing profits to shareholders, use their assets for a **stated charitable goal set out** in the company's articles of incorporation. In many common law countries, NPOs are given favorable tax treatment as a result of their charitable activities. For example, they are often **exempted** from corporation and other taxes and thus enjoy a reduced **tax burden**. In the UK, NPOs frequently take the form of a company limited by guarantee. Such a company is a private company, very like a private company limited by shares, but one which does not have a share capital. Instead the members undertake to contribute an agreed amount to the assets of the company in the event of winding up. This type of company is usually

---

[7] Thirty years appears to be an example of their average lifespan.
[8] Up to the amount they actually invest in the partnership. Investing partners must not be actively involved in the business, if their liability is to be limited to the amount of their investment.

adopted only for non-profit making entities, such as charities or members clubs, community enterprises and some co-operatives.

There is also a relatively new form of charitable formation in the UK called a Community Interest Company (CIC). CICs take the form of a private company limited by shares but can only be registered with the stated aim of carrying out projects which are for the good of the community. The CIC is a non-profit making entity and must be committed, in its constitution, to operating solely in the interests of some form of community enterprise. The two main features that distinguish CICs from *normal* charitable companies are the *asset lock mechanism* and the requirement of a Community Interest Statement and Report. Under the asset lock provisions, the assets and profits of the CIC must be permanently retained within the CIC, and used solely for the identified community benefit. Further, with every application to form a CIC, a Community Interest Statement must be lodged, with the usual documents, when seeking company registration. This statement, signed by all the directors, must describe the company's objectives and certify that the company is formed to serve the community, rather than for private profit. CICs can be limited by shares or by guarantee.

General partnerships

A **general partnership** (GP) is a pass-through business in which the **partners**, who are also the business's owners, share directly in its profits and losses. From a tax **point of view** GPs are more advantageous than corporations, **insofar as** the partners are only taxed once on the **profits** of the partnership. As we have seen, corporations must pay corporate tax on their profits, which are then distributed to their shareholders, who must also pay **income tax** on the money they receive. However, a negative aspect of a GP is that the partners, unlike the owners of a corporation, do not enjoy limited liability and thus are **exposed** financially, should the business begin to lose money. Moreover, they are **jointly and severally liable** for the actions of other partners. Consequently, if one of the partners decides to take all the money out of the business and disappear to *an island in the sun*, the remaining partners will be liable for the missing **monies**. In common law countries, partnerships are normally established **pursuant to** a partnership contract **drawn up** between the partners, who are free to agree to any terms they wish.

Sole proprietorships/sole trader

Like a partnership, a sole proprietorship is also a pass-through business that has no legal existence separate from its owner. **Accordingly**, the sole proprietor or sole trader does not enjoy limited liability as regards the debts of the business and is considered *solely* responsible for the same. Sole proprietorships often carry on business under a different **trade name**. This explains why in many common law jurisdictions one often sees the name of a business followed by the words "*John Smith trading as ...*". This is required by law so as to **prevent** a sole proprietor from being able to hide his/her identity behind a trade name. The advantage that a sole proprietorship has over a company is that it is easy to establish and is frequently **unregulated** in common law jurisdictions. Moreover, the owner only pays tax on profits once and thus is not a victim of double taxation. However, such business models frequently find it difficult to **raise capital**; moreover, hiring employees can become complicated as the owner is effectively entering into a personal contract with the employee.

Winding up/liquidation of companies

Winding up is the name given to the process pursuant to which a company **ceases to trade** and the **assets** and property of the business are redistributed **amongst** the company's investors and/or creditors. Winding up can also be referred to as a **dissolution** or liquidation of the business. The winding up may be a:

- *compulsory liquidation* **Compulsory liquidation**, also known as creditors' liquidation, is a process whereby the company's **unpaid creditors** apply for a court order to have the company declared **bankrupt**. Instead of forcing the company to cease trading, the court can alternatively order that it be put into **receivership**;
- *administration and receivership* Administration is a process whereby an expert administrator is appointed to the business to see if it is possible to **restructure** it and keep it functioning as **a going concern**, **whilst** at the same time ensuring that creditors get paid. In comparison, the aim of a receivership is to secure repayment of debt for secured creditors;
- *voluntary liquidation* **Voluntary liquidation**, also known as **shareholders' liquidation**, occurs when a company's board of directors adopts a **resolution** to that effect. The company officially stops trading upon adoption of the resolution. If at this time there are **outstanding monies owed** to creditors, it is necessary to hold a **creditors' meeting** and **appoint** a **liquidator** to distribute the assets of the company.

VOCABULARY

Sole-trader – *empresa em nome individual*
High street – *rua de comércio*
Multinational – *multinacional*
Public limited corporation – *sociedade anônima*
Undertaking – *empreendimento (to give an undertaking – dar um empreendimento)*
Company – *sociedade (companhia)*
To regulate – *regular*
Company law – *direito comercial*
Term – *termo*
Corporation – *corporação, sociedade em comandita por ações (ou mais comumente, sociedade anônima)*
Separate legal personality – *personalidade jurídica separada*
Pass through company – *empresa que permite a tributação direta aos seus associados e que desta forma evita uma dupla tributação*
Partner – *sócio*

Profit – *lucro*
Owner – *proprietário*
Separate business entity corporation – *empresa que possui personalidade jurídica separada (o contrário de uma « pass through company »)*
Attributable – *atribuível*
Category – *categoria*
Such as – *tal qual*
Partnership – *sociedade*
Sole proprietorship – *empresa em nome individual*
Jurisdiction – *jurisdição*
Share – *ação*
Characteristic – *característica*
Limited liability – *responsabilidade limitada*
Transferable share – *partes transferível*
Worth – *valor*
Management – *direção*
Board of directors – *conselho administrativo*
Legal entity – *entidade jurídica*
Indefinitely – *indefinidamente*
To wind-up (a company) – *liqüidar (uma empresa)*
To liquidate – *liqüidar*
Creditor – *credor*
To enjoy – *desfrutar*
Shareholder – *acionista*
To fail – *ir à falência (neste caso)*
Debt – *dívida*
To be aware of – *estar consciente de*
To deal with – *lidar com*
Abbreviation– *abreviação*
Limited – *limitado*
Incorporated – *sociedade anônima (verbo: to incorporate – estabelecer uma empresa que possui personalidade jurídica)*
Double tax burden – *dupla tributação*
Corporation tax – *imposto sobre sociedades*
Thereafter – *posteriormente*
To distribute – *distribuir*
By way of – *através de*
Dividend – *dividendos*
Legal capacity – *capacidade jurídica*
Right – *direito*
To investigate – *investigar*
Competition authority – *autoridade sobre a concorrência*
Tax authority – *administração fiscal*
Human rights – *direitos humanos*
(Right to a) fair hearing – *(direito ao) devido processo legal*
To invalidate – *invalidar, anular*
To avoid – *evitar*
Fine – *multa*

To impose – *impor*
To interact – *interagir*
Group – *grupo*
Employee – *empregado*
Investor – *investidor*
Customer – *cliente*
To register (a company) – *registrar (uma empresa)*
To file – *arquivar*
Articles of Incorporation, Association, Organization – *contrato social, estatuto da empresa*
Memorandum of Association – *ato constitutivo da empresa*
Companies Office – *autoridade responsável pelo registro das empresas*
Constitution – *constituição*
Briefly – *brevemente*
Purpose – *objeto*
Director – *diretor*
Board meeting – *reunião do conselho de administração*
To be issued – *ser emitido*
To carry out – *executar, pôr em prática*
Respect – *respeito*
Regulatory rules – *normas de regulação*
Emphasis – *ênfase*
To restrict – *restringir*
Worker – *trabalhador*
Host state – *país anfitrião*
Favors employee right – *favorecer os direitos do trabalhador*
In turn – *por sua vez*
Revenue – *renda*
Reduced tax rate – *juros reduzidos*
Tax base – *base tributária*
Tax return – *declaração de renda*
To compete – *competir*
Regulatory regime – *quadro regulamentar*
Delaware effect – *"efeito Delaware"*
Enabling legislation – *legislação que permite às empresas de funcionar sob quadro regulamentar menos restritivo ; enabling legislation can also mean legislation allowing the executive branch to adopt secondary legislation – legislação que permite a adoção de legislação secundária (por decreto)*
Private limited (liability) company – *sociedade limitada*
To be traded – *ser vendidos (ações)*
Over the counter (OTC) – *mercado livre de ações*
Stock exchange – *bolsa de valores*
To raise funds – *levanter fundos*
To purchase – *comprar*
Closed corporation – *sociedade "fechada", onde a aquisição de ações é restrita a seus membros*
Non-profit organization – *organização sem fins lucrativos*
Stated charitable goal – *objetivo de caridade estabelecido*

To set out – *anunciar*
To exempt – *isentar*
Tax burden – *carga tributária*
General partnership – *sociedade em nome coletivo*
Point of view – *ponto de vista*
Insofar as – *na medida em que*
Profit – *lucro*
Income tax – *imposto de renda*
To be exposed – *ser exposto a*
Joint and several liability – *responsabilidade coletiva e solidária*
Monies – *dinheiro*
Pursuant to – *segundo, de acordo com*
To draw-up – *redigir*
Limited liability partnership – *sociedade limitada*
To overcome – *ultrapassar, superar*
Accordingly – *conseqüentemente*
Trade name – *nome comercial*
To prevent – *impedir, prevenir*
Unregulated – *não regulado*
To raise capital – *levantar capital*
Winding up, liquidation – *liqüidação*
To cease to trade – *encerrar as atividades comerciais*
Asset – *bem, ativo*
Amongst – *entre*
Dissolution – *dissolução*
Compulsory liquidation – *liqüidação compulsória*
Unpaid creditor – *credor não pago*
To be bankrupt – *ir à falência*
Receivership – *administração judicial*
To restructure – *reestruturar*
A going concern – *uma empresa próspera*
Whilst – *enquanto, ao passo que*
Voluntary liquidation, shareholders' liquidation – *liqüidação voluntária*
Company resolution – *resolução da empresa*
Outstanding monies – *somas devidas*
To be owed – *ser credor (de uma soma em dinheiro)*
Creditors meeting – *reunião de credores*
To appoint – *nomear*
Liquidator – *liqüidante*

PART 1 – TEXT 2 – EXERCISES

1. Definitions

Write a sentence defining each of the following terms – one sentence per term

a)   Limited Liability Company
b)   Limited liability
c)   Double taxation burden

d) Board of directors
e) Corporation tax
f) Winding up
g) Delaware effect
h) Jointly and severally liable

2. Sentences

Write sentences with the following pairs of words demonstrating your knowledge of the relationship between them

a) Tax burden/sole proprietorship
b) Shareholder/corporation
c) Partnership/limited liability
d) Closed corporation/OTC
e) Enabling legislation/Delaware effect
f) NPO/tax burden
g) Sole proprietorship/trade name
h) Limited partnership/general partnership
i) Voluntary liquidation/bankrupt
j) LLP/jointly and severally liable

3. Fill in the missing words

Using the vocabulary in Text 2, fill in the missing words

a) Although a type of corporation _____ have limited lifespans; to the contrary separate business entity corporations only come to an end in the case of bankruptcy or when they are _____.
b) Partners in a general _____ are _____ liable, while in the case of an LLP they enjoy limited liability.
c) To create a corporation it is necessary to file the company's _____ with the _____.
d) Unlimited liability _____ offer their _____ greater secrecy but deny them the benefit of _____.
e) The _____ describes the process whereby regulatory competition occurs between different _____ in the US.

4. Knowledge test

The following questions may be answered in writing or by way of discussion

a) Do LLCs exist in your country? If not is there an equivalent type of company entity?
b) Do you think that the Delaware effect causes negative competition or does it lead to the creation of a more efficient pro-business regulatory environment?
c) Why do you think some businesses are allowed to benefit from limited liability?
d) Is it fair to impose a double tax burden on corporations?

e)   Should corporations be allowed to benefit from the provisions of human rights law?

PART 2 – QUICK LOOK GRAMMAR REVISION

Construction of a sentence in English

1. Constructing a sentence

Every sentence is made up of words organized into one or a number of clauses.

There are three basic types of sentence in English:
- simple sentences;
- compound sentences;
- complex sentences.

Simple sentences have one clause, while compound or complex sentences will have at least two if not more clauses. A sentence will normally have a subject and an object and will involve the subject doing something (by way of a verb) to the object.

Thus a sentence will normally be formed around the subject, the verb and finally the object, for example:

The lawyer hit his client.

If we want to describe the manner in which the meeting took place, then more information can be added by way of adjectives or adverbs, for example:

*The **old** lawyer walked **slowly** to work.*

The more information we put in the sentence, the more information the listener or reader receives. However, in English sentences are normally kept short, each sentence building upon the information contained in the sentence. For example:

The lawyer went to work. He was old and walked slowly.

In this way ambiguity can be limited and, as a general rule, good English is simple English and simple English is best guaranteed by short clear sentences.

> **Note:**
>
> Sentences are made up of a number of different parts, each of which has a name. Some of these are always present and some, such as adjectives, are optional:
> - subject: the person who is the *subject* of the sentence, i.e. who is performing the act;
> - object: the *thing* or *person* on whom the act is being performed;

- verb: providing the action in the sentence;
- definite (the) or indefinite (a, an) article;
- adjective: describing the context/qualifying the noun;
- adverb: qualifying the verb or possibly another adverb;
- noun: naming things (a proper noun is the actual name of a person or a place);
- preposition: relating one part of the sentence to another.

2. Different types of sentences

As we have seen there are three types of sentence in English: simple, compound and complex sentences.

Simple sentence Simple sentences contain a subject and a predicate[9]. A simple sentence normally has only one verb and describes only one action or idea.

Example:
> *John walked to the courthouse.*
> *Old John walked slowly to the old decrepit courthouse.*

Compound sentences Compound sentences are composed of two or more simple sentences with a conjunction placed in the middle, for example *but* or *and*.

Example:
> *John walked to the courthouse but his partner took a taxi to the courthouse.*

Complex sentences Complex sentences have more than one verb and describe more than one action or idea. Unlike compound sentences, which in reality are made up of two independent clauses that can stand alone, a complex sentence is made up of an independent clause that can stand alone and a subordinate or dependent clause that cannot.

Example:
> *John likes pleading before judges **that are nice**.*[10]

> **Note:**
>
> In compound sentences, each of the two clauses making up the sentence can stand alone as a simple sentence.
> **Example:**
> > *I may stay at work **or** I may go home.*

---

[9] A predicate is the part of the sentence (including the verb) that tells us something about the subject: John ran to work – here the subject of the sentence is John and the predicate is that he *ran to work* (the simple predicate is the verb *ran*).

[10] The dependent clause is in bold and, as it describes something, it is referred to as an adjectival subordinate clause.

Note:

Imperative sentences ordering someone to do something are unlike ordinary sentences, insofar as the subject "you" is usually understood and not expressed.

Example:

Go to work now.

3. Deconstructing a sentence

As we have seen, sentences are made up of different parts, for example the subject, verb, predicate, object etc. How do we identify each of these parts?

Subject The subject of a sentence is the "thing" to which the sentence refers. It is frequently but not necessarily found at the start of the sentence. To identify the subject of the verb, it is necessary to first isolate the verb and then ask *who* or *what* did it….

Example:

John walked to the courthouse.
Who walked to the courthouse? Answer: John.
Consequently John is the subject of the sentence.

Verb Verbs can take the form of either *action/dynamic verbs* or *state/stative verbs*:
John is working in his office – dynamic verb.
John works in an office – stative verb.

There may be a number of verbs in the sentence but every sentence has what is called a main verb.

Example:

Working all week on the pleadings made John happier.
Made is the main verb in the sentence and expresses the main action or the state of being of the object of the sentence – i.e. John.

The predicate Remove the subject and the predicate makes up the remainder of the sentence.

Example:

John pleaded the case before the court.
The predicate: *pleaded the case before the court.*
In this sentence the subject is John.

Object The object is the *thing* concerned by the action described in the verb. There are either direct or indirect objects.

Example:

John pleaded the case – the direct object is the *case.*

John pleaded the case before the judge – the direct object is the case, the indirect object is the *judge*.

Adverbs or adverbial phrases Adverbs or adverbial phrases tell us how the action of the verb was done.

Example:

John pleaded the case *three times* before different judges.

PART 2 – GRAMMAR EXERCISES

1. Identify the sentence

Identify the sentences below as simple, compound or complex sentences ……

a) Find me the file now.
b) I like to plead before younger judges as they are less demanding.
c) Ronnie chose to specialize in competition law as he hoped to make a lot of money.
d) I will go home now and go to bed.
e) The old lawyer with the big long white beard is very nice.
f) Bring in two coffees please and then order a taxi for 11:30am.
g) John was promoted because he works very hard.
h) Bill always smoked a cigarette during his morning break.
i) If I plead your case I will not be able to go on holiday.

2. Deconstruct the sentence ……

Identify the component parts of the following sentences……

a) I am tired.
b) John quickly finished working on the case.
c) Associates have to bill 1,400 hours a year.
d) John has always gone to the Algarve on holidays.
e) Translate the contract into English.

PART 3 – AUDIO AND ORAL – LISTENING AND SPEAKING

Comprehension

Listen to the following conversation, make notes of all the relevant facts and then answer the questions below. If you have trouble understanding, follow the conversation while also reading the text.

Conversation between Bob Jones, solicitor and James who wants to establish a business

Bob: "So James, you are thinking of becoming a businessman?"
James: "Well yes …. Nothing spectacular of course, I don't want to become Bill Gates or anything, but I do intend to start a business."

Bob: "And what type of business do you want to get involved in? Are you already trading or is it a start-up?"

James: "A start-up?"

Bob: "Yes, establishing the business from scratch, I mean from the beginning."

James: "I suppose you could say it's a start-up."

Bob: "So what do you want to do, that is if it's not a secret?"

James: "No, it is not a secret but obviously I would appreciate your discretion; I want to start up a restaurant."

Bob: "OK ... as your lawyer I should probably ask you a couple of questions just to make sure you are on the right track, so as to speak."

James: "The right track?"

Bob: "Well, yes ... just to see if it is a sustainable idea."

James: "Oh yes of course, ask away ..."

Bob: "The first question I would have to ask you is whether you have any experience in the restaurant business?"

James: "Sorry?"

Bob: "I asked whether you had any actual experience working in the restaurant business."

James: "Yes and no."

Bob: "Could you be a little more specific?"

James: "Well I love cooking."

Bob: "Is that it?"

James: "Well yes, isn't it enough?"

Bob: "You do realize that experience of cooking and experience of running a restaurant is not exactly the same thing. It is a little like if you told me you want to have an airline because you like flying."

James: "I believe that they are pretty close."

Bob: "There is no doubt a relationship between cooking and restaurants it is true ... but you don't if I understand correctly have any actual experience of working as a professional cook? You just like to cook .... like many people."

James: "Yes, but I am a good cook."

Bob: "Says who?"

James: "Pardon?"

Bob: "Look, I'm not here to tell you what should do but I would not be doing my job if I did not point out to you the risks of starting a business in an area in which you have little to no actual experience."

James: "But I know I will make a success of it."

Bob: "OK, it obviously is your decision."

James: "Yes it is."

Bob: "So what form do you want the business to take?"

James: "What do you mean?"

Bob: "Do you want the restaurant to be a business separate from you, i.e. do you want to establish a separate company and benefit from limited liability as regards any potential debts that the business may have or would you prefer to operate as a sole trader?"

James: "What do you think?"

Bob: "On the basis of your lack of experience and the notoriously high failure rate for restaurants, I'd be inclined to take the limited liability option somehow."

James: "Are you being smart?"
Bob: "No, just realistic!"

PART 3 – AUDIO COMPREHENSION – EXERCISES

1. Comprehension

From the notes you have taken, answer the following questions

    a)   Is James' business a start-up?
    b)   What form does Bob think the business should take?
    c)   What experience has James?
    d)   Does James want to be like Bill Gates?
    e)   Does Bob think James will be successful? In your answer state why.
    f)   What kind of cooking does James do?

2. Speaking practice

In the following series of conversation couplets develop suitable responses to the questions asked

    a)   Bob: "Hello James so what type of business do you want to start?"
            James: "_____."
    b)   Bob: "Have you ever managed or owned a restaurant before?"
            James: "_____."
    c)   Bob: "What experience of cooking do you have if any?"
            James: "_____"
    d)   Bob: "Do you know the success rate for new restaurants?"
            James: "_____."
    e)   Bob: "What form do you want your business to take?"
            James: "_____."
    f)   Bob: "Is your business a start-up?"
            James: "_____."
    g)   Bob: "What type of restaurant are you thinking of opening?"
            James: "_____."
    h)   Bob: "How big will your restaurant be?"
            James: "_____."
    i)   Bob: "Are you starting your business from scratch?"
            James: "_____."
    j)   Bob: "I hope you will invite me to the opening night."
            Charles: "_____."

3. Speaking practice continued ......

Create five other conversation couplets using in each couplet at least one word from the vocabulary found in Part 1, Text 1 or Text 2.

4. Speaking practice continued ......

Listen to the suggested replies and repeat

a)   Bob: "Hello James, so what type of business do you want to start?"
     James: "I would like to open up a restaurant."

b)   Bob: "Have you ever managed or owned a restaurant before?"
     James: "No I have no actual experience of running a restaurant."

c)   Bob: "What experience of cooking do you have, if any?"
     James: "I have never worked as a professional cook but I do love to cook."

d)   Bob: "Do you know the success rate for new restaurants?"
     James: "Not exactly but I believe it is rather low."

e)   Bob: "What form do you want your business to take?"
     James: "I would like to ensure that I would benefit from limited liability as regards the restaurant's debts."

f)   Bob: "Why do you want to start a restaurant?"
     James: "I have always loved cooking and having guests."

g)   Bob: "What type of restaurant are you thinking of opening?"
     James: "I would like to open a pizza restaurant."

h)   Bob: "How big will your restaurant be?"
     James: "I hope it will be big enough to be able to have at least fifty clients at any one time."

i)   Bob: "Are you starting your business from scratch?"
     James: "Yes, I am starting the business from the beginning."

j)   Bob: "I hope you will invite me to the opening night."
     Charles: "Of course I will and I hope you will give me a reduction as regards my legal costs!"

5. Associated questions

Discuss the following questions

a)   What business form could a restaurant take in your country? State the advantages and/or disadvantages of the different available forms the business might take?

b)   Is there a good regulatory environment in your country for setting up businesses? What are the good and bad points about your regulatory system?

c)   Would you like to go into business; what are the advantages and disadvantages?

d)   In general do you consider that businesses exploit their workers or is it a mutually beneficial relationship?

PART 4 – TRANSLATION EXERCISES

When carrying out the translations it is not necessary to translate directly word for word; rather the emphasis should be on translating the sense of the text. Language is not directly interchangeable and so direct translations do not always convey the meaning in the text.

Translate the following texts from English to Portuguese

A. What is a company?

A company is a form of business organization. The English word company comes from the latin *companio*. In medieval times, the word was used to refer to the trade guilds that were popular at that time. A company often takes the form of an "artificial legal person" enjoying perpetual succession. Thus, it is not affected by the death of its creators or members. Nor will a company be inconvenienced by the insolvency of its members, except indirectly, where a member has acted as guarantor for the company's debts.

B. A corporation is a legal entity distinct from its owners – Salomon v Salomon, 1897

Salomon's case is universally recognized in common law countries as authority for the principle that a corporation is a legal entity separate from its owners. The case firmly established that, upon incorporation, a new and separate artificial entity comes into existence. At law, a corporation is a distinct person with its own personality separate from and independent of the persons who formed it, who invest money in it and who direct and manage its operations. It follows that the rights and duties of a corporation are not the same as the rights and duties of its directors or members. The recognition that a corporation is a separate legal entity in its own right is the foundation of modern corporate law and business in western economies. A corporation is said to be *shrouded* in a corporate veil.

C. Lifting the corporate veil

Lifting or piercing the corporate veil describes the decision by the courts to look beyond the separate legal personality of a company and to apply the rights or liabilities normally attributed to the company to its owners or directors. Usually a corporation is treated as a separate legal person; however, in exceptional situations a court may decide to pierce/lift the corporate veil. A simple example would be where a company acts illegally, for instance bribing a public official. In such a case, the courts will pierce the corporate veil, considering the company's officers or owners criminally responsible for the actions entered into in the company's name.

Translate the following texts from Portuguese to English

A. Levantar o véu social é a única maneira de manter a responsabilidade dos administradores da empresa pelos atos da sociedade?

Perfurar o véu social não é o único meio de responsabilizar o administrador de uma empresa pelas ações desta. A responsabilidade da empresa pode ser estabelecida com base em teorias tradicionais do contrato, da representação e do direito da responsabilidade civil. Por exemplo, nas situações em que o dirigente ou administrador agindo em nome da empresa comete um delito, ele e a sociedade podem ser considerados responsáveis. Ademais, nos casos em que a sociedade cometeu um crime, a lei penal não hesitará em atribuir a responsabilidade penal dos administradores da empresa envolvidos.

B. O que é um prospectus?

Um prospectus é um documento desenvolvido originalmente no direito empresarial anglo-saxão e que foi criado para oferecer aos investidores um certo grau de proteção a seus investimentos. Na maior parte das jurisdições do common law, as empresas que emitirem títulos financeiros possuem a obrigação legal de emitir um prospectus que descreve a sociedade e as razões que explicam porque a sociedade emite ações. Um prospectus normalmente fornece aos investidores informações essenciais sobre a sociedade. Por exemplo, o propectus inclui uma descrição das atividades da sociedade e dos documentos contábeis, as biografias de seus administradores e dirigentes e informações detalhadas sobre a compensação, as ações judiciárias em curso envolvendo a empresa ou qualquer outra informação essencial.

C. A regras sobre o prospectus no Reino Unido

A publicação de qualquer informação ligada à emissão de títulos financeiros no Reino Unido é regida pela lei do Prospectus Rules, que coloca em prática a diretiva da União Européia sobre o prospectus. Um prospectus deve ser publicado por uma sociedade quando ela emite ações para a venda ao público ou quando uma empresa requere sua admissão em um mercado financeiro regulamentado. No Reino Unido, o único mercado financeiro regulamentado é o London Stock Exchange. O Alternative Investment Market (AIM) não é um mercado financeiro regulamentado.

PART 5 – ADVANCED READING

Why are certain business formations given the benefit of limited liability?

Pursuant to the doctrine of limited liability only corporations and not their members are responsible for the debts of a business, i.e. creditors are given no recourse to the personal assets of the corporation's shareholders. Thus, investors in a business entity benefit from limited liability and are only liable for the actual monies they have actually invested in the business. Fundamental to the doctrine of limited liability is the notion that upon incorporation a business develops a separate independent personality, and it is this legal entity and not its investors that actually incurs liabilities in the course of its business. This is said to be a veil that hangs around the entity, separating it from its members. Limited liability was introduced in the United Kingdom in the mid 1800s in order to encourage investment in UK industry. Although first introduced by Parliament under the Limited Liability Act, 1855, the courts in *Salomon v*

Salomon extended the principle to private companies. The result was the creation of a dynamic industrial economy that allowed the small island of Britain the economic flexibility to be at the heart of the industrial revolution. Its existence not only ensures easy access to investment for all sorts of business projects but also ensures the existence of a thriving investment market and stock exchange, where investors frequently compete to invest in specific business opportunities.

The doctrine of limited liability has been criticized by some as being morally suspect. After all, why should the creation of what is effectively an artificial legal entity allow promoters and investors to escape liability for the debts that they incur through their business? Why allow investors to avoid the debts of their business, so that others only indirectly connected to the activity, i.e. creditors, have to pay in their place? The answer to this is of course that you don't have to lend to a limited liability company if you do not want to. Moreover, if the existence of limited liability really was an issue for creditors, then companies would take an unlimited liability form in order to benefit from better lending arrangements. It must be recalled that the reason behind the introduction of limited liability was to encourage a culture of investment in business. Nonetheless, there are limits to the degree to which the members of a corporation can rely on the latter's separate legal status to avoid liability. In this regard the courts are willing to lift the corporate veil in which a corporation lies shrouded, if there is a suspicion of dishonesty or if the corporation is a mere façade, created to avoid liability.

For example in *Jones v Lipman* the defendant attempted to evade an order of specific performance made against him in equity, requiring him to transfer ownership of a property to the plaintiff. The defendant sought to avoid this by creating a limited liability company and transferring his title in the property to the newly created entity. The defendant was effectively the only shareholder in the new company. This way he hoped he would not have to transfer the property to the plaintiff and could instead make an equivalent payment in damages. However, the court considered the company to be merely a mask used by the defendant to escape his pre-established obligations in law. The corporate veil may not be used to hide illegal behavior. That said, there is nothing wrong with establishing a corporation in order to avoid future as yet not established liability, as long as such liability is legally incurred.

Chapter eight

INTELLECTUAL PROPERTY LAW

PART 1 – TEXT 1 – INFORMATION

What is intellectual property law?

The **law of intellectual property** exists to **promote creativity** and **innovation**. Different types of protection are granted depending on the nature of the *element* that one is **seeking** to protect. For example:

- an inventor can **protect** his **novel** inventions **by way of** registered patents;
- a business can protect its name or **logo** by way of **registered trademarks** and the tort law of **passing off**;
- a **draftsman** can protect his/her designs by relying on **design rights**;
- **literary and artistic works** and **computer software** can be protected under **copyright** law;
- **database rights** can be relied on to protect information lists held in databases.

How does one benefit from this protection?

Some of these rights exist automatically, whilst for others it is necessary to make an **application** to the appropriate authority. For example, once a design, literary or artistic work is created, then a right to prevent the copying of that work automatically exists, without the need to make an application to the authorities. However, other rights concerning trademarks, patents and registered designs need to be applied for and are **granted** by the relevant authorities existing both at national, European Union and international level.

A closer look at different types of intellectual property rights

As we have seen, there are different types of intellectual property rights such as patents, trademarks, passing off, copyright, design rights, database rights.

- *Patents* A patent seeks to protect an invention or a method of doing something that represents either a new product, an **improvement** on a previously existing product or a new or improved methodology or industrial process. Applying for a patent can be complicated and in common law countries the application will normally be made by a **patent attorney.** To be a patent attorney in the United Kingdom, it is necessary to be a member of the Charted Institute of Patent Attorneys.
- *Trademarks* A trademark signals the commercial origin of a good or a service, i.e. indicating that it is made or performed by a particular company. Thus, a trademark is often used to protect an image or

reputation that is encapsulated in a **brand**. Normally, in common law countries, applications for trademark protection are made by way of a **trademark attorney** registered with a national institute of trademark attorneys. In addition to the protection guaranteed under the heading of trademarks, **tort law** has developed a separate right, referred to as the tort of **passing off**. By bringing an action in passing off, a business can prevent another party from using its name or logo or a similar name or logo.

- *Copyright* Copyright is relied on to protect the expression of someone's ideas, whether they take literary, artistic or musical form. A person's copyright is infringed if someone else reproduces the work or a substantial part **thereof** without the consent of the copyright owner. Copyright gives automatic protection to artistic creators as regards their *works*; however, many artists can choose to apply to the authorities for formal copyright protection.
- *Database rights* Database rights protect the contents of a database where the act of compiling the database involves the active collection and verification of the data contained **therein**. **Thus** for a database to be capable of registration, it is necessary to show proof of such effort. **Consequently**, it does not normally suffice to take a list of people from the phonebook, if one is to successfully obtain IP protection over the collected information.

VOCABULARY

Law of intellectual property – *direito de propriedade intelectual*
To promote – *promover*
Creativity – *criatividade*
Innovation – *inovação*
To seek – *procurar*
To protect – *proteger*
Novel – *original*
By way of – *por meio de*
Logo – *logo*
Registered trademark – *marca registrada*
Passing-off – *comercialização fraudulenta*
Draftsman – *desenhista*
Design right – *proteção de desenhos e modelos*
Literary and artistic works – *obras literárias e artísticas*
Computer software – *programa de computador*
Copyright – *direito autoral*
Database right – *proteção de bases de dados*
Application – *pedido*
To be recorded – *ser registrado*
To grant – *conceder*
Improvement – *melhoria*
Patent Attorney – *advogado especialista em direito de patentes*

Brand – *marca*
Trademark Attorney – *advogado especialista em direito de marcas*
Law of Tort – *direito da responsabilidade civil*
To pass something off – *comercializar um produto de forma fraudulenta*
Thereof – *disso, daí*
Therein – *neste*
Thus – *assim, deste modo, portanto*
Consequently – *conseqüentemente*

PART 1 – TEXT 1 – EXERCISES

1. Vocabulary test

Fill in the missing words using the vocabulary in Text 1

a) Only _____ inventions can be _____ through the registration of a patent.
b) Pursuant to the tort of _____ it can be illegal to use names or _____ that are similar to those used by competitors.
c) In order for a database to be _____ protection, it is necessary that proof of effort be demonstrated as regards the collection of the _____.
d) Literary and _____ works can be protected under _____ law.
e) _____ are used to protect brands and can be obtained by going to see a trademark _____.
f) It is not necessary to _____ for copyright protection, as protection is considered to exist once the work in question is _____.
g) The role of _____ law is to promote _____

2. Vocabulary test

Write sentences with the following pairs of words. Your sentence should demonstrate your knowledge of the relationship between the words

a) Design rights/draftsman
b) Copyright/works
c) Brand/trademark attorney
d) Novel/patent
e) Database/protection
f) Passing off/trademark

3. Knowledge test

Each of the following statements is false; do you know why? Write a sentence stating why it is false

a) Copyright protection can be obtained by making an application to a registered trademark attorney.
b) Databases are the subject of automatic protection under the law of intellectual property.
c) The law of intellectual property exists primarily to allow people protection for their creations.

d)   Design rights can be protected under the law governing patents.
e)   In order to benefit from copyright protection it is necessary to apply to the appropriate authorities.

PART 1 – TEXT 2 – MORE INFORMATION

What is intellectual property law?

The **law of intellectual property** exists **above all** to **promote creativity** and **innovation**. It does this by **offering** *creators* protection **as regards** the exploitation of the results of their creation or innovation. The **extent** of the protection offered to **inventors** by the law **varies,** depending on the nature of the actual creation or innovation. For example, a different type of protection is granted depending on whether one is **seeking** to protect a **piece of writing** or a newly invented engine **part**. The extent of the protection granted is governed by the law of intellectual property, which **confers** different rights for different creations. Thus, and it is worth repeating, the primary **goal** of an intellectual property right is to promote innovation and it does this by **preventing** others from **copying** or profiting in some way from the creations of others.

By **relying on** an intellectual property right, a person can protect their creations, for example:
*   an inventor can **protect novel** inventions and the **methodology** behind their **manufacture** by way of a registered patent;
*   a business can protect its name or **logo** and the reputation developed **thereunder** by way of a **registered trademark** or more generally its rights can be protected under the law of **passing off**;
*   a **draftsman** can protect his designs by relying on the protection given to **design rights**;
*   **literary** and artistic works, **computer software** etc. can be protected through the law on **copyright**;
*   **database rights** can be relied on to protect information held in databases.

These different rights can on occasion **overlap**, offering complementary protection.

How does one benefit from this protection?

Some intellectual property rights exist or accrue automatically, while for others it is necessary to make an **application** to the appropriate authorities. For example, once a design, literary or artistic work is **recorded**, a right to prevent the copying of that work exists automatically. Coming under the heading of rights that arise automatically are rights such as copyrights, design rights and **performance rights**, i.e. the right to perform the creative musical work of another in public. With all these rights, the right to exploit the creation automatically rests with the author of the work. If, however, the author developed the work in the context of his/her employment, then, depending on the terms of the employment contract, the real beneficiary of the intellectual property right to exploit the work might well be the employer.

However, other IP rights such as registered trademarks, patents and registered designs need to be applied for and are **granted** by the relevant authorities. In Europe, such protection exists at national and European Union level. Registering a right with the national authorities of a country will only allow protection for the national territory of that country. In the same way, registering the right with a European Union authority will provide the right's holder with protection throughout the Union.

A **party** seeking to register a trademark, patent or design will need to contact the appropriate authorities: for example, the Patent Office in the United Kingdom or at European level the **Office for the Harmonization of the Internal Market** (OHIM) located in Alicante, Spain or the **European Patent Office** in Munich, Germany. Thereafter, to successfully register an application it is necessary for the:

- applicant to **fill in** an application form describing the nature of the right to be protected, accompanied by the appropriate **fee**;
- relevant authority to **process** the application and carry out **searches** to ensure that an earlier **conflicting right** has not already been registered; and
- right to be placed on a **register** with the applicant described as its legal owner. The advantage of recording ownership of the right on an official register is that the register proves ownership. Thus, in the case of a conflict with a **third party** that uses the right, the registered owner will not have to go before the court to establish ownership. **Rather**, any **action** before the court will immediately be centered on punishing the violation of the right. Moreover, should another party claim ownership of the registered right, the **burden of proof** as regards establishing ownership is placed on the claimant.

A closer look at different types of intellectual property rights

As we have seen, there are different types of intellectual property rights such as patents, trademarks, passing off, copyright, design rights and database rights. It is perhaps **worthwhile** to consider the nature of these rights in greater detail.

- *Patents* A patent seeks to protect a newly developed product or invention, or a new method of doing something that represents an **improvement** on the method previously used. Applying for a patent can be complicated and in common law countries the application will normally be made by a **Patent Attorney**. In the United Kingdom to work as a Patent Attorney, it is necessary to be a qualified lawyer and also a member of the **Chartered Institute of Patent Attorneys**. **Upon receipt** of the patent, the applicant is the only entity allowed to act **within the scope** of the patented right; for example to produce a specific type of product or to use a certain methodology in its creation. In other words, the patent holder enjoys the equivalent of a

monopoly and, **as such**, intellectual property rights can be considered an exception to the monopoly provisions of competition law. In return for this grant of exclusivity, the patent holder must make public the details of his/her invention. For Europe-wide patent protection, it is necessary to apply to the European Patents Office in Munich.

- *Trademarks* A trademark is an indication of the origin of a good or service. In other words, a trademark is used to protect a **brand**. Businesses frequently invest large sums of money in advertising, design and quality control in order to develop a brand, and intellectual property law allows them to prevent other businesses from seeking to benefit from that investment. Europe-wide trademark protection can be applied for from the Office for the Harmonization of the Internal Market (OHIM) or from the national offices in each of the member states. In the United Kingdom, applications for trademark protection are normally made by way of a **trademark attorney**, registered with the **Institute of Trademark Attorneys** (ITMA). Trademark applications tend to be less complicated than patent applications and in reality can in some cases be applied for without the necessity of legal assistance.

- *Passing off* In addition to the protection guaranteed under the heading of trademarks, **tort law** has developed protection under a right of action referred to as the law of passing off. By bringing an action in passing off, a business can prevent another party from **passing off** as his own a brand name or logo developed by the **plaintiff**. Passing off is thus a right of action providing protection for unregistered trademarks and may be brought before the courts once a business can establish that:
  - customers recognize or associate a name or logo as **denoting** the plaintiff's specific business; and
  - another business, by using that name or logo or one that is similar, is leading customers to believe that they are connected with the plaintiff's business.

  The main difference between trademark protection and rights existing under the heading of passing off is that the **former** establishes the existence of a right which can then be relied upon against third parties. However, in the case of passing off, it is necessary to **go before the courts** to first establish the existence of the right and then prove that it has been infringed. Thus, the burden of proof is on the business alleging the violation of its intellectual property right. Possession of a registered trademark overturns this burden of proof and consequently it is considered more valuable. This is important as in the common law possession is said to be nine-tenths of the law[11].

- *Copyright* Copyright is relied on to protect the expression of someone's ideas, whether they take literary, artistic or musical form. A copyright is infringed if a work or a substantial part **thereof** is

---

[11] By this is meant that the person who possesses a right normally wins a court case disputing the ownership of the right.

reproduced without the **consent** of the copyright owner. Copyright seeks to protect the expression of an idea rather than the idea itself. Thus, I may write a book about Charles de Gaulle and my ideas and the manner of their expression as regards Charles de Gaulle may be protected; however, I cannot prevent someone else writing about Charles de Gaulle discussing the same issues and even coming to the same conclusions. In the same way, if I take a photograph of Charles de Gaulle's house, I will enjoy copyright in the photo, which may not be reproduced and sold without my permission, but I will not be able to prevent another person taking a picture of the house from exactly the same position. Unlike patents or trademarks, a copyright is conferred automatically once some type of written, artistic or musical creation occurs. It is not necessary to demonstrate that the idea is a good one or that for example the painting in question is a work of art; the protection results from the work's existence, not from its value, which ultimately involves a subjective evaluation. Although a right in copyright exists automatically, it is also possible to formally register the right. As above, the advantage of registering copyright is that in the case of a subsequent conflict concerning ownership, the burden of proof is on the party reproducing the work without the registered owner's permission, to prove that (s)he has a right to do so. In the case of unregistered copyright, it is the party claiming ownership that must prove the existence of their right.

- *Design rights* Design rights protect the *design* of **three-dimensional** objects. As with copyright, design rights occur automatically and do not have to be registered. However, once registered, design rights grant the owner the exclusive right to use the design for the period of time stated in the grant of the right and create a presumption of ownership. As with patents and trademarks, a registered design right may be sought for a specific country or on a European or international basis. The Patent Office is responsible for registering design rights in the United Kingdom, while the OHIM carries out the same function on a EU-wide basis. There can be an overlap between trademark protection and design rights, with the major difference being that the former is not limited in time.

- *Database rights* Database rights protect the contents of a database, where **compilation** of the database required the active collection and verification of the data contained **therein. Thus**, for a database to be capable of registration, it is necessary to show proof of such effort in the compilation of the data. **Consequently**, it does not suffice to take a list of people from the phonebook, if one is to successfully obtain database protection over the list.

Vocabulary

Law of intellectual property – *direito de propriedade intelectual*
Above all – *acima de tudo*
To promote – *promover*

Creativity – *creatividade*
Innovation – *invenção*
To offer – *oferecer*
As regards – *quanto a, no que diz respeito*
Extent – *extenção, medida*
Inventor – *inventor*
To vary – *variar*
To seek – *procurar*
Piece of writing – *escrito*
(Spare) part – *peça (avulsa)*
To confer – *conferir*
Goal – *objetivo*
To prevent – *impedir*
To copy – *copiar*
To rely on – *contar com, depender de*
To protect – *proteger*
Novel – *original*
Methodology – *metodologia*
Manufacture – *fabricação*
Logo – *logo*
Thereunder – *estabelecido sob*
Registered trademark – *marca registrada*
Passing–*off* – *comercialização fraudulenta*
Draftsman – *desenhista*
Design right – *proteção de desenhos e modelos*
Literary – *literário*
Computer software – *programa de computador*
Copyright – *direito autoral*
Database right – *proteção de bases de dados*
To overlap – *sobrepor*
Application – *pedido*
To record – *registrar*
Performance right – *direito de representação*
To grant – *conceder*
Party – *parte*
Office for the Harmonization of the Internal Market – *instituto de harmonização do mercado interno (marcas, desenhos, modelos)*
European Patent Office – *Instituto Europeu de Patentes*
To fill in a form, to fill out a form – *preencher um formulário*
Fee – *pagamento (fees – honorários)*
To process – *tartar, preparar*
To search – *procurer, pesquisar*
Conflicting right – *conflito de direito*
Register – *registro*
Third party – *terceiros*
Rather (than) – *ao contrário, em vez de*
Action – *ação (judicial)*
Burden of proof – *ônus da prova*

Worthwhile – *valer a pena*
Improvement – *melhoria*
Patent Attorney – *advogado especialista em direito de patentes*
Chartered Institute of Patent Attorneys – *associação de advogados especialistas em direito de patentes*
Upon receipt – *a partir do recebimento de, após o recebimento de*
Coming within the scope – *entrar no âmbito da aplicação (da patente)*
Monopoly – *monopólio*
As such – *como tal*
Brand – *marca*
Trademark Attorney – *advogado especialista em direito de marcas*
Institute of Trademarks Attorneys – *instituto de advogados especialistas em direito de marcas*
Law of Tort – *direito da responsabilidade civil*
To pass something off – *comercializar um produto de forma fraudulenta*
Plaintiff – *demandante, requerente*
To denote – *denotar, indicar*
Former – *primeiro (elemento mencionado)*
To go before the courts – *ir perante os tribunais*
Thereof – *disso, daí*
Consent – *permissão*
Three dimensional – *tridimensional*
Compilation – *compilação (de uma base de dados) (To compile – compilar)*
Therein – *neste*
Thus – *assim, deste modo, portanto*
Consequently – *conseqüentemente*

PART 1 – TEXT 2 – EXERCISES

1. Definitions

Write a sentence defining each of the following terms – one sentence per term

- a)   Patent
- b)   Software
- c)   Passing off
- d)   Burden of proof
- e)   Trademark
- f)   Database
- g)   Novel

2. Sentences

Write sentences with the following pairs of words demonstrating your knowledge of the relationship between them

- a)   Register/trademark
- b)   Passing off/brand
- c)   To copy/protection
- d)   Europe/OHIM

   e)   Trademark attorney/patent
   f)   Monopoly/intellectual property law
   g)   Copyright/burden of proof
   h)   Design rights/three dimensional
   i)   Database/to compile

3. Fill in the missing words

Using the vocabulary in Text 2, fill in the missing words

   a)   The law of _____ seeks to guarantee _____ for inventors and
          creators of artistic works.
   b)   _____ law is relied on to provide protection for artists as regards
          their creations, whether they take _____ , artistic or musical form.
   c)   For European-wide _____ protection it is necessary to _____ to
          the Patent Office in Munich.
   d)   _____ is a common law tort that _____ one party misrepresenting
          their goods or services as being the goods and services of another.
   e)   Intellectual law provides protection under the headings of patent law
          and _____ law; the latter protects brands belonging to businesses,
          while the former protects _____ inventions.

4. Knowledge test

The following questions may be answered in writing or by way of discussion

   a)   Do you consider that intellectual property law offers too much
          protection or not enough?
   b)   Has the process of registration in the area of intellectual property law
          become too complicated?
   c)   What is the difference between the protection offered to businesses
          under the heading of passing off and under the law governing
          trademarks?
   d)   Why do you think there are limits on the amount of protection available
          under intellectual property law? After all, other property rights are
          not normally limited in this way.

PART 2 – QUICK LOOK GRAMMAR REVISION

Infinitives and gerunds

1. Forming infinitives and gerunds

The infinitive form of the verb =
   to + the base form of the verb.
   Example: *to go*
   I want *to go* to the office.

The base form of the verb =
   take away *to*, leaving the verb by itself.
   Example: *go*

I may *go* to the office.

The gerund of the verb =
> add *ing* to bare infinitive/base form of the verb.
> **Example:** *going*
> I like *going* to the office.

2. Verbs taking the infinitive, the base form and the gerund

Many verbs are automatically followed by either the infinitive, base form or gerund form

> ### Verbs and expressions taking the infinitive
> a)   *Verbs followed by the infinitive*

Agree, appear, choose, decide, expect, fail, hope, intend, learn, offer, plan, pretend, promise, refuse, seem ......
> **Example:**
> I will *agree to sign* the agreement if you will *promise to pay* me by the end of the month.

> b)   *Expressions followed by the infinitive*

Make up one's mind, do one's best
> **Example:**
> I *did my best to win* the case but the judge had *made up his mind to find* my client guilty.

> ### Verbs and expressions taking the base form
> a)   *Verbs followed by the base form*

Modal verbs such as can, may, must ......
> **Example:**
> I *can send* you the contract by courier, if you *must have* it by this evening.

> b)   *Expressions followed by the base form*

Had better, would rather ......
> **Example:**
> I *would rather go* to the meeting and you *had better go* too.

> ### Verbs and expressions taking the gerund
> a)   *Some verbs are always followed by the gerund*

Admit, dislike, enjoy, finish, imagine, miss, postpone, quit, risk ......
> **Example:**
> I *admit attending* some of the meetings but I *quit going* once I realized they were part of a cartel.

> b)   *The gerund is also used after all prepositions, and expressions ending in prepositions*

To be against, to give up, to be interested in, to look forward to, to put off ......

N.B. The gerund is also used after the structure "to be worth"
Example:
It is **worth studying** hard at school, if you are *interested in earning* a proper living.

> **Note:**
>
> Some verbs can take the infinitive or the gerund, example: ***like, begin, recommend, require, start, allow, intend, want, can't bear, continue, permit, dare ......***
> **Example:**
> He ***began to go*** the office ......
> He ***began going*** to the office ......

> **Note:**
>
> Verbs such as **recommend, permit, allow, advise** take the infinitive or the gerund form depending on the form of the sentence.
> If used with a direct object they are followed by the infinitive, otherwise the gerund form is used.
> **Example:**
> He ***advised*** the client ***to read*** the contract carefully.
> He ***advised reading*** the contract to all his clients.

3. Verbs that have a different meaning depending on whether the infinitive or gerund form is used

Sometimes the meaning of a sentence will change depending on whether the verb is in the infinitive or the gerund.
> **Example:**
> *I remember going to court.*
> *I remembered to go to court.*
>
> *I stopped smoking.*
> *I stopped to smoke.*
>
> *I am sorry for telling you that you lost the case.*
> *I am sorry to tell you that you lost the case.*

PART 2 – GRAMMAR EXERCISES

1. Identify the correct form of the verb .....

Write the sentence putting it in the correct form; some sentences may already be in the correct form ...

> He helped me preparing the case: *He helped me to prepare the case.*

a)   I enjoy to go to court.
b)   I hope pleading the case before the court.

c)   I set out to become the best lawyer in the world.
d)   I managed convincing the client to sign the contract.
e)   I can't bear to lose cases.

2. Using "it" and the infinitive......

Make a sentence using "it" and the infinitive form......

Working hard is important: *It is important to work hard.*

a)   Working without a secretary is difficult.
b)   Pleading in court is exhausting.
c)   Listening to clients can be boring.
d)   Drafting contracts takes a lot of time.
e)   Being in good humor is important at work.

3. Ask a question......

Fill in the blank ......

a)   Would you consider _____ (get) in touch with the client if he signed the agreement?
b)   He encouraged me _____ (work) harder.
c)   I am looking forward to _____ (go) on holidays.
d)   I am interested in _____ (work) in the area of tax law.
e)   I will try _____ (contact) the client one last time.

PART 3 – AUDIO AND ORAL – LISTENING AND SPEAKING

Comprehension

Listen to the following conversation, make notes of all the relevant facts and then answer the questions below. If you have trouble understanding, follow the conversation while also reading the text.

Conversation between Frank Smart, solicitor and Olivia Chisoli who wants to protect her business

Frank: "So Olivia, good to see you again; what can I do for you?"
Olivia: "Good to see you too Frank. As you know I am in the fashion business."
Frank: "Yes indeed I do, I am actually wearing one of your shirts; I will remove my jacket so you can see your logo, the funny looking dog."
Olivia: "That's the problem Frank, it seems that just because your shirt has my logo on it doesn't mean it is one of my company's shirts."
Frank: "What are you saying Olivia, is somebody counterfeiting your products?"
Olivia: "Yes, I am afraid that is what is happening."
Frank: "OK tell me everything."
Olivia: "I was at a market in London last weekend, on the Portobello Road, and there was a chap there selling our shirts out of the back of a van."
Frank: "So?"
Olivia: "So, I went up and had a look at the product and they were rip offs."

Frank: "Can you be sure they were counterfeit?"

Olivia: "Frank I manufacture these shirts; well I have them manufactured for me in India. The point is I know what my shirts look like and I can tell a genuine shirt from a copy. They were good copies; but the quality of the stitching was not as good and they were using cheaper buttons."

Frank: "Did you ask the guy where he got them?"

Olivia: "Yeah of course I did, I told him who I was and asked him where he was getting them from."

Frank: "And what did he do?"

Olivia: "He legged it Frank[12]. Jumped into his van and drove off."

Frank: "So we have nothing to go on....?"

Olivia: "Not so, I got the number of the van; a white Ford I think 337 BDH."

Frank: "OK that's something. I know a private investigator called Rockford, he is not too expensive... if you want I can ring him up and find out who this guy is."

Olivia: "Yes it would be a start but I don't really care about this guy Frank; I want to know who the supplier is... whoever it is they are breaking the law. As you know I registered a trademark to protect my brand and I want to find out who is violating it. You should remember this as you organized it for me and as I recall charged me enough money in legal fees to get it done."

Frank: "Of course I do Olivia. ... your trademark was registered under the WIPO (World Intellectual Property Organization) Madrid system[13]. The thing is you'll probably find out that these shirts are being manufactured in a country that does not necessarily enforce respect of intellectual property rules."

Olivia: "So what are you telling me, that I paid all that money for protection and now I don't have any at all?"

Frank: "Olivia you paid all that money to have *some* protection ... but it is not a perfect world; there are no absolutes. You have enough protection to allow us to go after the seller you saw on the Portobello Road. Once we find him and threaten him with prosecution we can hopefully find out who his supplier is. In this way we can try and work our way through the supply chain and find out who is manufacturing these shirts and in what jurisdiction. Then the matter turns into as much a political issue as a legal one."

Olivia: "So some guy can be manufacturing cheap shirts, passing them off as mine and despite the fact that I have a registered trademark nothing can be done about it?"

Frank: "I did not say that Olivia, I just said it was a possibility; it depends on the country involved. In any event, let's cross that bridge when we get to it. First thing to do is to stop them being sold in the markets here in this country."

Olivia: "So how much will it cost me?"

Frank: "Well it all depends on how much you want to stop it really."

Olivia: "Well I have to stop it, don't I? That little dog I use as a logo is worth a lot of money; I have spent over ten years and a lot of money in advertising and sponsorship deals developing the brand."

---

[12] *To leg it* – to run away.

[13] The Madrid system established under the Madrid Protocol (1891) and managed by the World Intellectual Property Organization (WIPO) allows applicants on the basis of their home country trademark registration to then register protection in other jurisdictions, thereby obtaining extended security, should they wish to have full global protection.

Frank: "Well then, we will have to have people go to markets all over the country to see how bad the problem is. Each time someone is found selling the shirts it will be necessary to video them and find out who they are."

Olivia: "OK, better start doing it I guess."

Frank: "Maybe to save money you can get your own employees to start visiting markets to locate any sellers of your shirts. In the meantime, I will phone Jim Rockford and try and get a line on the seller[14]. I will also contact the police. They have a special unit dealing with counterfeit goods."

Olivia: "OK let's nail[15] these guys Frank."

PART 3 – AUDIO COMPREHENSION – EXERCISES

1. Comprehension

From the notes you have taken, answer the following questions

    a)   What does Olivia do for a living?
    b)   What logo does Olivia have on her shirts?
    c)   Has Olivia tried to protect her brand?
    d)   What is the name of the private investigator Frank proposes to hire?
    e)   Where were the counterfeit shirts sold in London?
    f)   What does Frank recommend that Olivia should do?

2. Speaking practice

In the following series of conversation couplets develop suitable responses to the questions asked

    a)   Frank: "Can you tell me Olivia what product you manufacture?"
          Olivia: "_____."
    b)   Frank: "What happened when you were at the Portobello Road market?"
          Olivia: "_____."
    c)   Frank: "Do you know anything about the guy selling the shirts?"
          Olivia: "_____"
    d)   Frank: "What protection do you have for the brand?"
          Olivia: "_____."
    e)   Frank: "So what kind of logo do you have on your shirts?"
          Olivia: "_____."
    f)   Frank: "Do you want me to hire a private investigator to try and find out who the counterfeiters are?"
          Olivia: "_____."
    g)   Frank: "Have you invested in developing your brand Olivia?"
          Olivia: "_____."
    h)   Frank: "So what can I do for you Olivia?"
          Olivia: "_____."

---

[14]   *To get a line on someone* – to find out who they are.
[15]   *To nail someone* – to stop and/or catch someone.

3. Speaking practice continued ......

Create five other conversation couplets using in each couplet at least one word from the vocabulary found in Part 1, Text 1 or Text 2

4. Speaking practice continued ......

Listen to the suggested replies and repeat

a) Frank: "Can you tell me Olivia what product you manufacture?"
Olivia: "Yes of course, I manufacture shirts."

b) Frank: "So what happened when you were at the Portobello Road market?"
Olivia: "I was walking through the market when I saw a guy selling counterfeit shirts with my logo out of the back of a van."

c) Frank: "Do you know anything about the guy selling the shirts?"
Olivia: "No I don't know anything about him but I got the registration number of the van he was driving."

d) Frank: "What protection do you have for the brand?"
Olivia: "I registered the logo as a trademark under the Madrid system."

e) Frank: "So what kind of logo do you have on your shirts?"
Olivia: "A dog!"

f) Frank: "Do you want me to hire a private investigator to try and find out who the counterfeiters are?"
Olivia: "I guess we have no choice but I hope it won't cost a lot of money."

g) Frank: "So have you invested in developing your brand Olivia?"
Olivia: "Of course I have ... basically through advertising and sponsorship deals."

h) Frank: "What can I do for you Olivia?"
Olivia: "Hi I am the manufacturer of a brand of shirts protected by a registered trademark and my trademark is being violated by counterfeiters."

5. Associated questions

Discuss the following questions

a) Is there anything else that could be done to improve the functioning of the international trademark system?

b) Are there counterfeit goods available for sale in your country?

c) How do you think counterfeiters can be stopped?

d) Should brands receive protection under intellectual property law?

PART 4 – TRANSLATION EXERCISES

When carrying out the translations it is not necessary to translate directly word for word; rather the emphasis should be on translating the sense of the text. Language is not directly interchangeable and so direct translations do not always convey the meaning in the text.

Translate the following texts from English to Portuguese

A. What does the term intellectual property mean?

The term intellectual property dates from the late 18th century but it was not until the late 19th century that protection under this heading became more commonplace in common law countries. Intellectual property, or IP law as it is more commonly known, offers protection for a number of different types of creations concerning which specific property rights are recognized. Pursuant to the law of intellectual property, owners are granted certain rights to intangible assets, which they either created or paid someone to create on their behalf. Assets coming within this description include musical, literary and artistic works, inventions, words, phrases, symbols, and designs. Intellectual property law, depending on the nature of the asset to be protected, provides for the issuing of a copyright, trademark, patent, industrial design right or trade secret.

B. What do intellectual property rights do?

Intellectual property rights recognize the proprietary rights enjoyed by individuals in their creations. Intellectual property rights concern, in particular, non-rival goods, i.e. goods that may be used by a number of different people simultaneously without being exhausted. Rival goods, for example cars or clothing, may only be used by one person at any one time. On the contrary, any number of people may make use of a mathematical formula simultaneously, and thus a formula would be classed as a non-rival good. Some goods have both rival and non-rival characteristics; for example, a shirt made by a famous clothing designer. The shirt itself can only be worn by one person, but the brand may be used simultaneously for a number of different shirts.

C. Are intellectual property rights efficient for society?

The existence of intellectual property rights represents a trade-off between the interests of:

- inventors allowing them protection, so that they can benefit from their creations; and
- society, i.e. allowing the general population to benefit from the creations of others.

The real issue concerns not so much whether intellectual property rights should exist but rather determining the optimum period of protection, thereby ensuring maximum efficiency for society. The relevant benefits and costs to society provoked by the granting of intellectual property protection vary depending on the character of the invention. Indeed, it is for this reason that there are different categories of intellectual property rights and different corresponding protection periods.

Translate the following texts from Portuguese to English

A. Os direitos de propriedade intelectual conferem um monopólio?

Os direitos de propriedade intelectual conferem aos titulares desses direitos a reserva de mercado total ou parcial. Portanto, pode-se afirmar que a concessão de um direito de propriedade intelectual é o equivalente à concessão de monopólio. Entretanto, é provável que esta situação não constitua um monopólio tradicional, já que o direito é invocado para proteger algo que normalmente não existia antes da introdução da proteção. Deste modo, o direito não funciona como um monopólio comum, na medida que ele não busca privar a sociedade de um benefício de uma "coisa" existente. Sem essa proteção, a criação provavelmente não haveria existido.

B. A história da propriedade intelectual

A necessidade de uma proteção internacional da propriedade intelectual se tornou evidente no fim do século XIX, quando os expositores estrangeiros se recusaram a participar das exposições internacionais de inventores por medo de que suas idéias fossem roubadas ou exploradas comercialmente por outras pessoas. Esta situação levou à assinatura em 1883 da Convenção de Paris para a Proteção da Propriedade Industrial de 1883 e à posterior assinatura da Convenção de Berna em 1886. Esses dois tratados conduziram ao estabelecimento da Organização Mundial da Propriedade Intelectual (OMPI), em 1967.

C. Os períodos de proteção conferidos ao direito de propriedade intelectual são longos demais?

Uma crítica recorrente ao direito de propriedade intelectual diz respeito à uma aparente e crescente tendência à extensão da proteção concedida, tanto com relação à duração quanto ao alcance da proteção. Por exemplo, hoje é possível o registro de patentes de organismos vivos, e até mesmo cores começam a ser registradas como marcas. Alguns críticos da propriedade intelectual, como os que pertencem ao movimento social da cultura livre, denunciam a existência e a criação de monopólios intelectuais que não contribuem ao encorajamento da criação e que, ao contrário, são obstáculos ao progresso. Segundo estes críticos, os direitos de propriedade intelectual servem para beneficiar interesses privados em detrimento da sociedade em geral.

PART 5 – ADVANCED READING

Is IP protection a good thing?

Intellectual property (IP) protection has become an essential element in modern business and many businesses could not continue to function without the protection it affords. However, at first glance, IP law could appear to be anti-market insofar as it confers monopoly type protection to those who benefit from its provisions, allowing them to often charge inflated prices for what are sometimes very mediocre products. If true, this would not appear to promote an efficient allocation of resources and could be considered to undermine the existence of a truly efficient market. So, what theories can be advanced in favor of IP law?

The first and most obvious argument in favor of the existence of intellectual property rights for innovative ideas or processes is that, without such protection, people would not be willing to make the effort necessary for their development. Thus, the existence of IP protection works to stimulate the creative process and ensures the existence of an innovative and dynamic society. In competition law terms it could be said that without sufficient *recoupment (returned benefit)*, which is ensured by the protection granted by IP law, people and businesses would be unwilling to make the necessary investment in time and money to develop new intellectual property. It can also be argued that the protection granted by IP law in the area of trademarks allows consumers certainty when making a product choice. Thus, for example, the purchaser of a certain brand, without having any specific product knowledge as regards the actual process of manufacture, can rely on the brand as a guarantee of product quality. Therefore, IP law in this area not only protects the uninformed consumer but also prevents him from being ripped off by manufacturers using similar or identical branding processes but relying on substandard manufacturing processes.

On a more philosophical level, western capitalist society is partly founded on the notion of the right of private ownership. Indeed, the notion of private ownership is central to western society and it could be argued that consequently the western state has a duty to protect the innovator, so as to allow him/her benefit therefrom. Moreover, in this regard, the state does not do so without having some regard to the rights of society as well. As a result, and just as in the case of physical property, private ownership is not absolute and the extent of intellectual property rights can be limited, normally with regard to time. For example, in the case of patents, protection is given for a limited period of time in return for the inventor sharing the process behind the creation with society. In this way the interests of the individual and the group are balanced. Moreover, quite apart from the creator's right to benefit from his/her creation, there is the more fundamental question of his/her right of control over the creation, which can be considered as an extension of his/her personality. In this way the author of a song should, it can be argued, be allowed to prevent interpretations of that song, should (s)he find such an interpretation to be disturbing or undermining its artistic content.

Certainly, by promoting innovation and creation, IP rights assist in the development of a richer, more dynamic society, whilst also protecting the notion of private ownership central to western capitalist theory. Thus, the existence of some type of protection under this heading is accepted by most as a public good; while any argument over the rights and wrongs of IP protection is probably centered not so much on the actual existence of these rights as on the question of their duration. For example, it is normal that the author of a book should be able to benefit from its exploitation. However, it is another question whether that protection should extend decades after the author's death.

Chapter nine

LABOR LAW/EMPLOYMENT LAW

What is the extent of employment protection in common law countries?

In common law countries **employment law** or **labor law** is fundamentally **governed** or subject to the provisions of the **contract of employment** that is signed between the **employer** and the **employee**. **Nonetheless**, some minimum statutory protection does exist for employees, although each jurisdiction has its own rules. For example the right to:

- *a minimum period of holidays* This period is four weeks in the United Kingdom. In the USA there is no minimum statutory holiday right, although there are a number of public holidays available, ensuring that employees have limited holidays;
- *receive a **minimum wage*** In the United States the federal minimum wage is fixed at $7.25 an hour and £6.70 in the United Kingdom;
- ***parental leave*** *and **maternity leave*** Under European Union legislation common law countries within the EU, namely Ireland and the United Kingdom, have been required to allow fathers the possibility of taking *paternity* leave at the moment of a child's birth. Mothers have for a long time been allowed to take maternity leave;
- ***paid notice*** *in case of **dismissal*** In the United Kingdom, every employee is **entitled** to paid notice in the case of dismissal, if (s)he has worked with the business for more than one month.

Although the terms labor law and employment law are often used interchangeably, labor law tends to be used in reference to the statutory rules governing labor relations between employee organizations and employers, whilst the term employment law is used in the context of individual relations between employers and employees.

Dismissal of employees

In the United Kingdom, if a worker has been employed full-time for more than a year, (s)he may be only legally dismissed or **fired/sacked** for one of the following reasons.

- *Misconduct* If an employee refuses to respect the rules in force in the business in which (s)he works, (s)he may be dismissed. However, the rules must be reasonable and the non-respect of the rule in question must concern a **material matter** and not be **spurious**.
- *Redundancy* If a company shuts down completely, closes one of its divisions, reorganizes the way work is done or is restructured,

redundancies may result, i.e. employees can be **made redundant**. However, in theory at least, reorganizations cannot be used to **camouflage** replacing expensive workers with workers who cost less. Nonetheless, a firm remains free to organize its business as it wishes and in most common law countries a business cannot be compelled to employ someone where it is unprofitable for it to do so. The employer as part of the redundancy process must respect certain procedural rules concerning issues such as consultation with employees.

- *Ineptitude of the employee* If an employee is not doing his/her job properly or does not have a necessary qualification for the job, (s)he may be dismissed.

If an employee is dismissed for a reason other than those listed above, it is probable that the dismissal will be considered illegal. This will give the employee the right to receive **damages/compensation**. There are two types of illegal dismissal:

- *unfair dismissal* In the United Kingdom, a dismissal is considered to be unfair where an employee is employed for over one year with an employer and is dismissed for a reason not coming within one of the categories of misconduct, redundancy or inability.
- *wrongful dismissal* Wrongful dismissal occurs when an employer does not respect the rules linked to the dismissal process. For example, in the case of a redundancy, employers are meant to consult with staff representatives prior to **triggering** the redundancy process. Should they fail to do so, the resulting redundancies will be classified as wrongful dismissal.

Discrimination in the workplace

Discrimination may take many forms but two basic categories are recognized:

- *direct discrimination* **Direct discrimination** is said to occur when an employer directly treats an employee or future employee less well than other employees involved in the same or equivalent tasks. For example, a restaurant manager who refuses to hire an applicant for a position as waitress because she does not look young enough;
- *indirect discrimination* **Indirect discrimination** results from a business having in place a rule that is unfair to one group of employees and not another. For example, a rule that requires all employees to be over 180cm, which indirectly discriminates against the majority of women and smaller people in general.

VOCABULARY

Employment law/labor law – *direito do trabalho*
To be governed – *ser governado*
Contract of employment – *contrato de trabalho*
Employer – *empregador*

Employee – *empregado*
Nonetheless – *todavia, contudo, não obstante*
Minimum wage – *salário mínimo*
Parental leave – *licença parental*
Maternity leave – *licença maternidade*
Paid notice – *ávido prévio remunerado*
Dismissal – *demissão*
To be fired/sacked – *ser demitido*
Material matter – *aspecto substancial, fundamental*
Spurious – *falso, espúrio*
Redundancy – *demissão*
To be made redundant – *ser demitido*
To camouflage – *camuflar*
Damages/compensation – *danos, compensação*
Unfair dismissal – *demissão injusta*
Wrongful dismissal – *demissão irregular (desrespeito às formalidades de demissão)*
To trigger – *acionar*
Direct discrimination – *discriminação direta*
Indirect discrimination – *discriminação indireta*

PART 1 – TEXT 1 – EXERCISES

1. Vocabulary test

Fill in the missing words using the vocabulary in Text 1

a) The term _____ law refers to the statutory rules governing labor relations, while/whilst the term _____ law refers to individual relations between employers and employees, as per their contract of employment.

b) The term _____ wage, refers to a basic level of pay for _____.

c) _____ discrimination involves treating an employee less fairly than other employees involved in the same or equivalent circumstances, whilst _____ discrimination involves distinguishing between groups of employees.

d) Employees often have the right to be paid _____ in cases of dismissal.

e) To succeed in an action based on _____ dismissal, the employee must show that the _____ did not respect the rules governing the _____ process.

f) In the UK an employee may be legally dismissed in a number of cases: where it can be shown (s)he was guilty of _____, where the dismissal is part of a work reorganization or where the employee is unable to do his _____ properly.

g) In cases of wrongful or unfair _____, the employee has the right to receive _____ from the employer.

2. Vocabulary test

Write sentences with the following pairs of words. Your sentence should demonstrate your knowledge of the relationship between the words

a)   Unfair/trigger
b)   Spurious/misconduct
c)   Unfair dismissal/wrongful dismissal
d)   Notice/employer
e)   Spurious/compensation
f)   Maternity leave/labor law

3. Knowledge test

Each of the following statements is false; do you know why? Write a sentence stating why it is false

a)   In the United States employers are entirely free to fix their employees' salaries.
b)   Unfair dismissal occurs when an employer fails to respect the rules governing the dismissal process.
c)   Dismissal of an employee in the UK can only be justified in cases involving misconduct.
d)   There is no right to parental leave in the UK.
e)   Indirect discrimination is legal in the common law world.
f)   The terms employment law and labor law are interchangeable.

PART 1 – TEXT 2 – MORE INFORMATION

What is the extent of employment protection in common law countries?

The terms **labor law** and **employment law** are often used interchangeably. However, technically speaking, labor law refers to the statutory rules governing labor relations, whilst the term employment law refers to individual relations between employers and employees. In common law countries, employment law is fundamentally **governed** by the **contract of employment** signed between the **employer** and the **employee**. Unlike in some civil law jurisdictions, there are no **pre-established employment agreements** and thus each party is in principle free to enter into the agreement of their choice.

The **topic** of employment law is immense and **covers** issues **ranging** from dismissal of employees to broader social issues such as discrimination. **In this regard**, it is important to note that, although sharing the same basic system of law, many common law countries **employ** different **social models**. **Thus**, employees **enjoy** different levels of protection depending on the common law jurisdiction in which they work. However, from the **outset**, we can say that it is a general principle of all common law jurisdictions that a business is considered to exist primarily for the **benefit** of its **investors/shareholders** rather than for the benefit of its employees. The primary role of a business is profit maximization as opposed to ensuring social harmony and employment protection. This does not mean however, that employees have no rights or are offered no protection.

The general approach of common law jurisdictions in the area of employment law is not to define individual **conditions of employment** but **rather** to establish a **basic** minimum **level** of **statutory protection** applicable to all employees. One reason for this is because the principle of **freedom of contract goes to the heart** of the common law system and consequently people should be free to enter into the employment contract of their choice. Some examples of the minimum rights that must be respected by employers in common law jurisdictions include:

- *the right to a minimum period of holidays* For example, four weeks per year in the United Kingdom. There is no minimum statutory holiday right in the United States, although there are numerous public holidays ensuring that employees receive some holiday leave;
- *the right to receive a **minimum wage*** In the United States the minimum wage is fixed at $7.25 per hour, although the individual states may raise this amount if they wish. Minimum wage rates in the UK are dependent on the employee's age but start at £6.70;
- *the right to **parental leave** and **maternity leave*** In the United Kingdom there is a right to paid maternity leave of up to thirty-nine weeks when the employee has worked for over twenty-six weeks with the employer. In the United States there is much less protection on offer, with twelve weeks' compulsory maternity leave due to employees of companies with over fifty employees. For smaller companies in the US there is no **statutory guarantee** and some offer no guaranteed leave at all. Paid **paternity leave** of up to two weeks is guaranteed under the law of the United Kingdom but is non-existent under US law. The more generous **welfare allowances** of the United Kingdom system, as compared to those in the United States, partly result from the United Kingdom's membership of the European Union;
- ***paid notice** in the case of **dismissal*** In the United Kingdom every employee is **entitled** to paid notice in the case of dismissal, if (s)he has worked with the business for more than one month. **Thereafter**, the amount of paid notice an employee will receive depends on how long (s)he has worked with the business.

Of course, as previously mentioned, these are minimum guarantees and each employee is free to negotiate better terms with his/her employer; and many do, especially if they can demonstrate that their services are valuable to the business employing them.

Dismissal of employees

Dismissal is often a **reflection on** the inability of an employee to perform the job asked of him/her. However, more generally it can result from a change in the business direction of the **enterprise** in question or from a downturn in economic conditions. In most **business cycles** there are periods when employees are **hired** and periods when it is necessary that they be dismissed or **made**

redundant, if the business is to remain profitable for its investors. The laws of the different common law countries provide limited protection for employees, so as to **prevent** unfair dismissal.

In most US states, employees are **employed at will**. This means that an employee may be dismissed/**fired/sacked** at any time unless the employment contract provides to the contrary. However, even workers employed *at will* cannot be fired in breach of federal labor laws such as the Civil Rights Act, 1964 or the Americans with Disabilities Act, 1990. On top of the protection provided under the heading of federal law, individual states remain free to offer employees better protection, as is the case with the State of Montana for example. Although each American state offers different levels of employee protection in cases of dismissal, it can generally be said that employees enjoy greater statutory protection in the United Kingdom than they do in the United States.

In the United Kingdom, if a worker has been employed full-time for more than a year, (s)he may only be legally be dismissed for one of the following reasons:
- *Misconduct* Where an employee refuses to respect the rules in force in the business in which (s)he works (s)he may be dismissed. However, the non-respect of the rule must concern a **material** matter and not be **spurious**. Frequently, it is required that the employee be given a number of **warnings** before dismissal becomes acceptable. Moreover, the rule that has not been **complied with** by the employee, i.e. the basis of his/her misconduct, must be reasonable in character.
- *Redundancy* If a company shuts down completely, closes one of its divisions or restructures its business in any way, redundancies often result and employees may be made redundant. Such reorganization is normally a feature of larger companies, which often have a **syndicated workforce**, and the company will normally negotiate the redundancy program with the trade union in question before implementation of the reorganization program. If the redundancy concerns more than twenty employees, there is a legal duty on the employer to consult with the company's **trade union** or elected staff representatives where there is no trade union. In order for the redundancy program to be considered legally justifiable, the restructuring or reorganization must be genuine, i.e. there must no longer be any need for the worker to do the job entailed by the post that has been suppressed. Moreover, the selection for redundancy must be fair and efforts must be made to find the employee alternative employment. Finally, redundancy compensation must be paid to the employee. Reorganizations cannot be used to **camouflage** the replacing of expensive workers with workers who cost less. However, at the same time a firm is free to organize its business as it wishes and a business cannot be compelled to employ someone where it is unprofitable for it to do so.
- *Ineptitude/inability* If an employee is not doing his/her job properly or does not have the necessary qualifications for the job in question, (s)he may be dismissed. An employee may also be dismissed in the case of a chronic illness, which results in him/her being unable to do

his/her job. Moreover, where it becomes illegal to continue employing a person, for example because a truck driver loses his/her driving license, (s)he may be dismissed.

If an employee is dismissed for a reason other than those listed above, it is probable that the dismissal is illegal and consequently it will give the employee the right to receive **damages/compensation**. There are three categories of illegal dismissal but they are not mutually exclusive and in reality can overlap.

- *Unfair dismissal* In the UK, **unfair dismissal** is considered to occur when an employee is employed for a period of over one year – and is dismissed for a reason not coming within the three categories **set out** immediately above. Moreover, even if a dismissal does come under one of these headings, it is necessary that it be reasonable in the circumstances. Thus, firing an employee because (s)he has been late three times in one week, when (s)he has had an **exemplary** employment record for the previous five years, would probably be considered unreasonable and consequently unfair. The term *unfair dismissal* is relied on less in the US, but when used it normally refers to a situation where an employee is fired unfairly and not necessarily illegally (i.e. in breach of a specific legal provision). If an employee is let go in violation of a law, in the US the dismissal is often characterized as *wrongful*.

- *Wrongful dismissal* In the UK, **wrongful dismissal** normally occurs when an employee is dismissed in violation of the terms of his/her contract of employment, for example where an employee is fired without the employer respecting the applicable notice period. Unlike in cases of unfair dismissal, there is no requirement that the employee be in employment for a period of over one year. In the United States, the term wrongful dismissal can extend beyond situations linked to the employment contract, so as to include dismissal in violation of applicable statutory law. For example, if under law employers are meant to consult with staff representatives prior to **triggering** the redundancy process and they fail to do so, any resulting redundancies will be classified as a case of wrongful dismissal.

- *Constructive dismissal* Constructive dismissal is said to occur when an employee leaves his/her employment as a result of the hostile employment environment created, promoted or tolerated by the employer. In other words, it occurs when, as a result of the conditions of employment, the employee had no choice but to leave his/her job. Examples of constructive dismissal include bullying, failure to pay wages on time or generally inappropriate behavior on the part of the employer. Just as a case of unfair dismissal can also amount to a case of wrongful dismissal, in the same way a case of constructive dismissal may also be classified as being unfair or wrongful.

In the UK, if an employee has worked for an employer for less than one month, no entitlement to notice or compensation exists, unless the specific employment contract provides for such compensation. After having worked for one month with an employer, the right to at least one week's prior notice exists. Where fired **summarily** without being given the one-week's notice due, a worker has the right to receive payment for this week, i.e. **payment in lieu of notice**. Finally, in the case of a long-term employment relationship, the right to a minimum of one week's pay in compensation for every year worked, up to a maximum of twelve weeks, exists. However, if the dismissal is a result of **gross misconduct**, there is no entitlement to any notice period or pay in lieu of notice.

Disciplinary hearings

If **accused** of a **disciplinary offence** at work, for example stealing from colleagues, the right to a **disciplinary hearing** exists. In the UK, the procedure to be followed requires that the employee be:

- *given reasonable notice of the hearing, allowing for a sufficient preparation period* It is recommended that at least a couple of days notice should be given to an employee;
- *informed in detail as to the nature of the alleged **offence*** It is advised that the employer set out in writing the details of the accusation;
- *accompanied during the hearing by a **fellow member** of staff* The employee has a right to receive support during the hearing, either from a fellow employee or alternatively from his/her trade union representative;
- *shown any **evidence** supporting the accusation* Any evidence against the employee must be made available and the employee should be given the right to speak and to give his version of the events.

Discrimination in the workplace

No matter how **unpalatable,** discrimination is part of the reality of life and it is perhaps inevitable that discrimination of some kind occurs on occasion in the **workplace**. This does not mean that it should be tolerated and go unpunished. In this regard, Anglo-Saxon society has worked hard to create a work environment free of such **limiting** practices. In the United States, a general policy of *positive discrimination* has been in place for years in an attempt to **roll back** the effects of centuries of segregation policy put in place against members of the Afro-American community.

Discrimination may take many forms, but two basic categories of discrimination are recognized:

- *direct discrimination* **Direct discrimination** is said to occur when an employer behaves in such a way that his/her employee is directly treated less well than other employees. Normally, discrimination results from issues linked to gender, ethnicity or religion but it can concern any type of behavior once the discriminatory character of the behavior is established; for example, a restaurant manager who refuses to hire an applicant for a position as waitress because she does not look young enough;
- *indirect discrimination* **Indirect discrimination** results from a business having in place a rule that although applicable to everyone

is in reality unfair to one group of employees. For example, a rule that requires all waiters/waitresses to be over 180cm, which will indirectly discriminate against women and smaller people. Indirect discrimination is not always illegal, but the behavior must be capable of being **justified** and shown to be **unavoidable** from the point of view of the employer.

Damages available to employees resulting from discrimination can be significant, reflecting the importance given to **eradicating** this **blight** from society. This is particularly true in recognized sensitive areas such as racial or sexual discrimination. Compensation will normally be awarded under the following headings:

* *loss of wages* Any lost wages resulting from a dismissal that is qualified as discriminatory must be paid to the employee;
* *injury to feelings* It is only in cases of discrimination that damages are awarded under this heading. Damages are paid to compensate for any **feelings** of anger, **outrage** or **hurt** that the victim has suffered as a result of the discrimination;
* *personal injury* If as a result of the discrimination a victim suffers mental anguish or post-traumatic stress, the employer will have to compensate the employee for this. Damages under this heading can be significant.

VOCABULARY

Employment law/labor law – *direito do trabalho*
To be governed – *ser governado*
Contract of employment – *contrato de trabalho*
Employer – *empregador*
Employee – *emregado*
Pre-established employment agreement – *contrato de trabalho pré–estabelecido*
Topic – *geral (neste caso)*
To cover – *cobrir*
To range – *englobar*
In this regard – *a este respeito*
To employ – *empregar*
Social model – *modelo social*
Thus – *assim, deste modo, portanto*
To enjoy – *beneficiar*
Outset – *início*
To benefit – *beneficiar*
Investor, shareholder – *investidor, acionista*
Conditions of employment – *condições que dizem respeito à execução do contrato*
Rather (than) – *ao contrário, em vez de*
Basic level – *nível básico*
Statutory protection – *proteção legal*

Freedom of contract – *liberdade contratual*
To go to the heart – *ir à essência de*
Minimum wage – *salário mínimo*
Parental leave – *licença parental*
Maternity leave – *licence maternidade*
Statutory guarantee – *garantia legal*
Paternity leave – *licença paternidade*
Welfare allowance – *prestações pecuniárias relativas à proteção social*
Paid notice – *aviso prévio remunerado*
Dismissal – *demissão*
To be entitled – *ter direito a*
Thereafter – *posteriormente*
A reflection on – *o reflexo de*
Enterprise – *empresa*
Business cycle – *ciclo comercial*
To be hired – *ser contratado*
To be made redundant – *ser demitido*
To prevent – *impedir, prevenir*
Employed at will – *empregado à vontade*
To be fired, sacked – *ser demitido*
Material matter – *aspecto substancial, fundamental*
Spurious – *falso, espúrio*
Warning – *advertência*
To comply with – *respeitar*
Redundancy – *demissão*
Syndicated workforce – *força de trabalho sindicalizada*
Trade union – *sindicato*
To camouflage – *camuflar*
Damages, compensation – *danos, compensação*
Unfair dismissal – *demissão injusta*
Set out – *enunciado*
Wrongful dismissal – *demissão irregular (desrespeito às formalidades de demissão)*
Exemplary – *exemplar*
To trigger – *acionar*
Summarily – *de forma precipitada*
Pay in lieu of notice – *aviso prévio remunerado com dispensa do trabalho*
Gross misconduct – *falta grave*
To be accused of – *ser acusado de*
Disciplinary offence – *falta disciplinar*
Disciplinary hearing – *entrevista feita num procedimento disciplinar*
Offence – *falta (neste caso)*
Fellow member – *colega de trabalho (neste caso)*
Evidence – *evidências*
Unpalatable – *difícil de aceitar (engolir)*
Workplace – *ambiente de trabalho*
To limit – *limitar*
Roll-back – *remediar, apagar (neste caso)*

Direct discrimination – *discriminação direta*
Indirect discrimination – *discriminação indireta*
To be justified – *ser justificado*
Unavoidable – *inevitável*
To eradicate – *erradicar*
Blight – *ferrugem*
Feeling – *sentimento*
Outrage– *ultrage*
Hurt – *ferir*

PART 1 – TEXT 2 – EXERCISES

1. Definitions

Write a sentence defining each of the following terms – one sentence per term

   a)   Paternity leave
   b)   Gross misconduct
   c)   Direct discrimination
   d)   Labor law
   e)   Minimum wage
   f)   Trade union
   g)   Maternity leave
   h)   Unfair dismissal

2. Sentences

Write sentences with the following pairs of words demonstrating your knowledge of the relationship between them

   a)   Misconduct/sacked
   b)   Spurious/employee
   c)   Employer/summarily
   d)   Redundancy/restructuration
   e)   Gross misconduct/dismissal
   f)   Statutory guarantee/parental leave
   g)   Discrimination/workplace
   h)   Trade union/unfair dismissal
   i)   Disciplinary hearing/evidence

3. Fill in the missing words

Using the vocabulary in Text 2, fill in the missing words

   a)   As many _____ in the United States are employed at will, they have limited _____ and may be dismissed at any time.
   b)   Victims of _____ may receive _____ under three different headings: loss of wages; injury to feelings and personal injury.
   c)   Employees in the _____ have the right to receive a _____ of $7.25.
   d)   A business has the right to reorganize its workforce and as a result some _____ may occur; however, where more than 20 employees

are involved it is necessary to consult with the relevant _____ or staff representatives.

e) There are two types of discrimination _____ and _____ , the former is said to occur when a business seeks to discriminate against a class of employees.

4. Knowledge test

The following questions may be answered in writing or by way of discussion

a) Common law countries traditionally tend to have lower rates of unemployment than their European civil law counterparts. Do you think that this is a result of the labor law model they employ?

b) Should businesses be run for the benefit of their employees or their investors? Are the two goals mutually exclusive?

c) Is positive discrimination, whereby workers from certain ethnic backgrounds are favored over workers from other ethnic backgrounds, justifiable in order to promote equal opportunity?

d) Is it more important to have a job than to have a high level of job protection?

PART 2 – QUICK LOOK GRAMMAR REVISION

Dependent clauses

1. What is a dependent/subordinate clause?

As we have already seen, there are two types of sentence:
- simple sentence, i.e. a sentence containing just one clause:
  John loves to plead;
- complex sentence, i.e. a sentence containing a main clause and a dependent clause:
  John is a lawyer who loves to plead.

A sentence contains a subject (the who/what that 'does' the verb) and a predicate (the part of the clause that says something about the subject).

A dependent clause is a group of words with a subject and a verb, but that does not express a complete clause and thus cannot stand alone. A dependent clause normally takes one of two forms:
- subordinator (1), subject (2), predicate (3).
  Example: *that his car is very fast* – that (1) his car (2) is very fast (3);
- subordinator (1), predicate (2).
  Example: *who needs his car* – who (1) needs his car (2).

  Note:

  The relative pronoun is sometimes not included in the sentence
  Example:
  The car **that/which** he received for his birthday.

The car he received for his birthday.

Note:

A sentence containing a dependent clause with no supporting independent clause is considered to be a fragment and consequently is grammatically incorrect.

Thus, dependent clauses cannot stand-alone and must actually *depend* on something.

2. Adjective clause

The role of adjective clauses is to explain or modify the noun ......
Example:
> *The bike is not his*
> *The bike **that he is riding** is not his*:
> ***that he is riding*** = the adjective clause

Adjective clauses are used to give extra information about something without actually writing a new sentence.
Example:
> *I have a new client. He lives in London = I have a new client **who lives in London.***

The relative pronouns: *whom, who, that, which, whose, when, where*

- ***Who*** and ***whom*** replace nouns and pronouns referring to people.
  Who is the **subject** of the sentence, and in informal English can also be the object.
  Whom can never be the subject of the sentence, *only the object.*
  Who is used in both defining and non-defining relative clauses.
  Example:
  I know a lawyer ***who*** lives in Dubai.
  That lawyer, ***who*** studied in Paris, pleads really well.
  The lawyer ***who/whom*** I met yesterday is nice.
  The lawyer with ***whom*** I work is nice.
- **That** replaces nouns and pronouns that replace people, animals or things. It can be the object or subject of a verb.
  It is only used in defining relative clauses.
  Example:
  I know a lawyer ***that*** lives in Buenos Aires.
  Does he have a daughter ***that*** lives in London?
  The car ***that*** I bought works perfectly.
  The lawyer ***that*** I spoke to seemed pretty competent
- **Which** refers to things and animals and can be used in both defining and non-defining relative clauses:
  Example:
  The computer, ***which*** I bought last week, is useless. I prefer my old one.

This computer program, ***which*** is not expensive, makes my job much easier.

The non-defining relative clause is isolated from the rest of the sentence by the use of commas.

- **Whose** is used to replace possessive forms of nouns and pronouns. It can refer to people, animals and things and is used in both defining and non-defining relative clauses.
  Example:
  The man ***whose*** case I won is happy.
- **When** is used as a subordinator to replace reference to a time.
  Example:
  The lawyer felt ill ***when*** he was pleading before the court (i.e. at the time he was pleading before the court).
- **Where** is used as a subordinator to replace a place. It cannot be used as a subject.
  Example:
  The office ***where*** I work is located downtown.

Note:

Adjective clauses follow the noun, while adjectives precede the noun.
Example:
  - I know a **talented** lawyer
  - I know a lawyer **who is** good.

Note:

The relative pronoun ***that*** cannot follow a preposition … only ***whom, which*** and ***whose*** follow a preposition.
Example:
  - The man ***to whom*** I spoke agreed with me.
  - The business ***in which*** I invested made a profit.
  - The lawyer ***in whose*** company I spent the trip was very nice.
  - The car ***in that*** I invested did not work = WRONG.
  - The car ***in which*** I invested did not work = CORRECT.

PART 2 – GRAMMAR EXERCISES

1. Fill in the space …..

Find the appropriate subordinator relative pronoun ……

I met a lawyer _____ is very nice.
I met a lawyer *who* is very nice.

a) The lawyer _____ I met was very efficient.
b) The car _____ I rented did not work.
c) The lawyer _____ I hired was very expensive.
d) The barrister with _____ I talked explained the case to me.
e) The chair in _____ I am sitting is very comfortable.

2. Combine the sentences ......

Find the appropriate subordinator to link the following sentences ......

Do you know the lawyer? He works in the large office block.
Do you know the lawyer *who/that* works in the large office block?

a) Fred Sharpe is a lawyer. You can have confidence in him.
b) The lawyer was wonderful. He worked all night.
c) We went to see a court case. It was interesting.
d) The office is in the tall building. John works there.
e) The old lawyer is moving to Florida. I bought his practice[16].

3. Match the sentences ......

Match the appropriate sentences in column 1 with those in column 2 ......

Column 1

a) There is the sad lawyer ......
b) It is a tough puzzle ......
c) A contract is a document ......
d) There is the prison ......
e) Jack is a lazy lawyer ......

Column 2

a) which engages the responsibility of another.
b) that never gets his work done.
c) in which the prisoner is kept.
d) that is difficult to solve.
e) whose partner died.

PART 3 – AUDIO AND ORAL – LISTENING AND SPEAKING

Comprehension

Listen to the following conversation, make notes of all the relevant facts and then answer the questions below. If you have trouble understanding, follow the conversation while also reading the text.

Conversation between Bob Dylan and Michael Clarke

Bob: "Please take a seat Michael."
Michael: "Yes OK ... so what is this about?"
Bob: "OK Michael, in a word it's about you and your career here with Dylan & Dylan. You have been working with us for two years, is that correct?"
Michael: "What about it?"
Bob: "To be honest, we are not sure it is working out."
Michael: "What do you mean? Who is *we* exactly?"

---

[16] *Practice* is the name given to the business of a lawyer, doctor, accountant etc.

Bob: "Don't become aggressive Michael, that won't help things."

Michael: "I'm not becoming aggressive; I just want to know who exactly I'm dealing with here."

Bob: "You are dealing with me Bob, managing partner of Dylan & Dylan and I am telling you that after consulting with my partners, we have come to the conclusion that you are not perhaps the right ... the right fit for Dylan & Dylan."

Michael: "I am not the right fit for Dylan & Dylan, don't make me laugh."

Bob: "No one is laughing here Michael; I'm trying to have a serious discussion with you about your future."

Michael: "Oh no you are not ... you are trying to work up the nerve to fire me and let me tell you, you are not making a very good job of it."

Bob: "Please calm down Michael, there is no reason to get excited."

Michael: "Yes there is ... you are trying to fire me... of course I'm getting excited!"

Bob: "For the moment I am just trying to discuss the matter with you."

Michael: "Yeah sure you are ... what is that letter on the desk? Is it my dismissal letter ... already signed?"

Bob: "Why are you being so confrontational Michael?"

Michael: "Why am I being confrontational? Look, if you have something to say to me why not just come out and say it. But if this is a dismissal meeting I warn you that you have gone about it the wrong way."

Bob: "Really, why is that?"

Michael: "Because under my contract I have a right to have an employee representative present at all meetings of significance concerning the execution of my employment contract. Is this so unimportant to you that you did not even read my employment contract before beginning this farce?"

Bob: "Please calm down Michael ..."

Michael: "I'm perfectly calm Bob ... you are the one who appears to be a little flustered. Now coming back to my first question, why don't you tell me what this is about and let's cut out the song and dance[17]."

Bob: "OK, Bob, it is true we are looking closely at your employment with Dylan & Dylan."

Michael: "On what grounds?"

Bob: "Well you don't seem to be fitting in."

Michael: "You will have to do better than that Bob...."

Bob: "Will I Michael? To the best of my knowledge you are employed by our firm *at will*. Consequently you may be dismissed at any time."

Michael: "Why is it I'm not fitting in?"

Bob: "We'd prefer not to get into that Michael."

Michael: "I am sure you would prefer not to get into that as you say Bob but I want to *get into it*. Does it have anything to do with my new Rastafarian hairstyle?"

Bob: "As I said Michael, we'd prefer not to get into that."

Michael: "Rastafarianism is a religion ... did you know that Bob? Dylan & Dylan wouldn't be discriminating against me on religious grounds, would it Bob? You

---

[17] By saying *cut out the song and dance* Michael is saying ... get to the point and leave out all the blah blah blah ...

don't need me to tell you that discrimination is against the law; I might just have to bring an action against Dylan & Dylan on grounds of religious discrimination if you were to fire me. I am sure the newspapers would love to hear about this."

Bob: "Now Michael let's slow down ... nobody is necessarily talking about firing you ... this is above all a discussion about your future with the firm."

Michael: "Well it is a discussion you are going to have by yourself because I am not saying another word without my lawyer and employee representative being present. Have a good day Bob and I am sure you know where you can put your dismissal letter!"

PART 3 – AUDIO COMPREHENSION – EXERCISES

1. Comprehension

From the notes you have taken, answer the following questions

a)   What was the meeting between Bob and Michael about?
b)   Is Michael religious?
c)   What is Bob's position and what is the name of the business he works for?
d)   Why does Michael think he may be dismissed?
e)   What rights does Michael have under his employment contract with Dylan & Dylan?
f)   Under what conditions will Michael continue the discussion with Bob?

2. Speaking practice

In the following series of conversation couplets develop suitable responses to the questions asked

a)   Bob: "Why are you being so confrontational Michael?"
     Michael: "_____"
b)   Bob: "So Michael, how long have you been working with Dylan & Dylan?"
     Michael: "_____."
c)   Bob: "What are the conditions of your employment agreement with Dylan & Dylan?"
     Michael: "_____"
d)   Bob: "We are considering dismissing you Michael."
     Michael: "_____."
e)   Bob: "To be honest we do not like your new hairstyle Michael."
     Michael: "_____."
f)   Bob: "You are employed at will Michael, so we can do what we want."
     Michael: "_____."
g)   Michael: "Why are you firing me Bob?"
     Bob: "_____."

3. Speaking practice continued ......

Create five other conversation couplets using in each couplet at least one word from the vocabulary found in Part 1, Text 1 or Text 2

4. Speaking practice continued ......

Listen to the suggested replies and repeat

a) Bob: "Why are you being so confrontational, Michael?"
Michael: "I am not being confrontational; I just want to know what this is about."

b) Bob: "So Michael, how long have you been working with Dylan & Dylan?"
Michael: "I have been working with the Firm for two years."

c) Bob: "What are the conditions of your employment agreement with Dylan & Dylan?"
Michael: "I am employed at will."

d) Bob: "We are considering dismissing you Michael"
Michael: "On what grounds Bob?"

e) Bob: "To be honest we do not like your new hairstyle Michael."
Bob: "My hairstyle is part of my religious beliefs and so you are discriminating against me on religious grounds."

f) Bob: "You are employed at will Michael so we can do what we want."
Michael: "No you cannot, you are not allowed to fire me in breach of the law on religious discrimination."

g) Michael: "Why are you firing me Bob?"
Bob: "To be honest Michael, our clients don't like your new hairstyle; personally I like it but the clients don't and the clients are the only reason we have a business here."

5. Associated questions

Discuss the following questions

a) Would Michael be protected from dismissal under the law in your country?

b) Should businesses be free to choose their employees, especially in circumstances where the behavior of employees, even if linked to their personal beliefs, is upsetting for clients?

c) Should a Japanese restaurant that seeks to have a purely Japanese image, for example waitresses dressed in kimonos etc., have the right to employ only waitresses of Japanese origin?

d) In the context of a globalization, do you consider that overly protective labor laws promote unemployment?

PART 4 – TRANSLATION EXERCISES

When carrying out the translations it is not necessary to translate directly word for word; rather the emphasis should be on translating the sense of the text. Language is not directly interchangeable and so direct translations do not always convey the meaning in the text.

Translate the following texts from English to Portuguese

A. Trade Unions

Originating in Europe, trade unions became popular in many countries during the industrial revolution. It was at this time, with the movement from skilled to unskilled labor, that bargaining power moved predominantly to employers, leading to worker mistreatment and the imposition of ever-lower wages. Trade unions were a natural and necessary counterbalance to this process. Composed of individual workers, classes of workers or even the unemployed, trade unions became the mouthpiece of a disenfranchised class. The primary function of such organizations is to ensure that workers are guaranteed correct working conditions and pay during the course of their employment. Today, in many countries, trade unions have become key players in the political process, often punching far above the weight that their membership figures might imply.

B. The role of labor law

Labor law has been an integral part of the social and economic development of common law countries since the industrial revolution. The term labor law refers to the body of laws, administrative rulings and judicial precedents defining relations between employers and employees. Since the collapse of feudalism, the role of labor law in protecting employees has been one of the central influences in defining the nature and content of the *social contract*. Many of the terms and conditions of this social contract are established by statute law or by the common law rules developed by the courts. Labor law continues to be an area in constant evolution as geo-political movements and economic developments continue to introduce new economic realities for societies all over the world.

C. Labor law protection rules

Many laws are developed with the aim of protecting employees rather than employers, as the latter are generally viewed as being in a dominant bargaining position. Many countries, for example, have adopted precise rules establishing the minimum amount that workers are paid per hour. Minimum wage laws were first introduced nationally in the United States in 1938 and were later adopted by many other countries around the world. Another area subject to general regulation in many countries is the length of the working day or working week. Prior to the development of trade unions, European workers were working up to sixteen hours a day, six days a week. Moreover, many employees were children, effectively growing up chained to the factory in which they toiled. Slowly reforms were introduced, first in Germany and later throughout Europe and the world, to improve working conditions.

Translate the following texts from Portuguese to English

A. Ação industrial

A maior parte dos países exigem dos sindicatos o cumprimento de certos procedimentos antes de iniciar uma ação industrial (ou de protesto). Alguns países, por exemplo, exigem que os sindicatos realizem uma votação entre seus membros antes de entrar em greve. A greve é considerada como a arma mais poderosa do arsenal dos sindicatos. Entretanto, em diversos sistemas jurídicos tentar evitar a greve de certas categorias, como, por exemplo, as greves ilegais ou as greves em favor de outros trabalhadores em greve. Isto levou à quase total erradicação de greves gerais nestes países. Ademais, certas categorias de trabalhadores, como policiais, bombeiros e trabalhadores da área de saúde, são geralmente proibidos de entrar em greve. Ao invés de entrarem em greve, os trabalhadores normalmente adotam uma estratégia chamada "greve de zelo" ou "operação tartaruga". Alternativamente, eles podem tentar estabelecer uma política de boicote aos produtos da empresa.

B. As normas internacionais do trabalho

A Organização Internacional do Trabalho (OIT), sediada em Genebra, é o único órgão internacional ainda existente estabelecido no período da Liga das Nações. O princípio fundamental da organização é que o trabalho é mais que uma mercadoria e que não deve ser comercializado da mesma forma que um produto. A OIT produziu diversas convenções que foram assinadas e ratificadas pelos seus membros, e que permitiram a introdução de uma proteção de base para os trabalhadores através do mundo. Outras organizações, tais como a União Européia, exerceram um papel fundamental na melhoria da proteção dos trabalhadores ao introduzir novas regras, como a Diretiva Européia do Tempo de Trabalho, que limita a duração máxima da semana de trabalho para 48 horas.

C. O que significa o termo proteção social?

O termo proteção social pode referir-se a diversos elementos:
- Assistência financeira – implica a distribuição de dinheiro pelo Estado no caso de interrupção total ou parcial da atividade de trabalho devido a uma aposentadoria, um acidente ou deficiência física ou desemprego;
- O fornecimento de serviços sociais – implica o fornecimento de todos os tipos de serviços médicos e de assistência social em favor das pessoas desfavorecidas da sociedade.
- Seguro social – implica os benefícios e serviços que são fornecidos em troca da contribuição feita aos diversos regimes de seguro social, como, por exemplo, os regime de aposentadoria, de pensão por invalidez e viuvez e de seguro-desemprego.

PART 5 – ADVANCED READING

Trade unions and the problem of globalization

Workers' organizations are called trade unions in the United Kingdom and labor unions in the United States. A trade union can be defined as a collection of workers coming together under an organizational umbrella to achieve common goals centered on the notion of worker welfare. In an ideal world, workers and businesses cooperate and together develop mutually beneficial policy; however in reality their relations are often confrontational. Unions can be established to represent a specialized section of workers, for example railroad workers, or alternatively can seek to represent a cross-section of workers from various industries.

Trade unions began as a response to the dreadful working conditions imposed by employers on employees in the industrial revolution. Indeed, should anyone question the need for trade unions, it is only necessary to study the working conditions of workers during this period. In reality employers, under the influence of market mechanisms linked to efficiency and the resulting ever greater need for lower production costs, will, without the existence of some form of counterbalance, necessarily have to impose unreasonable working conditions on employees. An inefficient business is soon a bankrupt business and efficiencies that prejudice worker welfare are inevitable if a mechanism or counterbalance of some kind is not put in place to prevent this. There have always been two conflicting streams at the heart of trade unionism, namely should the activities of a trade union be:

- limited to its specific members; or
- should they seek to represent the mass of workers against employers in general.

The first interpretation is non-controversial and represents a recognizable tool in the capitalist system, in that the owner of an economically powerful asset, for example the production represented by a skilled workforce, uses that financial power to negotiate economic benefit. The second interpretation is far more controversial, as it threatens the very structure of the western capitalist system and explains the many years of conflict between the state and employers on one side and *radicalized* worker unions on the other. The dominant success of the western capitalist model post World War II diffused some of this tension, as most western economies and their businesses were sufficiently successful and worker numbers sufficiently low to ensure continuous improvement in working conditions. This period is identified as a particularly successful period in modern European history, referred to as *les années glorieuses* in France.

However, the process of globalization and the phenomenon of delocalization have meant that businesses, especially when it comes to non-skilled employment, are once more in a dominant position and are forced by the market reality of globalization to express that dominance by seeking greater financial efficiencies and profit maximization. The result is that European workers have lost much of the bargaining power they enjoyed in the second half of the last century and have had to face a choice between a reduction in working standards or conditions, for example zero-hours contracts, or unemployment. The alternative is that businesses will choose to move their labor-intensive activities to less expensive locations. In this regard, it should be recalled that businesses have little choice; if they are to remain financially solvent, they must always compete with the most efficient producer on the market. Success in a mass consumer market is more often than not defined by low production costs, which in turn partly implies lower employee costs. This is the reality of the western capitalist market and the *invisible hand* behind its financial success and sometimes corresponding social tensions.

Chapter ten

INTERNATIONAL LAW

PART 1 – TEXT 1 – INFORMATION

What does the term international law mean?

More and more our world resembles a **global village in which** business is **increasingly** international **in nature**. This process, known as **globalization**, has **occurred** as a result of dramatic technological **improvements** in **communication methods** and means of travel, but also as a result of a growing **network** of agreements and understandings between states, referred to collectively as international law. International law can be divided into two **fields**: public international law and private international law. Under the heading of public international law are found matters such as state **territorial disputes**, the Law of War and the control of **refugees**. **On the other hand**, private international law deals with conflicts between different national laws governing a whole **host** of **issues**, from divorce and contract disputes to **double taxation**.

What are the origins of international law?

The two main sources of international law are **custom** and treaties. Custom can be defined as an **accepted usage** between two states that has been in existence for so long that it has **taken** the **form** of **international customary law**. Today the major sources of international law are treaties and conventions. **Treaties** are legally binding agreements entered into between two or more states. **Conventions**, on the other hand, are legally binding agreements entered into by states, where the agreement is **drawn up in the context** of an **already** existing international organization such as the **United Nations**. International law should be distinguished from the notion of **comity**. Comity is the **term** that refers to the **accepted practice** or principle requiring states to **treat each other** and their **citizens** with **goodwill** and respect. Practices developed under the heading of comity include the rule that diplomats are not normally **prosecuted** for **infringements** of the law of their country of **posting**. Such a practice does not result from any actual rule in international law but **rather** is a simple principle of **mutual respect** that may in reality be violated or **broken** at any time.

What is the status of international law?

The status of international law is **to a certain extent dependent on** the tribunal or court that is **applying** it. Many international treaties or conventions provide for the establishment of an international court or tribunal to **police** the application of the agreement. **Not surprisingly**, international courts **established** under or **pursuant to** an international treaty will give the law of that treaty **great**

importance. However, national courts will only apply the provisions of an international treaty in place of their own national law provisions, where the law of the treaty is considered to actually **make up part of the national law** of the country **in question**. This will be considered to be the case when, in the United Kingdom for example, it has been incorporated into national law by way of an **Act of Parliament**.

To whom does international law apply?

As we have seen, public international law applies to states and recognizes three different types of state:

- *Independent State* An independent state can be defined as a state that is free from the control of other states and thus able to enter into agreements with other states of its choosing.
- *Dependent State* A **dependent state** is a state that has formally **surrendered** or **given up** some part or **aspect** of its **sovereignty** to another state or organization.
- *Inchoate State* An **inchoate state** is a territorial entity that is in the **process** of developing into a state, for example Palestine.

Private international law applies to people and businesses that are **carrying out** their activities on an international basis. It plays an **enormous** role in the **area** of international commerce, involving the import, export and general **transport of goods** across **borders**. Public international law applies primarily to relations between states.

VOCABULARY

More and more – *mais e mais*
Global village in which – *aldeia global na qual*
Increasingly – *de forma crescente, cada vez mais*
In nature – *in natura*
Globalization – *globalização*
To occur – *acontecer, ocorrer*
Improvement – *melhoria*
Communication method – *meio de comunicação*
Network – *rede*
Field – *setor, campo*
Territorial dispute refugee – *refugiado*
On the other hand – *por outro lado*
Host (a whole host of) – *um grande número de*
Issue – *questão*
Double taxation – *dupla tributação*
Custom – *costume*
Accepted usage – *uso reconhecido como obrigatório*
To take the form – *tomar a forma de, transformar–se*

International customary law – *regras não escritas de direito internacional, direito consuetudinário internacional*
Treaty – *tratado*
Convention – *convenção*
To draw up – *redigir*
In the context – *no contexto de*
Already – *já*
United Nations – *Organização das Nações Unidas (O.N.U.)*
Comity – *princípio da reciprocidade jurídica no que diz respeito ao reconhecimento de cada Estado com relação aos efeitos e à validade dos atos de outros Estados*
Term – *termo*
Accepted practice – *prática reconhecida*
To treat – *traitar*
Each other – *um ao outro*
Citizen – *cidadão*
Goodwill – *boa fé*
To prosecute – *processar judicialmente*
Infringement – *violação*
To be posted – *ser alocado (no exterior)*
Rather (than) – *ao contrário, em vez de*
Mutual respect – *respeito mútuo*
To break a rule – *violar uma regra*
To a certain extent – *numa certa medida*
To be dependent on – *depender de*
To apply a rule – *aplicar uma regra*
To police an agreement – *assegurar o respeito a um acordo*
Not surprisingly – *de forma pouco surpreendente*
To establish – *estabelecer*
Pursuant to – *segundo, de acordo com*
Great importance – *grande importância*
To make up part of the national law – *fazer parte do direito nacional*
In question – *em questão*
Act of Parliament – *lei (adotada pelo Parlamento)*
Dependent state – *Estado não soberano*
To surrender – *render–se*
To give-up – *desistir*
Aspect – *aspecto*
Sovereignty – *soberania*
Inchoate state – *Estado em formação*
In the process of – *num processo de*
To carry out – *efetuar*
Enormous – *enorme*
Area – *área*
Transport of goods – *transporte de mercadorias*
Border – *fronteira*

PART 1 – TEXT 1 – EXERCISES

1. Vocabulary test

Fill in the missing words using the vocabulary in Text 1

a) The term international law can be divided into two _____: public international law and _____ international law.

b) International law recognizes three basic types of state entity: _____, dependent states and _____ states.

c) The notion of _____ requires that states treat each other and their citizens with _____ and mutual respect.

d) The provisions of an international treaty or _____ only become part of the law of the United Kingdom upon the adoption of an Act of Parliament _____ the treaty into national law.

e) There are _____ main sources of international law: _____ and treaties.

f) A _____ is considered to be dependent when it has given part or all of its _____ to another state.

g) Pursuant to the notion of comity, states will not normally _____ diplomats who have _____ the law of the host state.

2. Vocabulary test

Write sentences with the following pairs of words. Your sentence should demonstrate your knowledge of the relationship between the words

a) Comity/diplomat
b) Inchoate/sovereignty
c) Double taxation/international law
d) Act of Parliament/incorporate
e) Treaty/convention
f) Public international law/private international law

3. Knowledge test

Each of the following statements is false; do you know why? Write a sentence stating why it is false

a) International law applies automatically in the domestic law of countries.

b) Comity is provided for under a number of different international conventions.

c) International law only recognizes independent states.

d) International law is limited to the area of public international law.

e) Treaties and conventions are the same thing.

f) Public international law applies to commercial matters and rules governing the transport of goods.

PART 1 – TEXT 2 – MORE INFORMATION

What does the term international law mean?

As our world **increasingly** resembles a **global village,** modern business has also become more **internationalized** as part of the **globalization** process. This has occurred for a number of reasons:

- *technical advances* On a **technical level**, inventions such as **faxes**, computers, internet and the digital revolution over the last forty years have **facilitated** greater international contact between people and businesses;
- *transport* Improved means of transport for people and goods have allowed the development of global distribution **networks** and consequently the development of **worldwide markets**;
- *removal of structural barriers* Globalization in the area of business has also been assisted by the removal of structural barriers, such as conflicting national **regulatory** rules **governing** product **manufacture** and sales. Harmonization of national regulatory rules has occurred on both a regional level, through organizations such as the European Union or the **North American Free Trade Association** (NAFTA), and on a global level through organizations such as the **World Trade Organization**. These organizations have promoted fiscal harmonization and the adoption of common rules and **standards**, leading to the establishment of global **common markets** for the benefit of both business and consumers **alike**.

In response to these **rapid** changes, international law has had to try to keep **pace**. International law **differs** fundamentally from national law, insofar as governments representing local interests develop national law. It is from this link with the **will of the people** that national laws draw their **moral force**. However, international law has more **dubious origins**; it results/evolves from practices and agreements entered into by states, frequently without any **formal** direct **sanction** by their populations.

The **notion** of international law is very **broad** and **extends to** areas as **diverse** as **human rights** violations and the resolution of **contractual disputes** between businesses. For this reason, international law is frequently divided into two basic areas:

- public international law; and
- private international law/conflict of laws.

Under the heading of public international law come matters such as state **territorial disputes**, maritime law, the law of War and the rules establishing rights for **refugees**. **On the other hand**, private international law deals with the resolution of problems resulting from the conflict between national laws, in areas such as marriage and divorce, **child custody** cases, intellectual property disputes and **double taxation**.

What are the sources of international law?

International law has a number of different **sources**. International law first **grew out of** an acceptance of general principles of **right and wrong** recognized by all civilized nations. Indeed, all the major systems of law share common general principles of right and wrong and it is on these basic principles that international law was built. The two main sources of international law are **custom** and treaties.

What is custom?

The first major source of international law is custom. Custom can be defined as an **accepted usage** that has been in existence for so long that it has **taken the form of customary international law**. For custom to become law, two conditions must be **fulfilled**:
*   firstly, the custom must be **regularly** and **consistently observed** by the states **in question**. This first obligation is a **behavioral** one and is called *usus* in legal terminology. For *usus* to be established, consistent and **recurring action** must be **shown** to **occur** as regards the application of the custom. Establishing *usus* is an **objective** factual **issue** and is normally **determined** by **making reference to** the acts of the government claiming the *usus* and those of the government against which the claim has been made. For example, if, by its past actions, a government has **recognized** the independence of an island **off its coast**, it may be **prevented** under custom from later attempting to **exercise sovereignty** over the island.
*   secondly, the state itself should feel **obligated** to **follow** or respect the custom or practice **in question**. This second requirement is psychological or subjective and requires **proof** that the state, against which the obligation is **claimed,** considers itself obliged to follow the practice in question. In law this requirement is referred to as *opinio juris sive necessitatis*. The necessity of this second requirement is less important when there is proof of consistent practice or *usus* as regards the custom. However, where there has only been **sporadic** practice, this requirement becomes more important.

Treaties and conventions

The modern sources of international law are treaties or conventions. **Treaties** are legally binding agreements entered into between two or more states. **Conventions**, on the other hand are legally binding agreements entered into by states, where the agreement is **drawn up** in the **context** of a previously established international organization. Many of the rules first established under the **heading** of customary international law are now **set out** in treaties, conventions or laws established by global international organizations such as the United Nations or regional **groupings** such as the European Union.

International law should be distinguished from the notion of **comity**. Comity refers to the **practice** or **requirement** that states **treat each other** with **goodwill** and respect. For example, traditionally diplomats have been allowed to travel between countries without being searched, hence the significance of the **diplomatic pouch** or bag. However, up until the **adoption of** the **Vienna Convention on Diplomatic Relations** in 1961, this practice only existed under the heading of comity, and thus was only an expression of a **non-binding courtesy between** states and not a legal right **guaranteed** by any **provision** of international law.

What is the status of international law?

The status of international law is **to a certain extent dependent on** the tribunal or court that is **applying** it and, more specifically, on whether it is an international or national court that is **hearing the matter** at issue.

i) When an international court is hearing the matter

Most international treaties or conventions provide for the establishment of an international court or tribunal to **police** the application of the agreement. **Not surprisingly**, for an international court **established pursuant to** an international convention or treaty, the law of that convention/treaty will be given great importance. Consequently, it will probably be considered to take **precedence** over the signatory state's national law, i.e. national law will be **subordinated** or thought **subservient** to the law of the convention/treaty. **Thus**, in **an action** before such an international tribunal, a state will frequently be **prevented** from **adducing** or **relying on** its own national law as a justification for **avoiding** an obligation **imposed** by international law.

ii) When a national court is hearing the matter

If the international law in question is considered to **make up part of** the national law and has been given precedence over the state's national law, then the national courts of that state will apply it in precedence over their own national law. Thus, the national court has to see if the international law at issue forms part of the national law and, if so, whether it has been given precedence to national law in the past. Whether an international law makes up part of a country's national law will **differ** depending on **whether** it **concerns** customary international law or an international law **emanating from** an international treaty or convention.

- *The application of customary international law as part of the national law of a country*

  In the case of customary international law there are two different theories as regards its application by national courts.

  - *Doctrine of incorporation* Pursuant to the **theory** or **doctrine of incorporation**, customary international law will be **considered** to make up part of the national law of a country where it is shown that the customary international law in question is not **inconsistent** with the state's national law or with the decisions of the state's national courts, i.e. national **case law**.

  - *Doctrine of transformation* Some national courts, **instead** of the doctrine of incorporation, apply the **doctrine of transformation**. **According to** this doctrine, customary international law can **only** be considered part of national law where it has **clearly** been adopted into national law by statute or court decisions.

- *The application of international treaties/conventions as part of national law*
In the case of international law **arising under** an international treaty or convention, the situation is a little different. Normally, a national court will only apply an international treaty in priority to a state's national law if the treaty has been **ratified** by the state. If it has not, then national law provisions will continue to apply. Some treaties are said to be **self-executing treaties** and **contain** a provision **stating** that the treaty will apply in the national law of the **signatory states** without it being necessary for such states to adopt domestic **enabling legislation**. However, even in the case of **so-called** self-executing treaties, if a state's domestic law **specifically** requires the general ratification of treaties, then such ratification will have to occur before the treaty or convention can be considered to make up part of national law.

To whom does international law apply?

As we have seen, public international law applies **mainly** to states. A state can be defined as a political **entity** with a recognized territory, a population and a government capable of carrying out its sovereign functions. International law recognizes three types of state.

- *Independent State* An independent state can be defined as **any** state free from the control of other states and thus free to enter into international agreements with any state of its choosing.
- *Dependent State* A **dependent state** is a state that has formally **surrendered** or **given-up** some **aspects** of its political and **governmental functions** to another state or **pan-national entity**.
- *Inchoate State* An **inchoate state** is an entity that is in the **process of** developing into a state; for example Palestine is generally referred to as a *territory* and in international law might be referred to as an inchoate state.

Private international law applies to people and businesses that are **carrying out** their private activities on an international basis. Obviously, international law has enormous importance as regards relations between states but it also plays an increasingly important role in the area of international commerce.

Vocabulary

Increasingly – *de forma crescente, cada vez mais*
Global village – *aldeia global*
Internationalized – *internacionalizado*
Globalization – *globalização*
Technical level – *nível técnico*
To fax – *enviar um fax*

To facilitate – *facilitar*
Network – *rede*
Worldwide market – *mercado de dimensões mundiais*
Structural barrier – *barreiras estruturais ou regulamentares*
Regulatory – *regulamentar*
To govern – *governar*
Manufacture – *manufatura*
North American Free Trade Association – *acordo de livre comércio norte-americano*
World Trade Organization – *Organização Mundial do Comércio*
Standards – *normas*
Common market – *mercado comum*
Alike – *da mesma forma*
In response – *em resposta*
Rapid – *rápido*
Pace – *passo*
To differ from – *diferir*
Will of the people – *vontade do povo*
Moral force – *força moral*
Dubious origin – *origem duvidosa*
Formal sanction – *sancionar formalmente*
Notion – *noção*
Broad – *amplo, largo*
To extend to – *se extender a*
Diverse – *diverso*
Human right – *direitos humanos*
Contractual dispute – *litígio contratual*
Territorial dispute – *litígio territorial*
Refugee – *refugiado*
On the other hand – *por outro lado*
Child custody – *guarda de menor*
Double taxation – *dupla tributação*
Source – *fonte*
To grow out of – *se desenvolver de*
Right and wrong – *certo e errado*
Custom – *costume*
Accepted usage – *uso reconhecido como obrigatório*
To take the form of – *tomar a forma de, transformar-se*
Customary international law – *direito consuetudinário internacional*
To fulfil a condition – *respeitar uma condição*
Regularly – *regularmente*
Consistently observed – *observado de forma sistemática*
In question – *em questão*
Behavioral condition – *condição ligada ao comportamento*
Usus – *prática confirmada*
Recurring action – *prática habitual*
To be shown – *demonstrar*
To occur – *acontecer, ocorrer*

Objective – *objetivo*
Issue – *questão*
Determined – *determinado*
To make reference to – *fazer referência a*
To recognize – *reconhecer*
Off the coast of a country – *ao largo da costa de um país*
To prevent – *prevenir*
To exercise sovereignty – *exercer a sua soberania*
To be obligated – *ser obrigado*
To follow – *seguir*
In question – *em questão*
Proof – *prova*
To claim – *revindicar*
Opinio juris sive necessitatis – *"convicção de direito ou de necessidade "*
(convicção de que um ato foi realizado porque ele era uma obrigação legal)
Sporadic – *esporádico*
Treaty – *tratado*
Convention – *convenção*
To be drawn-up – *ser redigido*
In the context of – *no contexto de*
Heading – *sob o contexto de*
To be set out in – *expor, descrever*
Grouping – *agrupamento*
Comity – *princípio da reciprocidade jurídica no que diz respeito ao*
reconhecimento de cada Estado com relação aos efeitos e à validade dos atos
de outros Estados
Practice – *prática*
Requirement – *condição*
To treat – *tratar*
Each other – *um ao outro*
Goodwill – *boa fé*
Diplomatic pouch – *bagagem diplomática*
Adoption of – *adoção de*
Vienna Convention on Diplomatic Relations – *Convenção de Viena sobre as*
relações diplomáticas
Non-binding – *não–vinculativo*
Courtesy – *cortesia*
Between – *entre*
To be guaranteed – *ser garantido*
Provision – *disposição*
To a certain extent – *numa certa medida*
To be dependent on – *ser dependente de*
To apply – *aplicar, colocar em prática*
To hear the matter – *julgar um caso*
To police (an agreement) – *assegurar o respeito de um acordo*
Not surprisingly – *de forma pouco surpreendente*
To be established – *ser estabelecido*
Pursuant to – *segundo, de acordo com*

To take precedence – *ter precedente sobre*
To be subordinated, subservient to – *ser subordinado a*
Thus – *então, portanto, deste modo*
An action before a court – *ação judicial*
To be prevented from – *ser impedido de*
To adduce – *citar, alegar*
To rely on – *se basear em*
To avoid – *evitar*
To be imposed – *ser imposto*
To make up part of the national law– *fazer parte do direito nacional*
To differ – *diferir*
Whether – *se*
To concern – *dizer respeito*
To emanate from – *emanar de*
Theory, doctrine of incorporation – *teoria, doutrina da incorporação*
To be considered – *ser considerado*
Inconsistent – *incompatível*
Case law – *jurisprudência*
Instead – *ao invés de*
Doctrine of transformation – *doutrina da transformação*
According to – *segundo, de acordo com*
Only – *somente*
Clearly – *claramente*
Act of Parliament – *ato legislativo*
To arise under – *deriver de*
To ratify, ratification – *ratificar, ratificação*
Self-executing treaty – *tratado auto–executório*
To contain – *conter*
To state – *declarar*
Signatory state – *Estado signatário*
Enabling legislation – *lei de autorização*
So-called – *assim chamado*
Specifically – *especificamente*
Mainly – *principalmente*
Entity – *entidade*
Dependent state – *Estado não soberano*
To surrender – *render–se*
To give-up – *desistir*
Aspect – *aspecto*
Governmental function – *função governamental*
Pan-national entity – *entidade panacional*
Inchoate state – *Estado em formação*
In the process of – *num processo de*
To carry out – *efetuar*
Enormous – *enorme*

PART 1 – TEXT 2 – EXERCISES

1. Definitions

Write a sentence defining each of the following terms – one sentence per term

a)   Comity
b)   Double taxation
c)   Globalization
d)   Customary international law
e)   Inchoate state
f)   *Usus*
g)   Ratification
h)   Convention
i)   Pan-national entities

2. Sentences

Write sentences with the following pairs of words demonstrating your knowledge of the relationship between them

a)   Custom/treaties
b)   *Usus*/condition
c)   Comity/diplomats
d)   Doctrine of incorporation/doctrine of transformation
e)   Dependent state/independent state
f)   Sovereignty/inchoate
g)   Convention/treaty

3. Fill in the missing words

Using the vocabulary in Text 2, fill in the missing words

a)   International law may arise under treaties or alternatively it may have been developed under the heading of _____ resulting from accepted _____.

b)   Customary international law may be considered to make up the law of an individual state pursuant to one of two theories: the doctrine of _____ or alternatively the doctrine of _____; pursuant to the latter doctrine it is necessary to demonstrate that the international law in question is not inconsistent with the national law of the state in question.

c)   A _____ treaty contains a provision whereby the treaty is said to apply in the _____ law of the signatory states without the need for formal ratification.

d)   A _____ state is one that has transferred part of its sovereignty to another state or some other pan- _____ organization involving a number of different states.

e)   For recognized rules to develop under the heading of custom it is necessary to demonstrate both _____ and proof that a state considers itself _____ to respect the rule in question.

4. Knowledge test

The following questions may be answered in writing or by way of discussion

a)   International law is only used as a tool by powerful states to defend acts that might otherwise be considered illegal.

b)   Although far from perfect, international law is the last line of protection before the breakdown of society.

c)   As a general rule, the international organizations formed after World War II have not lived up to the expectations of those who created them.

d)   The UN is only a talking shop[18] organized by the West, paid for by the West promoting a Western image of the world.

PART 2 – QUICK LOOK GRAMMAR REVISION

Dependent clauses continued …… adverb clauses & noun clauses

1. Adverb clauses

Adverb clauses provide information about what is going on in the main clause:
*   adverb clauses are normally introduced by words such as: *since, after, because, where, when*; and
*   usually answer questions asking "*where, when or why*".

Example:
> Question: *Why* did your client kill her husband?
> Answer: My client killed her husband *because he crashed her car*.

Note:

Sometimes the dependent clause may come before the independent clause
Example:
> Does Frank see his wife much?
> *Since he started working on the Simon v Schuster case*, Frank has not seen his wife much.
> *(if the adverb clause begins the sentence it will be followed by a comma)*

Note:

There are different kinds of adverb clauses:
> **time clauses** – *before, after, since, when, as long as …*
> Jim started to drink *after he lost an important case*.

> **reason clauses** – *because, since, as …*
> Jim is confident *because he knows the judge*.

---

[18]   The term "talking shop" is used to describe an organization that achieves little if nothing and spends most of its time just *talking*!

concessive clauses (used to make contrasting statements) – *though, although,   while ...*
I used to love to plead **although I was much younger at that time**.

purpose clauses – *in order to, so that ...*
I requested an adjournment *so that I could speak with the witness*.

condition clauses – *unless, if ...*
Unless things improve, I will have to fire my secretary.

2. Noun clauses

A noun clause generally takes the place of a noun in the sentence and will normally be the subject or object of the verb in the sentence.

It can be the object of a preposition ... and it can also be used as an adjective complement:
*Everyone is happy **that your client won***;

and as a subject complement:
*John's error was **that he failed to prepare for the case***.

Many of the words used to introduce adjective or adverb clauses are also relied on to introduce noun clauses, for example: *that, who, whom, why, when, where, whoever ...*

Examples of noun clauses acting as the subject of a verb:
- ***That Frank learned how to plead*** *is miraculous.*
- ***Whether John has enough clients to become partner*** *is questionable.*
- ***What the witness said*** *interested the barrister.*

Examples of noun clauses acting as the object of a verb:
- *Professor Smart's friends did not know **that he could not plead before the High Court**.*

Example of a noun clause as the object of a preposition:
- *The owner is not responsible for **what his employee did**.*

   Note:

   Sometimes the introductory word in a noun clause can be removed ...
   Example:
   – I know *that* the judge is here.
   – I know the judge is here.

Note:

Two independent clauses may be converted into an independent clause and a noun clause ...

Example:
- Barbara wonders ...
- Does James know how to plead?
- **Barbara wonders if James knows how to plead.**

Example:
- I know ...
- John did well.
- **I know that John did well.**

PART 2 – GRAMMAR EXERCISES

1. Choose the subordinator .....

Choose the appropriate subordinator from the list after each sentence ......

We keep the beer in the fridge _____ it does not get too hot.
since, so that, although
*We keep the beer in the fridge **so that** it does not get too hot.*

a) You need to study hard _____ the exams are very tough.
So that, since, because
b) Lawyers wear a gown and wig in court _____ impress their clients.
Because, in order to, after
c) You will have to pay higher insurance rates _____ you lose that case.
If, although, before
d) You may fall ill _____ you work too hard.
Because, if, so that

2. Combine the sentences ......

Identify the noun clauses in the following sentences ......

The judge ordered that the criminal be sent to jail.
***that the prisoner be sent to jail** – object of the verb ordered*

a) He said that he would not go to court.
b) It was good that he was present at the meeting.
c) The news that we won the case was confirmed.
d) I cannot rely on what he says.

3. Identify the dependent clause......

Identify the dependent clause ......

a) The book that the professor recommended is very expensive.
b) This is the place where I won my first case.

    c)   Unless the prosecution can make a better case, the accused will not be convicted.

    d)   He bought an expensive boat simply because he could.

PART 3 – AUDIO AND ORAL – LISTENING AND SPEAKING

Comprehension

Listen to the following conversation, make notes of all the relevant facts and then answer the questions below. If you have trouble understanding, follow the conversation while also reading the text.

Conversation between Mohamed and Professor Smart

Mohammed: "I was wondering if I might have a word with you Professor Smart."

Professor Smart: "Yes of course Mohammed, how can I help you?"

Mohammed: "Well, I was wondering if today we can really speak of a truly international system of law."

Professor Smart: "Why do you ask that?"

Mohammed: "To my mind the international system of law to which you refer could in fact be better described as the propagation of western values on an international basis."

Professor Smart: "But Mohammed, the United Nations is made up of the quasi totality of the states existing in the world today."

Mohammed: "I don't deny that."

Professor Smart: "Then where is the problem?"

Mohammed: "The problem is that most of them are just spectators sitting in the UN General Assembly in a process dominated by the West."

Professor Smart: "Well I suppose that is right, but that reflects the dominance of western values surely. And it is not just the West, Mohammed, there are also countries such as China and Russia and the Europeans that are all strong and influential."

Mohammed: "Well that explains their economic and political dominance but it does not explain their moral dominance. In fact they have no moral legitimacy and hence no moral dominance. The majority of the people living in the world today do not share those values … values that are being foisted[19] upon them by the Western powers by way of a supposedly international complex."

Professor Smart: "Well you are not completely wrong, Mohammed, it is true that the present system is far from perfect but I could counter your argument. Firstly, it is true that international law reflects the dominance of the western agenda that led to its development; but have you an alternative? It is one thing to tell me what is wrong, but another to tell me how it could be better. *Don't reject, suggest*; do you have a better alternative that would actually work?"

Mohammed: "Yes, the United Nations should be truly democratic with each nation having one vote. That way its decisions would be legitimate and truly international in character."

Professor Smart: "Yes it would be truly democratic, but it would also be a mess. Moreover, why should a country like the United States or China, which between

---

[19]   Foisted – when something is forced upon a person.

them possess much of the world's economic, political and military power, agree to have the same influence as a small island nation such as the Seychelles? You have to be practical, Mohammed. Countries like the United States, China or Russia demand the representation their economic and military power implies. Also, to speak of entities such as the United States or China as countries is a false description; you cannot compare them to an independent island in the Caribbean. Countries like this are huge melting pots of different ethnic groups representing millions of people. It is normal that they have greater influence."

Mohammed: "Greater influence, OK, but total domination, that is another thing."

Professor Smart: "Is there really total domination?"

Mohammed: "Well it looks like that to me."

Professor Smart: "Example?"

Mohammed: "The second Iraqi War. I believe an international coalition was developed to promote the domestic agenda of one state ... and it appears international law was manipulated to promote this end."

Professor Smart: "But is not all law at heart a manifestation of political power? Justice is an attribute of a successful legal system but it is not necessary for its actual creation."

Mohammed: "Perhaps ... but then stop telling me it is a system of international law. It is a system promoting western interests that are applied internationally."

Professor Smart: "Well that is certainly partly true but perhaps the success of international law is to be found in the very weaknesses that you pointed to as justification."

Mohammed: "How?"

Professor Smart: "Well you mentioned how the US manipulated the international system to promote its own ends. Even accepting that it is true, which I do not necessarily accept, surely the fact that a country as powerful as the USA considered it necessary to establish a coalition and canvass the United Nations is proof that international law is increasingly important. The US could have invaded Iraq on its own, which in any event it effectively did, without having to consult with the United Nations but it didn't, because it felt constrained by international law."

Mohammed: "Well, it is not ideal Professor."

Professor Smart: "No it is not, Mohammed, but nothing is perfect; we are on a road and we are getting there. Political realities have to be reflected in the character of any system we create. Indeed, as US power is on the wane, we are seeing the increasing presence of BRIC economies[20] in the international process. This is inevitable; indeed, I think the high water mark of western influence has been reached. Perhaps, for some systems this has occurred after the "damage" has been done. But this is the nature of evolution Mohammed."

Mohammed: "Mmmnnn I'm not sure I'm convinced by everything you say."

---

[20] BRIC: Brazil, Russia, India and China.

PART 3 – AUDIO COMPREHENSION – EXERCISES

1. Comprehension

From the notes you have taken, answer the following questions

a) Does Mohammed think the United Nations is an effective organization?
b) What countries does Professor Smart consider as being particularly influential internationally?
c) What example does Mohammed give of US dominance over the international system?
d) Does Professor Smart believe that justice is an essential element in the creation of a legal system?
e) Does Professor Smart consider that the US dominates international law?
f) What reform of the United Nations does Mohammed suggest?

2. Speaking practice

In the following series of conversation couplets, develop suitable responses to the questions asked

a) Mohammed: "The United Nations is just a talking shop dominated by the United States?"
   Professor Smart: "_____"
b) Mohammed: "Is it right Professor Smart that the United Nations is dominated by a western agenda?"
   Professor Smart: "_____."
c) Mohammed: "Why is the United Nations not more democratic?"
   Professor Smart: "_____"
d) Mohammed: "Why shouldn't the Seychelles have the same influence as Russia in the United Nations?"
   Professor Smart: "_____."
e) Mohammed: "Do you ever think we will see a truly fair system of international law developed?"
   Professor Smart: "_____."
f) Professor Smart: "How could the United Nations be made more democratic?"
   Mohammed: "_____."
g) Mohammed: "What do you think will be the consequence of the BRIC economies becoming wealthier and more advanced?"
   Professor Smart: "_____."
h) Professor Smart: "How do you think the area of international law can be improved?"
   Mohammed: "_____."

3. Speaking practice continued ......

Create five other conversation couplets using in each couplet at least one word from the vocabulary found in Part 1, Text 1 or Text 2

4. Speaking practice continued ......

Listen to the suggested replies and repeat ...

a) Mohammed: "The United Nations is just a talking shop dominated by the United States?"
Professor Smart: "Not just by the United States Mohammed, the emerging BRIC economies and Europe are also influential."

b) Mohammed: "Is it right Professor Smart that the United Nations is dominated by a specific number of countries?"
Professor Smart: "It is neither right nor wrong Mohammed; it merely reflects the influence and size of these countries."

c) Mohammed: "Why is the United Nations not more democratic?"
Professor Smart: "Countries like the US, China, Russia and Europe have very large populations and so their influence is not as undemocratic as it might first appear."

d) Mohammed: "Why shouldn't the Seychelles have the same influence as Russia in the United Nations?"
Professor Smart: "Because the Seychelles has a small population, little economic power or valuable resources; why should it have the same influence as Russia?"

e) Mohammed: "Do you ever think we will see a truly fair system of international law developed?"
Professor Smart: "No system of law is ever truly fair. Fairness is ultimately something we aspire to."

f) Professor Smart: "How could the United Nations be made more democratic?"
Mohammed: "Each member state should be given a vote that reflects its economic and political importance."

g) Mohammed: "What do you think will be the consequence of the BRIC economies becoming wealthier and more advanced?"
Professor Smart: "As these economies advance they will insist on participating in the development of international law, making it more representative and truly international in character."

h) Professor Smart: "How do you think the area of international law can be improved?"
Mohammed: "International law should be more representative of the different values existing in the world today."

5. Associated questions

Discuss the following questions

a) Is it realistic of Mohammed to think that it is possible to develop a system of international law that represents the interests of the world as a whole?

b)   Is Professor Smart correct when he says that the notion of justice is not a necessary ingredient for the creation of a system of international law?

c)   Should every member of the United Nations be given an equal vote?

d)   Is it correct that members of the UN Security Council should enjoy a right of veto?

PART 4 – TRANSLATION EXERCISES

When carrying out the translations it is not necessary to translate directly word for word; rather the emphasis should be on translating the sense of the text. Language is not directly interchangeable and so direct translations do not always convey the meaning in the text.

Translate the following texts from English to Portuguese

A. Private international law

Private international law is made up of the different rules governing the application of private law in an international context, above all in cases where there is a conflict of laws. National law applies to situations occurring in a purely internal context, when all the elements of a given legal issue concern that particular state. On the other hand, the rules of private international law apply once the elements making up a particular issue involve the potential application of a number of different national rules, frequently resulting from the involvement of parties coming from different states.

B. International public law

International law can be divided into two categories: international public law and international private law, governing relations between individuals of different nationality. If one speaks generally of international law, normally it is thought to refer to public international law. International public law governs relations between states, international organizations and quasi-states. The dominant sources of such law today are treaties and conventions. Other sources are international custom, general legal principles and the theories of leading academics.

C. The Universal Declaration of Human Rights

The Universal Declaration of Human Rights, adopted by the United Nations General Assembly on 10 December 1948, clearly signaled the establishment of an international movement for the protection of human rights. The Declaration established, for the first time in the history of humanity, the fundamental civil, political and cultural rights that should be enjoyed by all mankind. Over the years, its status as a fundamental standard of human rights that all should protect and respect has been largely recognized.

Translate the following texts from Portuguese to English

A. A noção de crime contra a humanidade

Um crime contra a humanidade é uma violação deliberada e atroz dos direitos fundamentais de um indivíduo ou grupo de indivíduos. A noção de crime contra a humanidade apareceu pela primeira vez como conceito jurídico reconhecido em 1945 na Carta de Londres (artigo 6(c)), que estabeleceu o tribunal militar internacional de Nuremberg. Este desenvolvimento é o resultado do desejo dos vencedores de obrigar os vencidos a prestar contas perante um tribunal sobre as atrocidades cometidas na Europa durante a Segunda Guerra Mundial. Esta noção foi igualmente invocada para julgar os líderes do regime Shõwa perante o tribunal de Tóquio. Este conceito é portanto fortemente ligado a um contexto histórico particular.

B. O direito do comércio internacional

O direito do comércio internacional, também conhecido como direito comercial internacional ou direito empresarial internacional, foi desenvolvido antes de tudo ao curso do século passado como resposta à crescente internacionalização do comércio. O direito comercial internacional deve ser normalmente diferenciado do direito econômico internacional, que diz respeito a questões como fusões, ofertas públicas ou operações fiscais internacionais. O objetivo do direito comercial internacional é mais geral e a sua extensão é mais difícil de definir de forma precisa. Entretanto, pode-se dizer que o direito comercial internacional procura governar as relações comerciais internacionais entre os operadores do mercado.

C. O trabalho dos escritórios de advocacia especializados em direito comercial internacional

As áreas de especialização dos escritórios de advocacia de direito comercial internacional são múltiplas e envolvem, entre outras:
- o pleito perante órgãos internacionais de resolução de conflitos tais como a Organização Mundial de Comércio;
- a atuação em casos que envolvem as leis de arbitragem internacional;
- as fusões e as aquisições;
- a defesa e a impetração de ações judiciais que envolvem leis antidumping; e
- a criação e a aplicação de acordos de comércio internacional.

De forma mais tradicional, estes escritórios também oferecem serviços que dizem respeito ao direito aduaneiro, à gestão de licenças para exportação e qualquer outra matéria que envolva legislação aduaneira.

PART 5 – ADVANCED READING

The legitimacy of international law

The increasingly international character of human interaction has called for corresponding developments in the field of international law. However, the predominance of western powers in this process has left a question mark hanging over just how international in content our system of international law really is. Indeed, the dominance of western values can to a certain extent be viewed as an attempt to impose a new *pax romana*, using horizontally developed physical structures such as the United Nations to channel vertically developed western regulatory values. Partly as a result of this, the present system of international law can actually promote tension between nations, instead of diffusing it.

Public international law

Public international law is aimed not so much at controlling the acts of individuals but rather at regulating the behavior of states. A state represents an aggregate of individuals and is held together by a multitude of links that are political, economic and social in character. The aggregate is dominated by the state, which wields authority domestically and represents the aggregate as regards dealings with other states. Unlike local national systems that have effectively been developing in tandem with advances in society, public international law, as we know it today, is a relatively new tool. Moreover, it has been developed primarily by the winners of the globalization process, and thus one of the main allegations against the present system of public international law is that it favors the richer nations to the detriment of poorer nations, and even that it is a Trojan horse for western values. Indeed, the overtly political character of global forums such as the United Nations, and the dominance given to structures such as the Security Council operating at its heart, certainly serve to partly negate the true international potential of public *international* law. In this regard, the area of private international law has perhaps been more successful, especially in the area of business and contract law; maybe because business by its very nature is effectively the same the world over, i.e. profit-driven.

Private international law

Private international law also referred to as the *conflict of laws*, deals with relations and interactions between private persons, including businesses operating across different jurisdictions. It governs private social situations having an international character and also international commercial relations. A successful example of private international law is the UN Convention on Contracts for the International Sale of Goods (CISG), which gives businesses operating in an international context a harmonized uniform set of rules, on which they can rely in the context of their transactions. The CISG applies to commercial international contracts (i.e. non-consumer contracts) for the sale of goods entered into between parties located in different jurisdictions. The provisions of the CISG are not obligatory on companies operating in signatory states and can be excluded by the parties in their contract document, if they so wish. The success of the CISG reflects the need for private international law mechanisms in an age in which national borders and conflicting legal jurisdictions often only serve to hamper international trade.

As increasingly the world is faced with problems that are global in character, the regulatory answers we develop to deal with these issues will have to be equally international if successful lasting solutions are to be found; thus the area of international law has a future.

EXERCISE ANSWERS

CHAPTER 1 – WHAT IS A CONTRACT?

Answers Chapter 1 – Part I – Text 1–Exercise 1

a) Enforceable, requirements. b) Courts, implied. c) Void/illegal, law. d) Implied, fact, quasi contracts. e) Capacity, bound. f) Enforceable/binding, unenforceable. g) Parties, consideration. h) Voidable, enforceable. i) Imply, enrichment. j) Offeror, acceptance, offeree.

Answers Chapter 1 – Part I – Text 1–Exercise 2

a) No, a contract to prevent unjust enrichment is not based on the behavior of the parties but is an implied in law contract, created by the courts in order to prevent a party gaining an unfair advantage over the other. b) No, an agreement without consideration is not a contract and thus is deemed to be an unenforceable agreement; it cannot be considered to be a void contract as it is not even a contract c) No, an intoxicated person is thought capable of entering into a contract where it can be shown that (s)he understood the nature of his/her commitment despite the intoxication. d) No, the offeror is the person who makes the offer and the offeree is the person to whom the offer is made. e) No, a quasi-contract is the name given a contract implied in law.

******

Answers Chapter 1 – Part I – Text 2 – Exercise 3

a) Offeror, offeree. b) Capacity, binding/enforceable. c) Void, voidable. d) Counteroffer, offer. e) Parties, implied, implied in fact.

******

Answers Chapter 1 – Part 2 – Exercise 1

c), e) and i) take "to".

******

Answers Chapter 1 – Part 4 – Translations

A. É possível aceitar uma oferta feita a outrem?–Boulton contra Jones, 1857

Fatos: O senhor Boulton comprou uma empresa de fornecimento de materiais de construção do senhor Brocklehurst. O senhor Jones, um cliente anterior à venda da empresa, deveria receber dinheiro do antigo proprietário, o senhor Brocklehurst. Antes da venda da empresa, Brocklehurst estipulou com Jones que pagaria a este o valor devido através do fornecimento gratuito de materiais de construção. Com base no acordo, Jones emitiu um pedido de encanamentos sem saber que a empresa havia sido vendida a Boulton. Boulton, o novo proprietário, entregou os encanamentos, ainda que o pedido não tivesse sido feito em seu nome, e cobrou de Jones o valor dos materiais fornecidos. Jones se recusou a pagar afirmando que a oferta foi dirigida a Brocklehurst, com quem ele tinha um acordo de pagamento da divida em mercadorias. Boulton processou Jones exigindo o pagamento dos materiais fornecidos.

Julgado: Na opinião do Tribunal, Jones endereçou o pedido especificamente ao senhor Brocklehurst, não ao senhor Boulton. Conseqüentemente, Jones não era legalmente obrigado a pagar os materiais que Boulton erroneamente forneceu.

B. A distinção entre oferta e convite para negociação–Heathecote Ball & Co. contra Barry, 2000

Fatos: Barry, um leiloeiro, anuncia o leilão sem reserva de dois motores novos. O preço recomendado pelo fabricante pelos dois motores era de 14 mil libras. Durante o leilão, um representante do requerente Heathecote Ball & Co. deu um lance de 200 libras. Como este foi o único lance dado, o representante considerou que a oferta do leiloeiro de venda sem reserva, ou seja, pelo maior preço oferecido, foi aceita. O leiloeiro declarou que ao colocar os motores à venda, ele não fez uma proposta para vender os bens, mas simplesmente um convite para negociação. Conseqüentemente, em sua opinião, foi o requerente quem fez uma oferta para comprar as maquinas por 200 libras, e que ele possuía o direito de recusar ou não a oferta e de portanto retirar os bens do leilão. O requerente argumentou que o uso das palavras "sem reserva" transformou o que normalmente seria considerado um convite para negociação em oferta.

Julgado: Na visão do Tribunal, o uso das palavras "sem reserva" configurou uma oferta do leiloeiro Barry para vender pelo o maior lance dado, independentemente do seu valor.

C. Ir além do dever exigido é uma contrapartida válida–Glasbrook Bros. contra Glamorgan Counti Council, 1926

Fatos: Os proprietários de uma mina de carvão, durante uma greve de seus funcionários, fizeram um pedido de proteção policial. A policia concordou em patrulhar a área, mas os patrões, com medo de ver sua propriedade depredada, solicitaram a presença constante da policia na mina, se oferecendo inclusive a pagar pelos custos extras desse serviço. Entretanto, posteriormente, os proprietários da mina se recusaram a pagar os policiais com base no argumento que a contrapartida feita pela policia, de manter-se presente na mina, não foi uma contrapartida válida, uma vez que eles estavam somente cumprindo o seu dever. Na opinião dos proprietários da mina, a policia já possuía o dever de proteger a área.

Julgado: De acordo com o Tribunal, a realização de um dever já existente não pode ser considerada uma contrapartida válida para formar uma relação contratual. Entretanto, com base nos fatos do presente caso, o Tribunal considerou que a policia atuou além de seu dever quando aquartelou oficiais de polícia na área. Por conseqüência, os proprietários da mina deviam pagar pela prestação do serviço extra.

A. Past consideration is not good consideration – ReMcArdle, 1951

Facts: A husband and wife were living with the husband's mother. The husband carried out extensive renovations to the house and the mother promised him payment of a certain sum of money after her death. After she died the son sought payment of the money promised to him. However, the executor of the will refused to pay the money to the son, claiming that the mother's estate was not bound by the promise. In the executor's opinion, the consideration offered by the son was *past consideration*, as the work had been performed prior to the mother making her promise to pay the son.

Held: The court agreed, considering that a promise to do something in return for something that has already been done is not binding in law. Thus the mother's estate was not bound by her promise and consequently the son was unable to recover the money[21].

B. The courts are sometimes willing to imply terms into a contract leading to the existence of a quasi-contract–The Moorcock, 1889

Facts: The plaintiff entered into a contract to use the defendant's wharf to load his boat. The wharf was located on the River Thames close to the ocean and so, when the tide was out, boats moored at the wharf rested on the riverbed. The riverbed at the defendant's wharf was bumpy/uneven and as a result the plaintiff's boat broke in two when the tide went out. The defendant claimed that he was not liable for the plaintiff's loss, as he had given no guarantee as to the state of the riverbed. The plaintiff sued the defendant on the basis that there was an implied clause in their contract that the riverbed was in suitable condition to allow the contract to be performed.

Held: The courts will imply such clauses into a contract where it is required for business efficacy. Consequently, in this case it was held to be a clause of the contract that the riverbed was in a condition necessary to allow the contract to be performed[22].

---

[21] Children do not have an automatic right to inherit from their parents in most common law countries.

[22] Thus a clause was implied into the contract guaranteeing the "suitable" condition of the river bed for mooring boats. As the riverbed was not in a suitable condition in this case, the court considered that the defendant had breached the clause implied by the court into the contract.

C. What is the Sherman Act?

The Sherman Antitrust Act authorizes the United States Federal government to investigate businesses suspected of anticompetitive behavior. It was the first national competition law that sought to limit cartels and monopolies and is the model used by most competition law authorities today. Passed in 1890, the Sherman Act prohibits:

- agreements or conspiracies between businesses seeking to restrict trade;
- monopolizing or attempting to monopolize trade.

CHAPTER 2 – VITIATING FACTORS AND THE MEETING OF THE MINDS

Answers Chapter 2 – Part I – Text 1–Exercise 1

a) Superior, adhesion/standard form. b) Minds, parties. c) Undue, relationship. d) Misrepresentation, fraudulent misrepresentation, innocent misrepresentation. e) Duress, free will. f) Mistake, material/fundamental. g) Fraudulent, rescinded. h) Presumption, rebutted.

Answers Chapter 2 – Part I – Text 1–Exercise 3

a) No, there is only a presumption of undue influence if the parties are in a special fiduciary relationship, such as doctor and patient. b) No, in many common law jurisdictions it is only possible to apply to have a contract rescinded in cases of innocent misrepresentation. c) No, in order for duress to be actionable[23], it is necessary to show that the duress complained of, actually caused the other party to decide to enter into the contract. d) No, in order to bring an action based on unconscionability, it is necessary to show that one party was in a greatly superior position to the other and excessively abused that position. e) No, for a mistake to invalidate a contract, it must concern an important matter going to the heart of the agreement.

******

Answers Chapter 2 – Part I – Text 2 – Exercise 3

a) Knowingly, material/important. b) Duress, will. c) Imposition, adhesion/ standard form. d) Repudiate, damages. e) Mistake, heart.

******

Answers Chapter 2 – Part 2 – Exercise 2

a) He ought to call his lawyer. He should not ring his lawyer. Should he ring his lawyer?

b) You had better send another bill to the client. You ought not to send another bill to the client. Should you send another bill to the client?

---

[23] To be the subject of a legal action before the courts.

c) You ought to ask the court for an adjournment. You had better not ask the court for an adjournment. Should you ask the court for an adjournment?

d) You should draft new pleadings. You should not draft new pleadings. Should you draft new pleadings?

e) You had better translate the contract into English. You should not translate the contract into English. Should you translate the contract into English?

Answers Chapter 2 – Part 2 – Exercise 3

a) Because he has a meeting. b) You have to speak English. c) I have to go to court. e) He had to work. f) I had to study a lot.

******

Answers Chapter 2 – Part 4 – Translations

A. Um erro quanto à identidade da pessoa pode levar à declaração de nulidade do contrato: Cundy contra Lindsay & Co, 1878

Fatos: O senhor Blenkarn, un estalionatário, envia uma comanda pelo correio a Lindsay & Co., com a assinatura falsa de um dos clientes mais importantes da empresa. A empresa envia os bens encomendados a Blenkarn, que imediatamente os vende a Cundy. Lindsay & Co. tenta então recuperar os bens de Cundy, sob o argumento de que o contrato original de venda de bens entre Lidsay e Blenkarn era nulo, uma vez que foi celebrado em erro provocado pela fraude de Blenkarn. Já que o contrato era nulo, Blenkarn não possuía o direito de propriedade necessário para a venda dos bens à Cundy, e, portanto, Cundy não era proprietário dos bens.

Julgado: De acordo com o tribunal, o contrato firmado entre Lindsay e Blenkarn era nulo devido ao erro de identidade provocado pela fraude. Consequentemente, Cundy não possuía direito de propriedade algum sobre os bens vendidos por Blenkarn e teve então que retornar os bens a Lindsay.

B. Para ser considerada fraudulenta, a deturpação dos fatos deve ser consciente: Derry contra Peek, 1889

Fatos: A sociedade Plymouth Tramways possuía a autorização legal do Parlamento para construir bondes. De acordo com as disposições desta lei, a sociedade tinha a permissão para:
- construir imediatamente bondes movidos a cavalo; e
- caso tenha recebido consentimento prévio da Junta Comercial, construir bondes movidos a vapor.

Entretanto, a empresa publicou um prospecto que anunciava que o direito de produzir bondes a vapor era uma das mais importantes especialidades da sociedade. Deste modo, o requerente comprou ações da empresa com base nesta declaração, que na realidade era falsa, pois a empresa necessitava da autorização prévia da Junta Comercial para a construção de bonde a vapor. Posteriormente, a Junta recusou o pedido de autorização, o que provocou a falência e o encerramento das atividades da empresa. Entretanto, na época da publicação do prospecto, a empresa acreditava honestamente que a autorização da Junta seria concedida.

Julgado: De acordo com a decisão do tribunal, Plymouth Tramways Co. não era culpada por deturpação fraudulenta dos fatos, já razoavelmente e honestamente entendia que suas afirmações eram corretas.

C. Para que haja deturpação fraudulenta, esta deve dizer respeito a fatos e não opiniões–Bisset contra Wilkinson–1927

Fatos: Wilkinson estava vendendo um terreno a Bisset. Durante as negociações, Wilkinson disse a Bisset que o terreno podia facilmente conter 2 mil ovelhas. Quando esta declaração foi feita, o terreno não estava sendo utilizado para a criação de ovelhas, e Bisset sabia que Wilkinson não possuía conhecimento algum na área. Após a compra do terreno, Bisset percebeu que o terreno não poderia conter 2 mil ovelhas e ensejou um ação judicial para anular o contrato sob o argumento de que Wilkinson forneceu uma informação fraudulenta sobre a capacidade de do terreno para a criação de ovelhas.

Julgado: A ação judicial de Bisset era impertinente e o Tribunal considerou que a declaração de Wilkinson constituía apenas uma opinião e não uma informação sobre fatos.

A. For the defense of duress to succeed it is necessary that the duress cause the decision to enter the contract–Barton v Armstrong, 1975

Facts: Armstrong was the chairman of Landmark Corporation Ltd. and Barton was the managing director and also had a substantial shareholding in the company. There was a history of bad feeling between the parties. Armstrong wished to leave the company and he made a number of death threats to Barton pressurizing him into purchasing Armstrong's holding in the company. Barton consequently agreed to buy Armstrong's share of the business, partly due to the threats, but also because he wanted to get rid of Armstrong and take control of the company. The company became insolvent shortly after this agreement and Barton sought to have the contract buying Armstrong's share set aside, on the grounds that he entered into the agreement under the duress caused by Armstrong's death threats. Armstrong claimed that Barton signed the agreement not because of the threat to kill him but because he wanted control of the business.

Held: On appeal, and overturning the decision of a lower court[24], the Court ordered that the contract be set aside on grounds of duress. In the opinion of the

---

[24]   The court of first instance agreed with Armstrong and claimed that although death threats had been made, they were not the real motivating factor behind Barton's decision to buy Armstrong's shares in the business. Consequently, the court refused to set the contract aside.

appeal court, it was sufficient to show that the death threats were partly behind the reason to enter into the contract in order to prove duress.

B. When will the courts recognize the existence of undue influence?–Lloyds Bank v Bundy, 1975

Facts: Mr. Bundy was an elderly farmer who for a number of years had relied on his bank manager at Lloyds Bank to take care of his financial dealings. Bundy's son was also a customer of Lloyd's Bank and owed the bank money. The bank manager convinced Bundy to mortgage his house in order to guarantee his son's debts to the bank. When the son's business failed the bank sought to take possession of Bundy's house. Mr. Bundy contested the action by the bank, claiming undue influence by the bank manager in convincing him to enter the agreement.

Held: The Court held that on the facts of the present case there was a special fiduciary relationship between the parties that robbed Bundy of his free will. Consequently Mr. Bundy was not bound by his agreement to guarantee his son's debts.

C. When does unconscionability arise?

Unconscionability is most frequently found in circumstances where one party is in an excessively dominant bargaining position *vis-à-vis* the other and then abuses that position by applying extremely unfair business terms. Unconscionability is often found to exist in transactions where:
- the subject-matter of the contract is highly complicated and one of the parties has no specialist knowledge. For example, when a bank introduces a disclaimer of liability into an investment contract with a consumer;
- a vendor/seller sells goods considered to be *necessaries*, for example white goods[25] on the basis of a contract of adhesion[26];
- a vendor vastly inflates the price of goods through the use of mechanisms such as unreasonable credit terms, whereby the *victim* pays an unreasonable price for the goods purchased.

CHAPTER 3 – UNFORCEABILITY, DISCHARGE AND REMEDIES FOR BREACH OF CONTRACT

Answers Chapter 3 – Part I – Text 1–Exercise 1

a) Duties, damages. b) Capacity, intoxicated. c) Simple, speciality. d) Contract, voidable. e) Recorded, exchanged. f) Performed, discharged. g) Declared, void. h) Renders, frustrated.

---

[25] Fridges, washing machines etc.

[26] A contract of adhesion is a contract containing standard terms that are not subject to negotiation. For example, when one buys "white goods" (fridges, cookers etc.), normally such purchases are done by way of an adhesion contract between the consumer and the seller/manufacturer.

Answers Chapter 3 – Part I – Text 1–Exercise 3

a) No, if there is a radical change in the conditions governing the performance of a contract, it is possible that the contract will be considered to have been frustrated. b) No, in the case of speciality contracts, it is not necessary to show the existence of consideration, as there is a presumption as to its existence. c) No, other remedies such as specific performance may be available in equity. d) No, speciality contracts have a statute of limitations period of 12 years, while simple contracts have a six-year prescription period. e) No, an injunction is a court order made in equity, preventing a party from acting in a certain way.

******

Answers Chapter 3 – Part I – Text 2 – Exercise 3

a) Recorded, orally. b) Minors, capacity. c) Substantial, damages. d) Frustration, bound. e) Irrebuttable, consideration.

******

Answers Chapter 3 – Part 2 – Exercise 1

a) Do you go to court every day? Yes, I do. b) Can you find a job? No, I can't. c) Did you meet the client yesterday? Yes, I did. d) Did you study/have you studied legal English? Yes I did/have. e) Will you be in court tomorrow? Yes, I will.

Answers Chapter 3 – Part 2 – Exercise 2

a) Does she work there? Where does she work? b) Are you working there? Where are you working? c) Was he working there? Where was he working? d) Are they going to work there? Where are they going to work? e) Should Bob work there? Where should Bob work?

Answers Chapter 3 – Part 2 – Exercise 3

a) Who went to court? b) Whom did Mohammed see? c) What happened? d) Whom did Bob see? e) What did Bob see?

******

Answers Chapter 3 – Part 4 – Translations

A. Deturpação negligente dos fatos: Hedley Byrne Co. Ltd. contra Heller Partners, 1967

Fatos: Hedley Byrne (HB) era uma agência de publicidade. Um de seus clientes, Easipower Ltd., fez uma grande encomenda a HB, que conseqüentemente decidiu verificar a situação financeira de Easipower. Eles questionarem o banco de Easipower, Heller & Partners Ltd., sobre a solvabilidade da empresa e o banco respondeu que Easipower poderia ser considerado capaz de cumprir as suas obrigações comerciais quotidianas. A carta do banco continha em seu cabeçalho a seguinte declaração: "sem responsabilidade por parte deste banco". Posteriorment, Easipower foi liquidada e HB perdeu 17000 libras esterlinas. HB propõe então uma ação contra contra o banco por deturpação negligente dos fatos.

Julgado: O Tribunal considerou que Heller & Partners era culpado por deturpação negligente dos fatos.

B. O que os Tribunais entendem pelo termo "necessidades"?–Nash contra Inman, 1908

Fatos: Inman era um estudante de graduação da universidade de Cambridge. Ele era bastante gastador e considerou necessário comprar 12 casacos caros do senhor Nash, um alfaiate. Entretanto, antes da entrega dos casacos, o rapaz tentou anular o contrato alegando que ele era menor e portanto não poderia ser submetido aos seus termos. O senhor Nash alegou que os elegantes casacos eram uma "necessidade" para o menor e que o contrato era portanto um contrato de necessidade o que, conseqüentemente, o tronava aplicável.

Julgado: Na opinião do Tribunal, Inman não era obrigado a pagar os casacos de acordo com as evidências fornecidas pelo pai do rapaz de que este dispunha de uma ampla quantidade de roupas.

C. Limites impostos pelos tribunais relativos à noção de "necessidades": Valentini contra Canali–1889

Fatos: Valentini, um menor, comprou móveis para seu apartamento. Após ter usufruído destes bens durante alguns meses, ele tentou devolver os móveis sob a alegação de que havia firmado contrato sendo menor. Canali se opôs às afirmações de Valentini considerando que este havia pago o valor normal de mercado pelos móveis e que portanto ele não foi explorado pela loja, ainda que fosse menor no momento em que firmou o contrato.

Julgado: Seria injusto se Valentini, após ter usufruído dos móveis durante meses, fosse de repente capaz de retornar os produtos a Canali e ainda recebesse o reembolso do valor pago. Foi particularmente importante para o Tribunal o fato de Valentini não ter sido explorado por Canali e que ele pagou o preço normal pelos móveis.

A. How do the courts interpret the concept of anticipatory breach?–Hochster v de la Tour, 1853

Anticipatory breach occurs when one of the parties to a contract informs the other party that they will not be performing their duties under the contract prior to the actual date that performance falls due. In the case of Hochster v de la Tour, Mr. de la Tour agreed to employ Hochster as a courier from June 1st onward. However, on May 11th, de la Tour informed Hochster that he did not need his services and would no longer be employing him as agreed. Hochster immediately began an action for damages; however, de la Tour claimed that he could not bring such an action until June 1st.

Held: Hochster could bring the action from the date de la Tour informed him that he was no longer going to perform his contractual obligations and did not have to wait until the date that performance fell due.

B. Discharge by waiver

At any time after entering into an agreement, the parties may subsequently agree to bring the contract to an end prior to the performance by one of the parties of his/her contractual duties. In such a case a party is said to waive the necessity for performance. However, it is important to note that any agreement to waive performance is a new agreement and thus in order to be legally binding, it must satisfy the four basic requirements of offer, acceptance, consideration and intention to create legal relations. If it does not, the agreement by one party to waive performance by the other will not be binding.

C. Equitable remedies – specific performance and injunctions

As the only remedy available under common law is an action for damages, should a party want the other party to actually perform the contract, it is necessary to apply to the court for an order of specific performance in equity. An order for specific performance is an order requiring a party to perform their contractual duty as set out under contract. However, equity is a discretionary remedy and the court will only award a solution in equity where it is shown that damages would not be just. Another equitable remedy is an injunction. An injunction is an order from the court requiring a party to refrain from doing something.

CHAPTER 4 – TORT LAW

Answers Chapter 4 – Part I – Text 1–Exercise 1

a) Res ipsa loquitur, self-evident. b) Non-intentional, strict liability. c) Breach, causal link. d) Plaintiff, contributory/comparative. e) Statutory, product. f) Tortfeasor/defendant, intended. g) Redress, wrongs. h) Strict liability, negligent.

Answers Chapter 4 – Part I – Text 1–Exercise 2

a) No, the amount of compensation received by the plaintiff from the defendant will be reduced to reflect the fact that the plaintiff, through his actions, contributed to the loss suffered. b) No, although primarily resulting from the case law of the common law courts, the legislative power has created statutory protection under this heading. c) No, pursuant to the doctrine of res ipsa loquitur the burden of proof is shifted from the plaintiff to the defendant in certain limited circumstances. d) No, in negligence actions it is necessary to establish a direct connection between the acts of the defendant and the loss suffered by the plaintiff. e) No, in the area of strict liability torts, the defendant is liable even where it is shown that (s)he was not negligent and regardless of whether (s)he intended the harm or not.

******

Answers Chapter 4 – Part I – Text 2 – Exercise 3

a) Duty, foresee. b) Wrong, loss. c) Res ipsa loquitur, defendant. d) Compensate, punish. e) Vicarious, employees.

******

Answers Chapter 4 – Part 2 – Exercise 1

a) What did you do last night? b) What are you going to do tomorrow? c) What do you want to do tomorrow? d) What do you need to do tomorrow? e) What would you like to do tomorrow? f) What should I do to improve my English?

Answers Chapter 4 – Part 2 – Exercise 2

a) Which case/one do you want/Which do you want? b) What did you bring last Saturday? c) Which file did Barbara borrow? d) Tell me which one you want? e) Which city did you like most in Europe?

******

Answers Chapter 4 – Part 4 – Translations

A. Qual é o escopo do dever de cuidado?–Smolden contra White, 1997

Fatos: Smolden era um jogador de rúgbi que se feriu durante uma partida na qual participou. Smolden alegou que o árbitro, o senhor White, falhou no seu dever de arbitragem correta da partida e que foi por conseqüência desta falha que o jogador se feriu. Conseqüentemente, ele processa o senhor White por negligência, exigindo uma compensação pelo dano que sofreu.

Julgado: Segundo o julgamento do tribunal, todo o árbitro possui um dever de cuidado sobre os jogadores nos jogos em que atuar, assegurando que as regras do jogo sejam aplicadas corretamente. Ao falhar neste dever, White se tornou responsável pelo dano sofrido por Smolden durante o jogo.

B. Quando um evento pode quebrar o nexo de causalidade? - Regina contra Blaue, 1975 ?

Fatos: O réu esfaqueou uma mulher de 18 anos de idade e perfurou o seu pulmão. No hospital, informaram à votima que ela necessitava de uma transfusão de sangue para sobreviver. Entretanto, por motivos religiosos, ela recusa a transfusão, o que provocou a sua morte no dia seguinte.

Julgado: Na opinião do Tribunal, quem é violento contra outrem deve aceitar a sua vítima como ela é. Este princípio se aplica tanto às características mentais quanto físicas da vítima. O Tribunal decidiu portanto que o réu era culpado por assassinato ainda que a vítima tenha morrido por causa de sua decisão de não receber uma transfusão, decisão esta baseada em sua crença religiosa extremista.

A. Does the notion of the duty of care extend to nervous shock?–McLoughlin v O'Brian, 1983

Facts: One of the claimant's children was killed and her husband and other child were injured in an accident caused by the defendant's (O'Brian's) negligence. The claimant did not witness the accident and was actually in her house when she was informed that her family had been in an accident. She immediately went to the hospital and suffered nervous shock on hearing that her daughter was dead. She sued the defendant in negligence, seeking compensation for the nervous shock she suffered.

Held: In the opinion of the Court, the defendant should have reasonably foreseen that the complainant would have suffered nervous shock as a result of his negligence, and thus he was liable to her for the damage she suffered.

B. Do the rights of a tort victim persist after his/her death?

It is a fundamental rule of the common law that a personal action is normally deemed to end with the death of the tort victim. Thus, where X dies as a result of Y's negligence, the right to bring an action under the common law is considered to end with X's death. However, statute law has intervened to temper the negative consequences of this common law rule. Under the 1976 Fatal Accidents Act, close relatives of the deceased may sue Y in X's name, where they can demonstrate that as a result of the accident they have suffered pecuniary loss. However, where Y, the tortfeasor, also dies in the accident, no action will continue to exist against his/her estate.

C. How should we understand the term vicarious liability?

If, when working for Y, X negligently injures Z, Z may bring an action against both X and Y. Y is said to be vicariously liable to Z for the actions of X. However, it is necessary to consider two separate situations where:
- X is an employee of Y; and
- X is employed as an independent contractor by Y.

The general rule is that an employer is responsible for all the acts of his/her employees carried out in the normal course of their employment. In the case of an independent contractor, the employer will only be liable for the acts he expressly or impliedly instructed the independent contractor to do.

CHAPTER 5 – INTENTIONAL AND STRICT LIABILITY TORTS

Answers Chapter 5 – Part I – Text 1–Exercise 1

a) Defamation, redress. b) Land, person. c) Liability, inherently. d) Tortious, commit. e) Public, private, damage(s)/loss. f) Liability, element. g) Person, assault. h) Confining, false imprisonment.

Answers Chapter 5 – Part I – Text 1–Exercise 2

a) No, the tort of assault involves putting a person in fear of attack but does not involve their being physically touched. b) No, to establish liability under the heading of strict liability, it is necessary to demonstrate that the element that caused the damage was under the defendant's control. c) No, an action in defamation can only succeed if the statement made is untrue. d) No, strict liability will not be engaged where the damage results from an Act of God or from an act of a stranger. e) No, the defendant will not be held liable if the act of trespass was necessary for the defendant's protection.

******

Answers Chapter 5 – Part I – Text 2 – Exercise 3

a) False, confining, will. b) Land, permission. c) Defamation, slandered. d) Nuisance, private. e) Light, true.

******

Answers Chapter 5 – Part 2 – Exercise 1

a) Whose files are these? b) Whose file is that? c) Whose notes are those? d) Whose briefcase is this? e) Whose car did you borrow last night?

Answers Chapter 5 – Part 2 – Exercise 2

a) How do you get to work? b) How do you speak English? c) How did you get to the office today? d) How fast do you usually drive? e) How did you become a lawyer?

Answers Chapter 5 – Part 2 – Exercise 3

a) How often do you go to the movies? b) How often do you read the newspaper? c) How often do you go swimming? d) How often do you eat out? e) How often are you late for work?

Answers Chapter 1 – Part 2 – Exercise 4

a) How far is it from Manchester to Liverpool? b) How far away is New York? c) How far away is the nearest bank? d) How far do you live from the University? e) How far do you jog every day/For how far do you jog every day?

Answers Chapter 1 – Part 2 – Exercise 5

a) How long does it take you to walk to your office? b) How long did it take John to draft the contract? c) For how long will the meeting last/The meeting will last for how long? d) For how long will you be in court/How long will it take you to finish in court? e) How long did it take you to fly to New York?

******

Answers Chapter 5 – Part 4 – Translations

A. A diferença entre perturbação e invasão de imóvel

Os delitos de perturbação e invasão de bem imóvel são bastante próximos, e muitas vezes é difícil diferenciá-los. Entretanto, existem algumas diferenças fundamentais entre os dois. Primeiramente, a invasão é passível de gerar uma ação judicial pela sua simples existência, sendo desnecessária a prova de que houve dano. Por outro lado, para poder ingressar com uma ação por perturbação, é necessária a prova de que o ato de perturbação resultou em dano real. O invasão envolve a entrada efetiva na propriedade de outrem, enquanto a perturbação não envolve necessariamente uma invasão efetiva à propriedade alheia. Na realidade, a perturbação se produz primeiramente na propriedade do réu antes de provocar resultados na propriedade do autor da ação, como, por exemplo, um vizinho que toca música muito alta durante a noite. Em resumo, a invasão precisa somente da simples ocorrência para ser passível de ação judicial. Já no caso da perturbação, é necessário demonstrar que a perturbação possui caráter repetitivo para que a ação judicial seja considerada procedente.

B. Limites da defesa volenti non fit injuria (nenhum dano pode ser provocado sobre aquele que consente): Bowater c/ Rowley Regis Corporation (1945)

Fatos: O requerente, um empregado da prefeitura, recebeu uma da seu patrão para utilizar um cavalo que no passado havia demonstrado ser perigoso. Diante de tal ordem, o empregado protestou, mas seu chefe insistiu. Algumas semanas mais tarde, o cavalo fugiu e o empregado foi ferido. A prefeitura argumentou que a ação movida pelo empregado por danos seria improcedente, já que ele havia concordado em utilizar o cavalo.

Julgado: Segundo a doutrina do *volenti non fit injuria*, não se pode considerar que um homem consentiu sem que este tenha a possibilidade de escolher livremente, e esta liberdade de escolha supõe a ausência de todo o tipo de coação. Este tipo de liberdade de escolha normalmente não existe numa relação empregado/ empregador.

C. A noção do privilégio do comerciante

A noção de privilégio do comerciante é reconhecida por diversas jurisdições anglo-saxônicas. Segundo esta regra, um comerciante pode deter uma pessoa suspeita de furto de mercadoria durante um período de tempo razoável. Entretanto, o comerciante só poderá agir dessa forma se ele demonstrar indícios razoáveis de que a pessoa retida cometeu ou tentou cometer um furto de mercadorias da loja. Ademais, comerciantes que detiverem clientes inocentes sob esta alegação foram processados por detenção arbitrária. Conseqüentemente, este direito não pode ser comparado com o direito da polícia de reter suspeitos de crimes.

A. The infliction of emotional distress

The infliction of emotional distress is a controversial tort, whether it occurs negligently or intentionally. However, it is the negligent infliction of emotional suffering that is the more controversial of the two. As a cause of action, it is available in most common law countries but is interpreted restrictively. The underlying concept of the action is that we all have a legal duty to use reasonable care to avoid causing emotional distress to another individual. This tort is to be contrasted with the tort of *intentional* infliction of emotional distress, insofar as there is no need to prove an actual intent to inflict distress.

B. Defamation and defenses

In common law countries, if one is to succeed in an action in defamation it must be shown that the alleged defamatory statement is false. Consequently, proving that the contested statement is true is often the best defense against an action in defamation. Statements made in good faith and in the reasonable belief that they are true are generally treated the same as true statements; however, a court may inquire into the reasonableness of the belief or opinion in question. The notion of privilege, such as parliamentary privilege, provides a complete bar to defamation actions in most common law countries. Moreover, special rules apply in the case of public figures. In most jurisdictions, in order for a public figure to win a libel case, the statement must have been published in circumstances where the author either clearly knew that it was false or was reckless with regard to reviewing its veracity.

C. Assault and battery – when is it allowed?

In order not to be liable for an assault or battery, the defendant must demonstrate privilege, i.e. that (s)he had the right to threaten or "touch" the plaintiff, for example in cases of self defense. Privilege will be considered to exist in the case of police officers, where it is shown that the force used was necessary to carry out a lawful arrest. The large majority of common law jurisdictions allow the use of some amount of force by a person seeking to protect their property from theft or damage. Indeed, some jurisdictions in the United States have extraordinarily broad laws, permitting the use of significant and even deadly force to prevent the theft of property. Finally, in many common law countries parents are legally authorized to apply reasonable physical discipline when bringing up their children.

CHAPTER 6 – CRIMINAL LAW IN COMMON LAW COUNTRIES

Answers Chapter 6 – Part I – Text 1–Exercise 1

a) Crown Prosecution Service, District Attorney; b) non-indictable/felonies, Crown Court c) accused, jury; d) triable either way, summary; e) lies, Criminal Court of Appeal; f) reasonable suspicion, offence; g) suspect/accused, lawyer/ solicitor; h) interrogating/interviewing, interview/interrogation; i) evidence/ committed; j) charge.

Answers Chapter 6 – Part I – Text 1–Exercise 2

a) The CPS takes the decision to prosecute. b) Speeding and other motoring offences of that kind are considered minor offences and must be tried in the Magistrates' Court c) Appeal normally lies from the Magistrates' Court to the Crown Court. d) The police must have reasonable suspicion before they can arrest someone. e) The time limit for filing an appeal in criminal matters is 21 days. f) Although the decision to prosecute is normally taken by the CPS, in exceptional cases a prosecution may be brought by private parties.

******

Answers Chapter 6 – Part I – Text 2 – Exercise 3

a) Triable either way offence, summary, jury, Crown; b) Duty Solicitors', custody; c) Accused, senior police officer, entitled; d) bail, court, security, witnesses e) charged, Crown Prosecution Service (CPS), plea bargain, offence.

******

Answers Chapter 6 – Part 2 – Exercise 1

a) Does b) Wasn't c) Will d) Will be e) Should f) Hasn't g) Hasn't.

Answers Chapter 6 – Part 2 – Exercise 2

a) Isn't b) Has c) Doesn't d) Would e) Doesn't e) Does f) Have.

Answers Chapter 6 – Part 2 – Exercise 3

a) Doesn't he? b) Isn't he? c) Won't he? d) Doesn't he? e) Can't he?

******

Answers Chapter 6 – Part 4 – Translations

A. A confissão de culpa

A negociação da pena, também chamada de confissão de culpa, « plea deal » ou « copping a plea » ocorre quando o protomor oferece ao réu a oportunidade de confessar a sua culpa em troca de uma pena mais leve. Por exemplo, um réu acusado de crime grave pode ter a oportunidade de confessar uma contravenção, o que pode não ser punível com pena de prisão. O Ministério Público aceitará este acordo para garantir uma condenação e de evitar os custos associados a uma ação penal por um crime grave. Entretanto, a confissão de culpa pode significar um dilema para o acusado; mesmo se ele não for culpado ele pode ser tentado a declara-se culpado de uma infração menos grave para evitar a pena de prisão.

B. O que significa mens rea?

O *mens rea* deve ser estabelecido para que o réu seja condenado por uma infração penal. O *mens rea* exige que o acusado tenha cometido o crime com intenção criminosa ou com "espírito criminoso". O teste do common Law para estabelecer a responsabilidade penal pode ser resumido pela frase "*actus non facit reum nisi mens sit rea*", ou seja, o ato não torna a pessoa culpada a menos que sua mente também seja culpada. Portanto, o acusado deve ter tido a intenção de cometer o crime. Na realidade, o *mens rea* é presumido na maior parte dos casos, e cabe ao acusado o ônus de provar a ausência de *mens rea* para evitar uma condenação.

C. O desconhecimento da lei pode ser utilizado como defesa?

A regra de que o desconhecimento da lei não exclui a ação penal é uma regra geral do common law. Entretanto, caso se trate de uma lei particularmente complexa, os tribunais às vezes consideram que o desconhecimento da lei pode ser utilizado como atenuante ou até mesmo como defesa se a incompreensão for de boa-fé e a lei excessivamente complexa. De fato, o número crescente de leis e regulamentos às vezes torna quase impossível o conhecimento de todas as obrigações estabelecidas pela lei por um cidadão comum. Ademais, a confiança razoável do acusado numa declaração do governo sobre uma lei em particular que depois venha a ser incorreta normalmente autoriza o acusado a evitar uma condenação ou ter sua pena reduzida.

A. What is recklessness?

Recklessness is said to occur where there is clear evidence that the accused foresaw or should have foreseen a particular outcome as regards his/her actions, even if (s)he did not desire the outcome to occur. In deciding not to stop the behavior, the accused took the risk of causing the loss or damage and it is for this that (s)he is considered reckless. The accused, knowing the recklessness of his/her act, had a choice to continue the behavior or not. In the opinion of the common law, by deciding to proceed the accused manifested an intention to expose the victim to harm. In this regard, the greater the probability of harm occurring to the victim, the greater the degree of recklessness and, subsequently, the greater the punishment the accused will receive.

B. What is the role of motive in criminal law?

One of the primary issues in criminal proceedings is that of motive. If it is established that the accused had a motive consistent with what actually occurred, this will add to the level of probability that the actual crime was committed by the accused and will make the prosecutor's case more credible. On the contrary, where there is clear evidence that the accused had no motive or even had a motive not to do what actually occurred, this will often be fatal to the prosecutor's case. However, a supposed lack of motive cannot be relied on as a defense; rather its role is more general or circumstantial, discrediting the prosecution's overall case.

C. Motive is not to be confused with the notion of mens rea – Regina v Yip Chung, 1995

Facts: Yip Chung was convicted of smuggling heroin and appealed against his conviction. His appeal was based on the fact that the first-instance Court failed to consider that he did not have the necessary *mens rea*. Chung claimed that although he acted as a courier trafficking heroin into the United Kingdom, he did so seeking to bring the criminal gang behind the drug smuggling to justice and not to actually bring the drugs into the country.

Held: The House of Lords rejected his appeal. In the Court's opinion, he himself during the appeal admitted that his intention was to carry out the crime. For the court, his motive in so doing, i.e., the capture of the other criminals, was irrelevant and could not be relied on as a defense.

CHAPTER 7 – COMPANY LAW

Answers Chapter 7 – Part I – Text 1–Exercise 1

a) Double taxation b) Legal entities, shareholders/owners c) Partners, limited liability d) Proprietorship, pass through e) Jointly or severally, partners. f) Corporations, Inc., Corp. g) Wound, trade, assets h) Limited liability partnerships, general partnerships.

Answers Chapter 7 – Part I – Text 1–Exercise 2

a) No, corporations are separate legal entities and thus are not pass through businesses for tax purposes. b) No, corporations may either be open to members of the public or not. c) No, if the partnership takes the form of an LLP, then the partners will enjoy limited liability. d) No, creditors of corporations have the right to receive payment out of the corporation's assets. e) NPOs, because they are non-profit organizations, normally receive favourable tax treatment. f) No, LLPs have the best of both worlds insofar as they enjoy limited liability but are taxed as pass through entities and thus are not subject to a double taxation burden.

******

Answers Chapter 7 – Part I – Text 2 – Exercise 3

a) LLC, wound up b) Partnership, jointly and severally liable c) Articles of incorporation, Companies Office d) Companies, shareholders/members, limited liability e) Delaware effect, jurisdictions/states.

******

Answers Chapter 7 – Part 2 – Exercise 1

a) Simple. b) Complex. c) Compound. d) Compound. e) Simple. f) Compound. g) Compound. h) Simple. i) Complex.

******

Answers Chapter 7 – Part 4 – Translations

A. O que é uma sociedade?

Uma sociedade é uma forma de organização comercial. A palavra "company" em inglês deriva do latim *companio*. Nos tempos medievais, esta palavra era utilizada para se referir às associações de comércio que eram populares naquela época. Uma sociedade freqüentemente adota a forma de uma "pessoa jurídica artificial", desfrutando de uma sucessão perpétua. Dessa forma, ela não é afetada pela morte de seus fundadores ou membros. Ademais, a empresa não será afetada pela insolvabilidade de seus membros a não ser que um membro tenha agido como fiador das dívidas da sociedade.

B. Uma corporação é uma entidade jurídica que possui uma personalidade separada de seus proprietários: Salomon contra Salomon, 1897

O caso Salomon é universalmente reconhecido nos países do common law como a jurisprudência que instituiu o princípio de que uma corporação é uma entidade jurídica separada de seus proprietários. Este caso estabeleceu de forma rígida que uma vez legalmente constituída, a corporação é uma pessoa distinta que possui personalidade jurídica separada e independente das pessoas que a formaram, que investiram o seu dinheiro na empresa e que dirigem e administram as suas operações. O princípio institui que os direitos e deveres de uma corporação não são idênticos aos direitos e deveres de seus dirigentes ou membros. O reconhecimento de que uma corporação é uma entidade jurídica separada de direito próprio é um fundamento do direito comercial e empresarial moderno dos países ocidentais. Considera-se que uma corporação está coberta por um véu corporativo.

C. Levantar o véu social

A expressão levantar ou perfurar o véu social descreve a decisão dos tribunais de enxergar além da personalidade jurídica separada de uma sociedade e de aplicar os direitos e obrigações, normalmente atribuídos à sociedade, aos seus proprietários e dirigentes. Habitualmente, uma corporação é tratada como personalidade jurídica separada. Entretanto, em circunstâncias excepcionais, o tribunal pode decidir levantar ou perfurar o véu social. Um exemplo simples é o de uma sociedade que age ilegalmente ao corromper um agente público. Neste caso, os tribunais perfurarão o véu social e considerarão os administradores ou proprietários como penalmente responsáveis pelas ações empregadas em nome da sociedade.

A. Is lifting the corporate veil the only way to hold the controllers of a company liable for the company's acts?

Piercing the corporate veil is not the only means by which a director of a corporation can be held liable for the actions of the corporation. Liability can be established through conventional theories of contract, agency, or tort law. For example, in situations where a director or officer acting on behalf of a corporation commits a tort, (s)he and the corporation may be considered jointly liable. Also, in cases where the company has committed a crime, criminal law will not hesitate to attribute criminal responsibility to the company officers involved.

B. What is a prospectus?

A prospectus is a document first developed in common law company law and was introduced to offer investors some level of protection as regards their investments. In most common law jurisdictions, companies issuing securities to the public are required by law to issue a prospectus describing the company and the reason why it is issuing the shares. A prospectus commonly provides investors with material information about the company; for example it will include a description of the company's business, financial statements, biographies of the company officers and directors, detailed information about their compensation, any litigation that is taking place involving the company and any other material information.

C. Rules concerning prospectuses in the United Kingdom

Publication of information in relation to the issue of securities in the United Kingdom is governed by the Prospectus Rules Act, implementing the European Union's Prospectus Directive. A company must publish a prospectus when it is issuing shares for sale to the public or where a company is requesting admission to a regulated stock market. In the United Kingdom, the only regulated market is the London Stock Exchange. The Alternative Investment Market (AIM) does not constitute a regulated market.

CHAPTER 8 – INTELLECTUAL PROPERTY LAW

Answers Chapter 8 – Part I – Text 1–Exercise 1

a) Novel, protected. b) Passing off, logos. c) Granted (capable of), data. d) Artistic, copyright. e) Trademarks, attorney. f) Apply, recorded (created). g) Intellectual, innovation.

Answers Chapter 8 – Part I – Text 1–Exercise 2

a) No, trademark attorneys are not specialized in copyright protection. b) No, in order to qualify for protection, it is necessary to demonstrate that the compilation of the database involved the active collection and verification of the data. c) No, the law of intellectual property exists to encourage innovation and this primary goal is achieved by allowing people to protect their creations. d) No, although there is sometimes an overlap between the law governing patents and copyright, design rights are protected by specific provisions governing this area. e) No, protection under the heading of copyright law is automatic, once the work in question is recorded.

******

A Answers Chapter 8 – Part I – Text 2 – Exercise 3

a) Intellectual property, protection. b) Copyright, literary. c) Patent, apply. d) Passing off, prevents. e) Trademark, novel.

******

Answers Chapter 8 – Part 2 – Exercise 1

a) I enjoy going to court. b) I hope to plead the case before the court. c) I set out to become the best lawyer in the world. d) I managed to convince the client to sign the contract. e) I can't bear to lose cases/I can't bear losing cases.

Answers Chapter 8 – Part 2 – Exercise 2

a) It is difficult to work without a secretary. b) It is exhausting to plead in court. c) It can be boring to listen to clients. d) It takes a lot of time to draft contracts. e) It is important to be in good humor at work.

Answers Chapter 8 – Part 2 – Exercise 3

a) Getting. b) To work. c) Going. d) Working. e) To contact.

******

Answers Chapter 8 – Part 4 – Translations

A. O que significa propriedade intelectual?

O termo propriedade intelectual existe desde o fim do século XVIII, mas foi somente após o fim do século XIX que a proteção da propriedade intelectual se tornou mais desenvolvida nos países do common law. A propriedade intelectual, ou "IP Law", como é mais comumente conhecida, protege alguns tipos de criações para as quais certos direitos de propriedade são reconhecidos. Segundo o direito de propriedade intelectual, é conferido aos titulares desses direitos alguns direitos sobre os bens móveis intangíveis que eles mesmos criaram ou que foram criados em seus nomes por pessoas que eles contrataram. Os bens cobertos por essa descrição incluem as obras musicais, literárias, artísticas, invenções, palavras, frases, símbolos, desenhos e modelos. A lei da propriedade intelectual, dependendo da natureza do bem a ser protegido, permite a proteção certos direitos tais como o direito autoral, as marcas registradas, as patentes, os desenhos e modelos industriais ou qualquer segredo comercial.

B. Quais são as funções do direito de propriedade intelectual?

O direito de propriedade intelectual reconhece os direitos de propriedade dos indivíduos sobre suas obras. O direito de propriedade intelectual envolve em particular os bens não rivais, ou seja, os bens que podem ser utilizados por um número diferente de pessoas de forma simultânea e sem se exaurir. Os bens rivais, como, por exemplo, carros e vestimentas, só podem ser utilizados por uma pessoa por vez. Por outro lado, uma fórmula matemática, por exemplo, pode ser utilizada por qualquer número de pessoas de forma simultânea. Portanto, esta fórmula pode ser classificada como bem não rival. Certos bens podem possuir características rivais e não rivais: por exemplo, uma blusa produzida por um estilista famoso. A blusa em si só pode ser usada por uma pessoa, mas a marca pode ser utilizada simultaneamente por um número de blusas diferentes.

C. Os direitos de propriedade intelectual são benéficos para a sociedade?

A existência de direitos de propriedade intelectual representa um exercício de conciliação entre os interesses:

- dos inventores, pois permite que eles se beneficiem de suas criações através da proteção destas;
- e da sociedade, para que o grande público possa se beneficiar das criações de terceiros.

O verdadeiro problema não é o de saber se os direitos de propriedade devem existir, mas é na realidade de determinar o período ideal de proteção para garantir o máximo de benefícios para a sociedade. Os benefícios e custos pertinentes para a sociedade provocados pela concessão de proteção à propriedade intelectual, variam conforme a natureza da invenção. De fato, é por este motivo que existem diferentes categorias de direitos de propriedade intelectual e diferentes períodos de proteção.

A. Do intellectual property rights grant a monopoly?

Intellectual property rights reserve markets or parts of markets for the owners of the right. Thus, it could be argued that the conferral of an intellectual property right is the equivalent of granting someone a monopoly. However, it probably does not constitute a monopoly in the traditional sense of the word, as the right is relied on to protect something that would not necessarily exist prior to the introduction of the protection. Thus, the right does not function as a normal monopoly, insofar as it does not seek to deprive society of the benefit of an existing "thing". Without the protection, the creation might probably not have occurred.

B. The history of intellectual property

The need for international protection of intellectual property became evident in the late 1800s when foreign exhibitors refused to attend international exhibitions for inventors for fear that their ideas would be stolen and exploited commercially by others. This led in 1883 to the signing of the Paris Convention for the Protection of Industrial Property and the later signing of the Bern Convention in 1886. These two treaties led directly to the establishment of the World Intellectual Property Organization (WIPO) in 1967.

C. Are the protection periods granted by intellectual property law too long?

A recurrent criticism of intellectual property law concerns what appears to be an increasing tendency to extend the protection granted, with regard to both the duration and the scope of the protection on offer. For example, patents are now being granted for living organisms, and even colors have begun to be trademarked. Some critics of intellectual property law, such as those in the free culture movement, point to the creation of intellectual property monopolies, which in their opinion, far from encouraging creation actually work to prevent progress. In their opinion, intellectual property rights serve largely to benefit private interests to the detriment of society in general.

CHAPTER 9 – LABOR LAW / EMPLOYMENT LAW

Answers Chapter 9 – Part I – Text 1–Exercise 1

a) Labor, employment. b) Minimum, employees. c) Direct, indirect. d) Compensation. e) Wrongful, employer, dismissal f) Misconduct, job. g) Dismissal, damages.

Answers Chapter 9 – Part I – Text 1–Exercise 2

a) No, US federal law has established a minimum wage for employees. b) No, when an employer fails to follow the rules governing the dismissal process, it is said to be a case of wrongful dismissal. c) No, the dismissal may also be justified if it can be shown that the employee was incapable of performing the job for which (s)he was hired or where the dismissal occurs in the context of a redundancy procedure. d). No, under European Union law as implemented into UK national law, employees have a right to parental leave. e) No, both direct and indirect discrimination are considered to be illegal in Anglo-Saxon countries. f) No, although often used interchangeably, labor law refers to the statutory protection established by the legislative power in order to protect employees, while employment law refers to specific relationships between employees and employers.

******

Answers Chapter 9 – Part I – Text 2 – Exercise 3

a) Employees, protection. b) Discrimination, damages. c) United States, minimum wage. d) Redundancies, trade union. e) Indirect discrimination, direct discrimination.

******

Answers Chapter 9 – Part 2 – Exercise 1

a) That/whom. b) That/which. c) That/whom. d) Whom. e) Which.

Answers Chapter 9 – Part 2 – Exercise 2

a) Fred Sharpe is a lawyer in whom you can have confidence. b) The lawyer who/that worked all night was wonderful. c) The court case that/which we went to see was interesting. d) John works in the office that is in the tall/high building. e) The old lawyer whose practice I bought is moving to Florida.

Answers Chapter 9 – Part 2 – Exercise 3

a) A+E b) B+D c) C+A d) D+C e) E+B

******

Answers Chapter 9 – Part 4 – Translations

A. Sindicados

Originários da Europa, os sindicatos ficaram populares em diversos países durante a revolução industrial. Foi neste período, com a mudança da mão-de-obra qualificada para a não qualificada, que o poder de negociação passou a favorecer os empregadores, o que levou à exploração dos trabalhadores e a imposição de salários cada vez mais baixos. Os sindicatos eram um contrapeso natural e necessário a este processo. Compostos de trabalhadores individuais, de categorias de trabalhadores e até mesmo de desempregados, os sindicatos se tornaram os porta-vozes de uma classe sem voz. A função primária dessas organizações é de garantir que os trabalhadores se beneficiem de condições de trabalho e de salários corretos no curso de seus empregos. Hoje em dia, em diversos países, os sindicatos se tornaram atores-chave do processos político e geralmente dispõem de uma influência maior que o número de aderentes pode nos fazer supor.

B. O papel do direito do trabalho

O direito do trabalho constitui uma parte integral do desenvolvimento social e econômico dos países do common law desde a revolução industrial. O termo direito do trabalho se refere ao conjunto de leis, normas administrativas e precedentes judiciais que definem as relações entre empregados e empregadores. Desde o colapso do feudalismo, o papel do direito do trabalho na proteção dos trabalhadores foi uma das influências centrais para a definição da natureza e do conteúdo do *contrato social*. A maior parte dos termos e condições desse contrato social são estabelecidos pelo legislador ou pelas regras do common law desenvolvidas nos tribunais. O direito do trabalho continua a ser uma área em constante evolução na medida em que os movimentos geopolíticos e o desenvolvimento econômico continuam a introduzir novas realidades econômicas nas sociedades em todo o mundo.

C. As regras de proteção do direito do trabalho

Muitas leis são desenvolvidas com o objetivo de proteger os empregados ao invés dos empregadores, já que estes são geralmente vistos como a parte que possui uma posição de negociação superior. Diversos países, por exemplo, adotaram regras precisas que estabelecem o valor mínimo que os trabalhadores devem receber por hora. As primeiras leis sobre o salário mínimo foram introduzidas no âmbito nacional pelos Estados Unidos em 1938 e foram posteriormente adotadas em outros países do mundo. Uma outra área coberta pelas regras gerais em diversos países é a que diz respeito à duração do dia ou da semana de trabalho. Antes da criação dos sindicatos, os trabalhadores europeus trabalhavam até dezesseis horas por dia, seis dias por semana. Ademais, vários empregados eram crianças que de fato cresciam acorrentados à fábrica em que trabalhavam duramente. Reformas foram lentamente introduzidas em primeiro lugar na Alemanha, e posteriormente na Europa e no mundo, com o objetivo de melhorar as condições de trabalho.

A. Industrial action

Most countries require that trade unions follow particular procedures before deciding to take industrial action. For example, some countries require that unions ballot their membership prior to striking. Strike action is considered the most powerful weapon in the trade union arsenal. However, many labor law systems seek to prevent certain categories of strike, for example wildcat strikes or sympathy strikes in favor of other striking workers. This has led to the near total eradication of general strikes in these countries. Moreover, certain categories of workers, such as policemen, fire fighters or health staff are often forbidden to strike. Instead of striking, workers sometimes adopt a go-slow or a work-to-rule policy. Alternatively, they might attempt to establish a general boycott of a company's products.

B. International labor rules

The International Labor Organization (ILO) headquartered in Geneva is the only surviving international body set up at the time of the League of Nations. The fundamental principle of the organization is that labor is more than a commodity and that it should not be traded in the same way as produce. The ILO has drafted numerous conventions that have been signed and ratified by its members, and which have introduced basic protection for workers throughout the world. Other organizations such as the European Union have played a fundamental role in enhancing worker protection by introducing new regulations, such as the European Working Time Directive limiting the maximum length of a working week to 48 hours.

C. What does the term social security mean?

The term social security may refer to a number of different things:
- *income assistance* This involves the distribution of money by the government in the case of full or partial cessation of employment resulting from retirement, disability or unemployment;
- *provision of social services* This involves the provision of medical care in all of its forms and social work assisting disadvantaged members of society;
- *social insurance* This refers to benefits or services provided in return for contributions made to various insurance schemes (social); for example, retirement pensions, disability insurance, survivor benefits and unemployment insurance.

CHAPTER 10 – INTERNATIONAL LAW

Answers Chapter 10 – Part I – Text 1–Exercise 1

a) Fields/areas, private. b) Independent states, inchoate. c) Comity, goodwill. d) Convention, incorporating. e) Two, custom. f) State, sovereignty. g) Prosecute, infringed/broken.

Answers Chapter 10 – Part I – Text 1–Exercise 2

a) No, normally international law will only apply in the law of a state that has actually incorporated the law in question into its national legislation. b) No, comity results from practice developed between states based upon notions of goodwill and mutual respect. c) No, international law recognizes three basic state entities: independent states, dependent states and inchoate states. d) No, international law is made up of both public and private international law. e) No, a treaty is a separate stand-alone document, whilst a convention is a document drawn-up in the context of an already existing international understanding or agreement. f) No, public international law is primarily concerned with relations between states.

******

Answers Chapter 10 – Part I – Text 2 – Exercise 3

a) Custom, usage. b) Incorporation, transformation. c) Self-executing, domestic. d) Dependent, national. e) Usage, obliged/obligated.

******

Answers Chapter 10 – Part 2 – Exercise 1

a) Because. b) In order to. c) If. d) If.

Answers Chapter 10 – Part 2 – Exercise 2

a) That he would not go to court – object of the verb "said". b) That he was present at the meeting – in apposition to the pronoun "it". c) that we won the case – in apposition to the noun "news". d) What he says – object of the preposition "on".

Answers Chapter 10 – Part 2 – Exercise 3

a) That the professor recommended: adjective clause. b) Where I won my first case: adjective clause. c) Unless the prosecution can make a better case – adverb clause. d) Because he could – adverb clause.

******

Answers Chapter 10 – Part 4 – Translations

A. Direito internacional privado

O direito internacional privado é um sistema de regras que governam a aplicação do direito privado no contexto internacional sobre todos os casos onde há conflito de leis. O papel do direito nacional é de reger as situações que ocorrem num contexto estritamente interno, ou seja, quando todos os elementos de uma lide jurídica dizem respeito a um Estado em particular. Por outro lado, as regras de direito internacional privado podem ser colocadas em prática uma vez que os elementos de um caso em particular envolvem diversas regras nacionais devido à presença de partes que possuem nacionalidades diferentes.

B. *Direito internacional público*

O direito internacional pode ser dividido entre duas categorias: o direito internacional público e o direito internacional privado, que regem as relações entre pessoas de nacionalidades diferentes. Quando se fala em direito internacional de uma forma geral, normalmente se faz referência ao direito internacional público. O direito internacional público rege as relações entre os Estados, as organizações internacionais e os quase-Estados. A fonte dominante deste direito hoje são os tratados e convenções. Outras fontes são os costumes internacionais, os princípios gerais do direito e a doutrina.

C. *A declaração universal dos direitos humanos*

A declaração universal dos direitos humanos, adotada pela Assembléia Geral das Nações Unidas em 10 de dezembro de 1948, marcou claramente o estabelecimento de um movimento internacional de proteção dos direitos humanos. A declaração forneceu pela primeira vez na história da humanidade os direitos civis, políticos e fundamentais que beneficiam toda a humanidade. Durante os anos, o status dos direitos humanos como regra fundamental que todos devem proteger e respeitar foi largamente reconhecido.

A. *The notion of a crime against humanity*

A crime against humanity can be defined as a deliberate and odious violation of the fundamental rights of an individual or group of individuals. The notion of a crime against humanity appeared for the first time as a recognized legal concept in 1945, in the Charter of London (article 6(c)) establishing the Nuremberg Military Tribunal. This development resulted from the desire of the victors to call to justice those on the losing side who were responsible for the atrocities committed during the Second World War in Europe. The notion was also relied on to try the leaders of the *Tojo regime* before the Tribunal of Tokyo. The concept is thus strongly anchored in a particular historical context.

B. *The law of international commerce*

The law of international commerce, also referred to as international business law or international commercial law, was primarily developed over the last century in response to the growing internationalization of business. International commercial law should probably be distinguished from international economic law, which applies to areas such as mergers, public offerings[27], international tax operations etc. The aim of international commercial law is more general and its scope is more difficult to define precisely. However, it can be said that international commercial law seeks to govern international commercial relations between market operators.

---

[27] By public offerings is meant the introduction of shares for sale to the general public.

C. The work of international commercial law firms

The areas of expertise of international commercial law firms are many and involve *inter alia*:

- pleading before internationally recognized dispute resolution bodies, such as the World Trade Organization;
- dealing with cases involving international arbitration law;
- mergers and acquisitions;
- defending and bringing antidumping law actions; and
- the creation and application of international commercial agreements.

On a more traditional level, these firms also offer services in the area of customs law, the management of export licenses and other matters concerning customs law.

www.ingramcontent.com/pod-product-compliance
Lightning Source LLC
Chambersburg PA
CBHW051416090426
42737CB00014B/2696